DURHAM INDOLOGICAL SERIES

SYMBOLS IN ART AND RELIGION

SCHOOL OF ORIENTAL STUDIES
UNIVERSITY OF DURHAM

DURHAM INDOLOGICAL SERIES

1. THE YOGI AND THE MYSTIC
Edited by Karel Werner

2. SYMBOLS IN ART AND RELIGION
Edited by Karel Werner

SYMBOLS IN ART AND RELIGION

The Indian and the Comparative Perspectives

Edited by
KAREL WERNER

MOTILAL BANARSIDASS PUBLISHERS PVT. LTD.
DELHI

First Indian Edition: Delhi, 1991

ISBN: 81-208-0833-9

Also available at:
MOTILAL BANARSIDASS
41 U.A., Bungalow Road, Jawahar Nagar, Delhi 110 007
120 Royapettah High Road, Mylapore, Madras 600 004
16 St. Mark's Road, Bangalore 560 001
Ashok Rajpath, Patna 800 004
Chowk, Varanasi 221 001

PRINTED IN INDIA
BY JAINENDRA PRAKASH JAIN AT SHRI JAINENDRA PRESS, A-45 NARAINA INDUSTRIAL AREA, PHASE I, NEW DELHI 110028 AND PUBLISHED BY NARENDRA PRAKASH JAIN FOR MOTILAL BANARSIDASS PUBLISHERS PVT. LTD., BUNGALOW ROAD, JAWAHAR NAGAR, DELHI 110 007

CONTENTS

ABBREVIATIONS

A — Aṅguttara Nikāya
AAr — Aitareya Āraṇnyaka
AB — Aitareya Brāhmaṇa
AV — Atharva Veda
BhG — Bhagavad Gītā
BP — Bhāgavata Purāṇa
BandP — Brahmāṇḍa Purāṇa
BM — British Museum
BU — Bṛhadāraṇyaka Upaniṣad
Bv — Buddhavaṁsa
CJSR — Canadian Journal of Studies in Religion
CU — Chāndogya Upaniṣad
D — Dīgha Nikāya
DA — Dīgha Nikāya Atthakathā
Dhp — Dhammapada
DhpA — Dhammapada Atthakathā
Dv — Divyāvadāna
ERE — Hasting's Encyclopaedia of Religions and Ethics
GP — Garuda Purāṇa
HR — History of Religions
IE — Indo-European
IHQ — Indian Historical Quarterly
IIJ — Indo-Iranian Journal
J — Jātaka
JAOS — Journal of the American Oriental Society
JIABS — Journal of the International Association of Buddhist Studies
JOIB — Journal of the Oriental Institute Baroda
JRAS — Journal of the Royal Asiatic Society
JUB — Jaiminīya Upaniṣad Brāhmaṇa
LP — Liṅga Purāṇa
M — Majjhima Nikāya
MaiU — Maitrī Upaniṣad
Mhb — Mahābhārata

MtsP — Matsya Purāṇa
Miln — Milindapañha
MuU — Muṇḍaka Upaniṣad
Mv — Mahāvaṁsa
N — Nidānakathā
PP — Padma Purāṇa
Ps — Patisaṁbhidāmagga
PTS — Pāli Text Society
R — Religion (Journal of Religion and Religions)
RV — Ṛg Veda
S — Samyutta Nikāya
SB — Śatapatha Brāhmaṇa
SBE — Sacred Books of the East
SCR — Studies in Comparative Religion
Sn — Suttanipāta
SP — Skanda Purāṇa
Thag — Theragāthā
TB — Taittirīya Brāhmaṇa
TS — Taittirīya Saṁhitā
VA — Vibhaṅga Atthakathā
V & A — Victoria and Albert Museum
VIN — Vinaya Piṭaka
VP — Viṣṇu Purāṇa
VmP — Vamana Purāṇa
VS — Vājasaneyi Saṁhitā
VyP — Vāyu Purāṇa
YV — Yajur Veda
WZKM — Wiener Zeitschrift für die Kunde Des Morgenlandes
ZDMG — Zeitschrift der Deutschen Morgenländischen Gesellschaft

THE EDITOR'S PREFACE

The hope expressed in the Preface to *The Yogi and the Mystic*, the first collection of papers in this series, namely that the publishers would be able and willing to bring out a second collection, this time dedicated to the theme of symbolism, is being realized by the appearance of this book.

As with the first volume, the contributions included in this one also stem from the harvest of the Symposia on Indian Religions which took place during the ten years of the editor's convenership (1975 – 84). It was the Seventh Symposium, housed in the Cherwell Centre, Oxford, in 1981, which was concerned with the theme of symbolism in Indian religions and, like the previous one-theme conference on mysticism, attracted much interest which enabled eventually the present publication.

In the case of mysticism, the editor could offer a general framework for the way in which the inquiry into the different varieties of mysticism in Indian religions could be conducted; it was outlined in his introductory paper whose extensive synopsis was made available to the participants invited to contribute, although it was left to them whether they would choose to relate their contributions to the theory outlined in the synopsis or not. In the event, the editor subsequently felt justified in claiming that the structural pattern of mystical doctrine, experience and path as outlined in his introductory paper had a virtually universal applicability and was recognizable even in papers which did not directly relate to his synopsis or, in one or two cases, were written without their authors' knowledge of it.

The editor could make no similar claim to having a generally applicable theory in the case of symbolism. He was therefore delighted to receive the offer of a paper from a colleague with a philosophical background who was preoccupied with general methodological problems of symbolism in religions. His paper was used to introduce the theme and some of its general implications to the Symposium and is published in this collection almost unaltered. Other contributors did not have a chance to read it beforehand and wrote their papers independently.

The imagination of one participant in the proceedings of the Symposium was fired enough to ponder over its theme for some time and to prepare a kind of 'footnote' to it for the subsequent year's Symposium. It was later finalized and published in a journal. The author reworked it again for the purposes of this collection after he had read all the other contributions.

Although this last paper tries to find some pattern in the creation, use and meaning of symbols and even suggests a theory which it attempts to illustrate with the materials of some of the other contributions, we can hardly claim to have a comprehensive grasp or clear understanding of the processes in human thought, experience and creative effort which lead to the birth of symbols and to their effectiveness. The assembled papers offer some valid, although only partial, insights into these processes, but their nature or essence is elusive and will require ever more attention and ever fresh attempts to elucidate them, without any guarantee that the problem will eventually be fully understood. This does not mean that effective use and new creation of symbols will not go on. It is as with language. One does not have to understand fully its nature in order to use it effectively and creatively, and the language itself, as well as its employment both in the creative process and in everyday affairs, will remain forever independent of the theories of language and of the contentions of linguistic philosophy.

The first paper, 'Symbols and Religious Language', takes as its starting point two clearly inadequate definitions of symbol, one ascribing the capacity of becoming a symbol to anything that has a meaning and the other one regarding the process by which a symbol comes into existence to be a matter of convention rather than of any intrinsic link between the symbol and the entity which it symbolizes. The author then proceeds to examine, first, the qualities which a symbol may be required to have, such as being 'acceptable' and having an 'innate power' or what is called 'necessary character', and, second, the relation a symbol has to what it symbolizes: whether it represents that entity and somehow participates in it, mediates its deeper meaning or even integrates into human life realities not normally encountered in everyday life, a point particularly relevant to symbols in religions. He then examines symbols as used in religious discourse, the claims Tillich makes for symbolic language as pointing to truth if it adequately expresses man's 'ultimate concern', and Wittgenstein's 'picture' theory of religious language — only to conclude that, symbols being the language of religion, we can never know the reality they point to; we can only elucidate the life which symbols have as a form of language.

Illuminating as the paper is in matters of theory of symbols and in the conceptual analysis of their place in the context of linguistic philosophy, it does little to prepare us for the way in which subsequent contributors take the reality of symbols and their effectiveness for granted and explain their meaning and role in their particular area of research.

This is immediately clear from the next paper, 'The Symbolism of Indian Art'. The author simply accepts that religions are founded on sets of symbols which structure man's intuitions about his world and its meaning and about destiny, and proceeds to show how the language of symbols has been incorporated not only in the scriptures, myths and legends of the Indian tradition, but most powerfully also in Indian religious art and even in the structural complexity of the Hindu temple. From here there is a direct link to the 'structural', or shall we rather say multidimensional, complexity of the 'temple' of the human personality itself which ranges from the gross level of the physical body through the suprasensory level of the 'subtle' body to the level of the divine energy, reaching even as far as the transcendental 'centre' of being itself, beyond 'the wasteful entropy of time'.

The editor's own paper, 'Symbolism in the Vedas and its Conceptualization', also unquestioningly accepts the obvious fact of the existence of powerful symbols and their multidimensional connection with the human world, both individual and social, and its link to the cosmic and transcendental realms. Focusing on a few examples as they were preserved in the ancient Vedic mythology of creation, it points out a further fact, expressed already in the title of the article, namely that, with time, the powerful mediation of subtle messages conveyed directly to the hearts of their recipients through the language of symbols wears out and they require interpretation in order to be understood. In this process of translating symbols into concepts, the message grows weaker, even to the point of becoming ineffective. The symbols which once shaped individual lives and even the social order are then no longer living forces. Does their interpretation help the original messages to become effective again? Does our conceptual knowledge of the meaning of symbols of so many ancient traditions influence our lives and society? One would have liked to have another paper which would address this problem, perhaps utilizing the insights of Jungian psychology.

In his search for the meaning of ancient religious monuments which almost invariably are also works, often great works, of art, John Irwin, too, has been faced with the problem of interpreting, i.e. conceptualizing, the message of archaic symbols rooted in the cosmogonic myth. As an art historian and a fine analyst of detail in archaeological materials he has never turned his effort towards systematic theorizing. Yet, as may be obvious from the included contribution, put together from the partial draft of his intended paper and from the editor's summaries of his earlier research, he is constantly groping after some kind of a unitary picture of the archaic man's vision of cosmos and of himself within it. What seems to be emerging from his occasional remarks and pointers is an idea, tantalizingly appealing and evocative but extremely vague, of a — possibly universal — prehistoric 'Cosmic Religion' with the central role of the *axis mundi* which is simultaneously seen to be identical with the highest deity. His ideas, scattered in many research articles which unfortunately suffer from too many repetitious restatements, are very important and stimulating and would merit a careful rethinking and a new systematic presentation in a monograph.

In contrast, Harvey concentrates on the interpretation of the symbols in the early Buddhist tradition from within it and as a result he tends to brush aside or underestimate the underlying continuity of subliminal symbolical messages from archaic times. His disagreement with Irwin over the interpretation of some of the symbolical meanings of monuments which Buddhism inherited from the pre-Buddhist past is a matter of different emphasis and of shift of standpoint rather than a real controversy. A specialist in one tradition is entitled to concentrate on meanings of its monuments 'closer to hand' and nourished from within it. A historian of art or religions must seek to uncover connections across whole epochs of time and boundaries of different traditions.

Miller's paper is an example of scholarly effort trying to unravel the perplexing complexities of late Hindu myth-making and to read from it (or read into it?) messages of moral significance universally valid and therefore relevant even for our time. Hence also her attempts to make use of Jungian guidelines for some of her conclusions. This is a highly commendable approach even if it may be regarded to be still in its infancy. By the nature of the prevailing methods of academic research it is also still quite controversial, but by the same token promising and potentially very fruitful.

The two following contributions seem to stand apart from the rest. One deals with fire symbolism in a court epic which is an example of a highly élitist, even artificial, variety of Sanskrit poetry. Its symbolism is therefore seemingly quite remote from the mainstream of the Hindu religious tradition. Indeed, poets do take liberties when using metaphors, which sometimes seem far-fetched or even arbitrary. Yet their metaphors do have some features in common with the mainstream use of symbols in religious art and may sometimes provide useful insight into the wider process of symbol-making. The other contribution, by Roebuck, is an example of a matter-of-fact approach of a museum worker faced with the task of identifying, placing in context and finally labelling exhibits. Here, one can hardly indulge in theorizing but has to research historical, religious and even literary sources for all available clues and be as sober and precise as possible. But there is in this work also a scope for wider issues as the author shows when she draws parallels with comparable approaches to the subject of weapon symbolism in European art.

Sutton's paper brings nearer to us the thinking on symbolism as it is reflected in the work of the great Indian art historian Coomaraswamy. Once highly acclaimed, he can now hardly be regarded as widely influential, despite the tribute paid to him not so long ago in the form of the commemorative edition of his selected works. There is much in his writings which deserves to be well remembered and utilized — as transpires also from Bastow's closing paper. Bastow tries to establish the necessary precondition for the relation between a symbol and the symbolized entity to be fruitful, and claims that their relation must be ontological and, particularly in the context of religions, even metaphysical. Here he parts company with the historian of religions and ventures into the deeper waters of philosophy of religion. This is enabled to him by his regard for religions as providers of a 'world view', a basically metaphysical feat. The role of the symbol is then to bridge, for the religious believer, the inevitable gulf between the 'focus' of his belief, which is transcendental and therefore incomprehensible, and himself, because the symbol is, although somehow related to the transcendental focus, approachable and comprehensible. Bastow further tries to classify symbols into 'deep' and 'superficial', not a happy terminological choice, while the reasons for this distinction need further investigation. The application of his ideas to materials presented in the other papers of this collection does, however, reveal certain variations in the way symbolism works in Indian religions which make the need for some kind of classification of varieties of symbolism appear justified.

It is hoped that readers will find that some valuable results have been brought to light through this publication. In the editor's view it certainly offers some new insights into the theme and clearly demonstrates the richness and the fascination of the field of symbolism as well as the importance of further and continuous research into it.

1

SYMBOLS AND RELIGIOUS LANGUAGE

Glyn Richards

If one were to seek a definition of a symbol, the view might be expressed that 'Whatever has meaning is a symbol and the meaning is whatever is expressed by the symbol.'[1] Given such a comprehensive definition it could be argued that all words and figures are symbols and similarly that all acts are symbols since words, figures and acts have meaning.

A more precise definition might be that 'the essence of a symbol is . . . that its importance, value or meaning is not inherent in the intrinsic properties of the symbol itself, but in the thing symbolized' and that the relationship between the symbol and the thing symbolized is conventional and arbitrary rather than intrinsically caused.[2] The implication of this definition is that symbols are conceived as developing within social structures and cultural environments, or within what might be called forms of life, and that we look in vain for what is called 'a cross-cultural, pan-human pattern of symbols.'[3] That is, the choice and development of a symbol is a result of the acceptability of that symbol and of decisions taken within particular social, religious or cultural contexts, and the relevance of a symbol, or its value, importance and meaning, is to be found within these contexts and is related to the thing symbolized. This leads us to consider views that have been expressed about the characteristics of symbols such as the following.

(A) ACCEPTABILITY, INNATE POWER AND NECESSARY CHARACTER

One characteristic of a symbol, it is claimed, is that it is 'acceptable', by which is meant that it is socially determined. The acceptance of a symbol is a social rather than an individual matter. An individual may conceive or indicate the idea of a symbol, but its creation is a social act. So the creation and maintenance of a symbol depends on group acceptance; it is by means of the reaction of a group that it becomes a symbol. This is what is meant by saying that the relation between a symbol and the thing symbolized is 'conventional and arbitrary'. Its meaning is what people who accept it determine.

A further characteristic of a symbol, it is claimed, is its 'innate power'.[4] But if the concept of 'innate power' means that symbols possess some kind of inherent power in the magical sense or that their meaning lies within themselves, then clearly that is at odds with the notion of acceptability of symbols and their value, importance and meaning as being related to the thing symbolized. It is not possible for symbols both to possess 'innate power' in the magical sense *and* to be socially determined or acceptable: If we take a flag (e.g. the Maple Leaf) as a symbol for a country (Canada), does the 'innate power' mean that no other flag could possibly serve the same symbolic purpose? A symbol then, like a sign, can be exchanged, contrary to Tillich's view, although it has to be admitted that in the case of the Canadian flag the creation of the new symbol was a social act acceptable to the community which continues to recognize itself in that symbol.

Another characteristic of symbol, it has been argued, is its 'necessary character'. This description suggests a view which escapes the magical connotation of 'innate power', on the one hand, and the conventional or arbitrary connotation of 'social determination', on the other. To say that a symbol has a 'necessary character' might point to the naturalness of a symbol within a culture. A willow tree, for example, might be taken to be or accepted as the symbol of unhappy life. Its naturalness as such a symbol is indicated by its drooping branches and its 'necessary character' might become evident if we tried to substitute a holly bush for it. The unacceptability of the holly bush would be related to the natural associations of the willow tree within a culture and would indicate the necessary character of the willow tree as a symbol for unhappy life.

The same point might be made about the maple leaf as the natural symbol for the Canadian flag. The predominance of the maple tree in Canada makes its leaf the natural symbol for the country's flag and its 'necessary character' might become evident if one substituted an oak leaf for it.

(B) REPRESENTATION AND PARTICIPATION

It is claimed that symbols are representational and participate in the reality of that to which they point. But what does this mean? Is it the case that 'participation' follows necessarily from the concept of 'representation'? If the essence of a symbol, its importance, value and meaning, lies not in itself but in what is symbolized, does this mean that its efficacy is determined by the way it participates in the reality of what is symbolized?

The ambiguity implicit in the idea of 'participation' may be clarified somewhat by the explanation that one who is chosen to represent an institution or a high-ranking person, for example, is said to participate in, or partake of, the honour of what or whom he represents. If so it would seem that it is representation which is the primary factor here and that it is simply in the sense of representing something other than itself that a symbol can be said to participate in the reality of what it symbolizes. 'It radiates the power of being and meaning of that for which it stands.'[5]

Preliminary questions that might be raised at this point in connection with the concept of representation and participation and the notion of acceptability are whether the value, meaning and importance of symbols depend solely on their relation to the thing symbolized or on their participation in the reality to which they point, or whether because of their shared application within a culture they manifest the life they have.

If we inquire further what life is manifested or what it is that symbols show, we might get the reply that they show themselves in such a way that those who accept them and live by them understand what it means to talk of such things as the holy, the ultimate or the aesthetic. The basic question being raised here is whether or not we understand what it means to speak of the ultimate from the use of concrete particulars or from the shared application of symbols in a form of life.

The relation of a symbol to what it shows may not be like the relation of a diagram or plan to a house. The symbol may itself be the object of thought and show itself in such a way that from the life it has and from its shared application within a culture we know what it means to speak of the ultimate or the holy. It is itself a picture of the holy and the whole weight is in the picture. I shall return to this viewpoint in our discussion of religious language.

(C) MEDIATION AND INTEGRATION

We might ask whether anything more is involved in saying that symbols are representative beyond the fact that they stand for what is symbolized. It is suggested that a basic characteristic of representative symbols is that they point beyond themselves to something which cannot be grasped immediately and has to be mediated.[6] That something could be what Lonergan calls 'the world of the adult mediated by meaning and motivated by values' as distinct from 'the world of mediacy of the infant'.[7]

The transition from the one world to the other involves, according to Lonergan, a process of learning which includes asking questions, reflecting, deliberating and formulating views about the nature of reality. But it is not always easy to formulate views clearly and precisely because of the obscure nature of the world. Symbols, therefore, intimate to us 'the kind of world in which we become our true selves'.[8]

Again, that something could be what is called 'a particular kind of reality, different from that of daily life subject to ordinary speech' which requires the use of symbols in order to speak about it at all.[9] It is for this reason that Ricoeur can refer to symbols as the meeting point of different realities.[10] Such dimensions of reality that need to be expressed in symbols are not normally encountered in ordinary day-to-day experience.

If it is accepted that symbols perform a mediatory function, then it is understandable that their integrating power should also be accepted.[11] The cohesive stabilizing effect of symbols in social groups might be illustrated, for example, by a document or an event in the political realm or by a holy book in the religious realm. But symbols could also have the opposite effect, depending on the nature of what is mediated. They could have disintegrating powers, e.g. the political symbol of the svastika or the golden calf in the history of Israel.

The same preliminary questions which were raised in connection with the notion of participation and acceptability may be asked again here in relation to what is described as the mediatory function of symbols. Lonergan, as we have seen, suggests that symbols intimate to us the kind of world in which self-realization is a possibility or the kind of reality which requires symbols to speak about it. It might be argued that we know what it might mean to speak of a world in which self-realization is a possibility or that we understand what it means to talk of a reality not normally encountered in everyday life, as Ricoeur suggests, *not* because symbols serve a mediatory function but rather because they constitute a form of language which enables us to understand what it means to talk of the kind of world, or kind of reality, Lonergan and Ricoeur speak of.

What needs to be recognized is the danger of assuming that symbols are *necessarily* means of communicating or mediating something. Do we say, for example, that we smash a picture of a loved one in order to express, communicate or mediate our anger — or is this the form our anger takes? Similarly, our understanding of the kind of reality or world referred to takes the form of symbolic language. To understand that reality we need to explore the grammar of our response; we need to see symbols as a form of language and seek to elucidate the life they have.

We may now turn to the examination of religious symbols as they find expression in religious language. If we ask at the outset what form religious language takes or what life it has for people or what its nature is, we may note that it has been referred to as analogical, as serving a moral purpose and as symbolic.

(A) ANALOGICAL PREDICATION

Those who refer to religious language as the language of analogy would argue that descriptions applied to God in religious discourse cannot be taken literally. There is a difference between what is called the ordinary use of language and the way language is used in religious discourse. The statement 'God is good', for example, does not have the same meaning as the statement 'John is good'. 'Goodness' as applied to God is not identical with 'goodness' as applied to John. Goodness is not being used univocally, or in the same sense, in these statements, but neither is it being used equivocally or in a completely different sense. The relation between 'goodness' as applied to God and 'goodness' as applied to John is analogical.

The doctrine of analogical predication, which is the way Aquinas attempts to resolve the problem of religious language, seeks to show that human 'goodness' only approximates to divine 'goodness' which is the ideal norm, and that we have an indication of what it might mean to talk about the 'goodness' of God by analogy with what we know about human 'goodness'; the one corresponds to the other. Human 'goodness' indicates what 'goodness' might mean when applied to God.[12]

The distinction here is between what might be called the literal and analogical use of language. In religious discourse language is used analogically rather than literally though the existence of God to whom descriptive terms are applied is presupposed by those who uphold the doctrine of analogy. What the doctrine of analogy does is to indicate how certain statements can be made about God without detracting from the mystery of the divine.[13]

It will be seen that the ordinary use of language is regarded as the paradigm of rationality. Or, as Hick describes it, the secular meaning of a word is primary in that it determines the definition of the word.[14] Religious language is seen as an adaptation of ordinary language and in order that ordinary language should not be stretched to breaking point, or eroded by a thousand qualifications, it is necessary in religious discourse to speak of 'analogical predication'.

It might be argued that the fundamental mistake here is to assume in the first place that there is a single paradigm of rationality to which all modes of discourse must conform, or that the secular meaning of a word is primary and that religious discourse is an adaptation of ordinary language. I shall return later to the conceptual confusion involved in imposing the grammar of one mode of discourse on another and failing to distinguish between what is called surface grammar and depth grammar. At this point we might look at the attempt that has been made to describe the nature of religious language as serving a moral purpose. It has been referred to also as follows.

(B) A PSYCHOLOGICAL AID

This particular theory of the nature of religious language is to be found in R. B. Braithwaite's lecture on the nature of religious belief which shows an awareness of the logical positivist belief that all meaningful statements are *either* logical or mathematical propositions on the one hand *or* empirical propositions on the other.

Now it is Braithwaite's view that religious statements do not belong to either of the two categories. They are not logical or mathematical propositions and they are not empirical propositions. They would forfeit the claim to be related to existence if they were placed in the former category and they would have to be in principle falsifiable if they were placed in the latter category. In what way then can they be regarded as meaningful assertions?

Braithwaite argues that they serve a moral function: they express the intention of the person who makes the assertions to act in a certain way. When a Christian asserts that God is love, he is indicating or expressing his 'intention to follow an agapeistic way of life'.[15] The stories associated with religions, such as those concerning the beginning of the world or the last judgment, need not be regarded as facts of past or future history. They are simply psychological aids to moral effort. They need not be believed to be true in the sense that 'the empirical propositions presented by the stories correspond to empirical fact'.[16] Rather the relation between religious stories and the moral way of life is a psychological and causal one. The stories help a man to pursue a moral course of action. The fact that they are not believed to be true makes no appreciable difference to their moral significance.[17]

It is not entirely clear whether Braithwaite considers the stories about creation and judgment to be empirical statements which need to be shown to be empirically false or whether he thinks they are accepted as empirically true by some religious believers when in fact they do not claim to be empirically true and ought not to be so characterized in the first place. In either case these stories should no longer be considered as empirical statements either in themselves or in the minds of the believers but rather as psychological aids to moral conduct.[18]

A similar criticism can be levelled against the empiricist view of the nature of religious language as was brought against the theory of 'analogical predication'. The fundamental presupposition of Braithwaite's theory is that for a religious assertion to be meaningful it must either be an empirical proposition or serve a moral function. For a story to be true it must consist of 'straightforward empirical propositions capable of empirical test'.[19] Stories about creation and judgment and assertion expressing belief in God cannot be considered true or meaningful in that sense, so they must be regarded as serving a moral function.

However, it might be argued that the fundamental mistake here again is to fail to distinguish between the surface grammar and depth grammar of religious discourse and to assume that there is a single paradigm of rationality to which all modes of discourse must conform. What Braithwaite fails to realize is that in religious belief 'the grammar of "belief" and "truth" is not the same as in the case of empirical propositions . . .'[20]

It might be argued further that far from serving a moral function or acting as psychological aids to moral conduct, religious stories are in fact *expressions* of moral outlook which is directly related to religious beliefs. Religious language is not contingently related to moral conduct as a kind of psychological aid; 'it is internally related to it in that it is in terms of this language that the believer's conduct is to be understood.[21]

Some critics of Braithwaite would insist on retaining the referential nature of religious language and they accuse him of being a reductionist when he fails to preserve it. Hick, for example, insists on the factual and not merely symbolic nature of belief in the love and power of God when he claims that 'religious beliefs must be regarded as assertions of fact, not merely as imaginative fictions'.[22] The 'symbolic' implies for Hick, it would seem, something less than real or at least something that is not on the same level as the 'factual'. This is quite a different view from that of Tillich who makes the claim that religious language is indeed symbolic.

(C) SYMBOLIC LANGUAGE

A very full and comprehensive examination of religicus symbols is to be found in Tillich's writings. For him the language of faith is the language of symbols.[23] His fundamental agreement with Otto's analysis of the holy means that he acknowledges the mysterious and fascinating character of the holy and the ambiguity which characterizes man's experience of it. To be aware of the holy is to be aware of the divine presence or of the nature of ultimate concern. The ambiguous character of the holy means that it has both the creative and destructive potential for man which is clearly manifested in the auspicious and threatening form of Śiva, the destroyer god of the Hindu triad. In order that the nature of the holy or the content of the ultimate concern might be truly expressed or communicated it is imperative, in Tillich's view, that it be expressed in symbolic form. Hence his claim that religious faith can only be adequately expressed in symbolic language.

If we inquire why the holy, or the ultimate concern, cannot be expressed immediately or directly rather than through the mediatory function of symbols, the answer would be that immediate or direct expressions do not succeed in communicating the power of the holy. Ultimate concern is that which we take with ultimate seriousness and which we would be ready to suffer and die for, and faith is the state of being grasped by ultimate concern. The character of ultimacy is such that it demands symbols in order to be adequately expressed, for a symbol points to the ultimate, unlocks dimensions of the soul we would not otherwise be aware of and 'opens up levels of reality' which would otherwise remain closed to us.[24]

Tillich uses Picasso's 'Guernica' as an example of the dual function of symbols. The painting starkly expresses man's predicament. In the destruction of the small town of Guernica by Fascist planes one may see manifested man's guilt, anxiety and despair. The expressive style of the painting has religious implications; it points to man's finitude, his bondage to demonic forces and his estrangement from the 'ground of being', a concept to which we shall return. In short, it is a symbol of the Cross, an expression of the human predicament, which raises existential questions about the meaning of existence. The painting offers no answers, but since the human predicament is courageously expressed, answers are anticipated. Depth dimensions are unlocked and levels of reality opened up.[25]

Religions themselves, according to Tillich, are concrete expressions of ultimate concern and these expressions take the form of words and events. One such word is 'God' which is the most fundamental symbol of the holy or of the unconditional. If we object that 'God' cannot be regarded as 'only a symbol',[26] Tillich's reply would be that the objection shows confusion about the true nature of a symbol. The implicit assumption of the statement 'only a symbol' is that the symbolic is somehow less real than the literal and empirical and therefore less true. But in fact the truth and reality of a religious symbol has nothing to do with empirical reality; it has to do with the ultimate and with dimensions of reality not open to the more literal approach. It is true when it is an adequate expression of ultimate concern. When it ceases to be so it dies.

If 'God' is a symbol, we need to examine further what it symbolizes. Tillich's claim is that it symbolizes God as 'ground of being'. That is, 'God' is the symbol for God as the 'ground of being' or 'being itself', which is the only non-symbolic term for the ultimate or unconditional.[27]

If we ask what precisely 'ground of being' or 'being itself' means in this context, we find ourselves facing further questions. What does it mean to say that one is ultimately concerned with the 'ground of being'? Again, if symbols 'participate in' the reality of that to which they point, is not everything symbolic, since everything participates in 'being itself' or the 'ground of the structure of being'?[28]

Can it be that for Tillich the concept of the 'ground of being' or the 'structure of being' preserves the character of ultimacy, and hence is less susceptible to the charge of idolatry, the essence of which is that finite, concrete concerns are elevated to the status of the ultimate concern? It is evident that it makes no sense to ask if God as the 'ground of being' exists or not; it would be like asking if existence exists, which is meaningless. The relevant question is whether the symbol 'God' is an adequate expression of God as ultimate concern or 'ground of being'.

From what has been said we can see that Tillich shares the belief that the language of religious discourse cannot be taken literally. The question that might be asked is whether, by making God the fundamental symbol for the 'ground of being', he is not seeking a form of meaning and intelligibility that corresponds to the paradigm of ordinary language. Does his use of the concept 'ground of being' indicate a desire to maintain the notion of something that might be referred to or something to which the symbol 'God' might point? It is clear that, for him, 'God' as symbol points to a reality and does not simply express the subjective outlook of a religious believer.[29] The subjective factor of religious symbols, he claims, is not 'unrelated to the objective referent of the symbols, but rather has an essential relation to it'.[30]

This being so it might be argued that the use of the phrase 'ground of being' in an objective, referential sense does not necessarily make religious discourse more meaningful. It is possible to make out a case for maintaining that the criteria of the meaningfulness and intelligibility of religious discourse are to be found within religion itself and that religious language does not require verification by either referential or empirical norms. Wittgenstein argues that through religious stories we are presented with a picture of divinity which is itself the reality of God. The picture is non-referential; it does not refer us to external facts, for the whole weight is in the picture. Neither is the picture symbolic in the sense that it points to a referential 'ground of being'. It is itself the reality of God. We shall return to this view.

Tillich resists the view of those who would insist on the factual and not 'merely symbolic' nature of belief in the love and power of God.[31] For him love, power, and justice ought not to be regarded as qualities or attributes of a divine being. They are symbols taken from finite experience and attributed to God as the symbol of the 'ground of being'. Similarly acts attributed to God do not refer to what God as a divine being did in the past or will do in the future.[32]

But the question is whether Tillich does not return to a similar referential use of language when he speaks of God as the symbol for the 'ground of being'. What he says about the subjective factor of a religious symbol bearing an essential relation to its objective referent and about the symbol's transparency to the referent for which it stands seems to suggest that he does. That is, the ultimate is hypostatized. In which case it might be argued that his theory of symbols does not prevent him ultimately from imposing the grammar of one mode of discourse on another and failing to distinguish between what is called the surface grammar and depth grammar of religious discourse.[33] His basic assumption seems to be that religious language has to be referential in some sense or another. The mediatory function and representational character of his theory of religious symbols enables him to retain the referential nature of religious language without having to accept the factual nature of religious discourse.

An alternative view of the nature of religious language is the view that religious beliefs play the kind of role a picture plays in a man's life. This view might be attributed to Wittgenstein who claims that religious stories, pictures and catechisms constitute the language of belief or the response of belief. This is the form belief takes and we understand the nature of belief when we explore the grammar of the response. To elucidate the language of belief is not to seek an explanation for belief, but to clarify the role it has within a culture. Wittgenstein, for example, says:

> Suppose we said that a certain picture might play the role of constantly admonishing me, or I always think of it. Here an enormous difference would be between those people for whom the picture is constantly in the foreground, and the others who just didn't use it at all.[34]

On this view it is suggested that religious stories introduce us to the reality of God. What we are presented with by the stories is a picture of divinity and the divinity is the reality of God. The fact that we do not see what the picture represents does not detract from the reality of God, because it is not the purpose of the picture to refer us to external facts nor does it depend on external facts. Rather the picture determines the attitude of believers to the facts.

According to Wittgenstein the term 'God' is among the earliest terms we learn. We understand its meaning through stories, pictures and catechisms. The picture reveals the reality of God and the 'whole *weight* may be in the picture'.[35]

What this means is that the criteria for the meaningfulness of religious discourse are to be found within religion itself and not in its verifiability or falsifiability in accordance with empirical norms. To insist that what is regarded as intelligible in one context must be intelligible in the same way in all contexts, or that the same criteria of intelligibility apply in all modes of discourse, may be regarded as philosophical prejudice. The attempt to posit general criteria of meaning that can be applied to all significant utterances points to the presupposition already referred to, namely that the ordinary use of language is the paradigm of rationality.

But what does 'the ordinary use of language' mean? Winch claims that philosophers are guilty of 'arbitrary linguistic legislation' when they insist on specifying the meaning a word must have:

> The 'must' is not a logical 'must' but simply the 'must' of their own preferences, or the 'must' of one context which they have elevated consciously or unconsciously to be a standard for all others.[36]

The same point applies when the claim is made that the secular use of a word is primary and that its religious use is an adaptation of secular use.

Both the theory of analogical predication and the empiricist view of religion as a psychological aid to moral endeavour share the common belief that the language of religious discourse cannot be taken literally. They differ in that those who uphold the doctrine of analogical predication presuppose the existence of God to whom descriptive terms are applied as, for example, in the statement 'God is good', while upholders of the empiricist view do not make the same assumption. For them the assertion 'God is love' is simply the declaration of an intention to live a life dedicated to love.

The theory of the symbolic nature of religious language shares the belief that the language of religious discourse cannot be taken literally. In common with the theory of analogical predication it holds that language is not being used univocally when applied to that which is ultimate. The question may be asked whether it is the case that if symbols do not point to a reality beyond themselves they must of necessity express the subjective outlook of religious believers? Can it not be maintained that symbols have a life of their own and that the unity of symbols is to be found in the language of religious discourse? They are related to one another more within the context of religious life than because they participate in the reality to which they point.

If that is the case, then the validity and truth of a religious symbol would not depend so much on its self-negating quality, or its transparency to the referent for which it stands, as on the life it has in the context of belief within a particular culture or tradition. What might be said then is that what Tillich calls the metaphysical ground of being gets its meaning from the symbols used in a particular form of life and not vice versa.

If this is so, it is a mistake to assume that we know the reality symbols point to, or participate in, prior to an analysis of the symbols themselves. To talk of the adequacy of symbols and the extent to which they represent the ultimate is to prejudge the issue. We know what is meant by the ultimate, or the reality of God, from an exploration of the grammar of the response. Symbols constitute the language of religion. We need to see them as a form of language and seek to elucidate the life they have.

NOTES

1 A. R. Radcliffe-Brown, *Structure and Function in Primitive Society*, London, 1952, p. 143, quoted by J. Skorupski, *Symbol and Theory*, Cambridge UP, 1976, p. 117.

2 T. Parsons, *The Structure of Social Action*, London, 1968, p. 416, quoted by Skorupski, op. cit., p. 118.

3 Mary Douglas, *Natural Symbols*, London, 1970, p. 11.

4 Paul Tillich, 'The Religious Symbol', pp. 301 – 2, *Religious Experience and Truth*, ed. Sidney Hook, New York UP, 1968, pp. 301 – 21.

5 Tillich, 'The Meaning and Justification of Religious Symbols', p. 4, *Rel. Exp. & Truth*, pp. 3 – 11.
6 Ibid. p. 4.
7 Bernard J. F. Lonergan, 'Reality, Myth, Symbol', p. 31; *Myth, Symbol and Reality*, ed. Alan M. Olsen, Notre Dame UP, 1980, pp. 31 – 7.
8 Ibid. p. 34.
9 Jacques Waardeburg, 'Symbolic Aspects of Myth', p. 43, *Myth, Symbol and Reality*, pp. 41 – 68.
10 Paul Ricoeur, *Interpretation Theory: Discourse and the Surplus of Meaning*, Texas Christian UP, Fort Worth, 1976, pp. 41 – 68. Quoted by Waardeburg, op. cit., p. 42.
11 Tillich 'The Meaning . . .', p. 5.
12 Cf. John Hick, *Philosophy of Religion*, Prentice-Hall, New Jersey, 1973, pp. 69 – 71.
13 Ibid. p. 71.
14 Ibid. p. 69.
15 R. B. Braithwaite, *An Empiricist's View of the Nature of Religious Belief*, Cambridge UP, 1955, p. 18.
16 Ibid. p. 24.
17 Ibid. p. 27.
18 Cf. D. Z. Phillips, *Religion Without Explanation*, Oxford, 1976, pp. 141 – 2.
19 Braithwaite, op. cit., p. 23.
20 Phillips, op. cit., p. 143.
21 Ibid. p. 144.
22 Hick, op. cit., p. 83.
23 Paul Tillich, *Dynamics of Faith*, New York, 1958, p. 45.
24 Ibid. p. 42.
25 Tillich, *Theology of Culture*, Oxford UP, 1959, p. 45.
26 Hick, for example, insists on the factual and not 'merely symbolic' nature of belief in the love and power of God. See his *Philosophy of Religion*, p. 83.
27 Tillich, *Dynamics of Faith*, p. 46.
28 Cf. Tillich, *Systematic Theology*, vol. I, London 1968, p. 265.
29 Tillich, 'The Religious Symbol', p. 304.
30 Ibid. p. 306.
31 Hick, *Philosophy of Religion*, p. 83.
32 Tillich, *Dynamics of Faith*, p. 47.
33 He is guilty of a similar misuse of language in his treatment of the historical Jesus. See my article 'Paul Tillich and the Historical Jesus', CJSR, 1974/5, pp. 120 – 8.
34 Ludwig Wittgenstein, *Lectures and conversations on Aesthetics, Psychology and Religious Belief*, Oxford, 1966, p. 56.
35 Ibid. p. 72.
36 See D. Z. Phillips, *Faith and Philosophical Enquiry*, London, 1970, p. 17.

2

THE SYMBOLISM OF INDIAN ART

Philip S. Rawson

Art symbolism in India can only be interpreted in broad and consistent terms across a range of different geographical and social conditions. We have to call those terms religious and metaphysical. It is a characteristic of Indian mind and culture that it focuses on constancies and is not fascinated or diverted by the multiplicity and variety of instances and individuals or by historical change.

All religions, including our own 'secular' ones, are founded upon a clutch of interwoven 'fossil' symbols whose metaphysical references serve to structure otherwise inexpressible intuitions about the origin, meaning and destiny of the human world, and guide people's behaviour as well as their spiritual effort. They link together experience at personal, social and cosmological levels. It is these we shall be looking into here, as a unified armature for cultural interpretation.

We must beware of falling into the fashionable error of interpreting other people's behaviour and ideas in terms of the reductive conceptual systems native to our own culture, thus translating them without understanding. If we do so and approach Indian art externally by trying to classify contributory aspects that are subsidiary as if they were somehow primary 'causes' giving meaning to the structures of the art, we will never see what their true meaning is. Michael Polanyi[1] has amply demonstrated the processes whereby we supersede subsidiary perceptions by a leap of the mind to grasp a focal meaning in any act of understanding, from the humblest to the most elevated.

This of course does not mean that there are no differences of theoretical conformation among the many Indian cultural expressions. Exactly the reverse. It implies that the meanings of all such differences can readily be accommodated within and contribute to the overall intuition.

At the root of Indian artistic symbolism lies the Indian conception of time. The West tends to think of time as a single dynamic process, a forward movement from a past beginning identified either as a divine act of creation via Genesis or a scientific 'big bang', towards a future end when 'there shall be no more time', again perhaps by divine act or by entropy — a state of total inertia. In our 'present' we ride an 'objective cosmic process' in which we have no real part.

This view of time is reflected under deep-rooted ideas of progress, revolution, Last Judgement, all within the same overall time-bracket, however much our relative apprehensions of remote regions and eras of the universe may be adrift. Because it is ours we tend to believe this is the only possible 'right' view of time.

Our art is populated by beings whom we can imagine to have come 'into frame' from somewhere and will pass on to somewhere else later on. We favour foregrounds filled with active entities and with events resulting from their interaction. Our principal symbols are bodies which are images of active wills or synthesized forces performing work along the same overall direction of time towards a single future horizon.

The Indian concept of time is quite different from this. Of course, the ordinary Indian sees himself performing in a broadly common time involving succession, shift and movement. But in the Indian imagination shapes of transience are seen as qualities arising within epochs, each of which is a whole. Nothing that happens alters the whole in any real sense. Appearance and change happen constantly, unfolding a series of ages (*yugas*) from an invisible source which maintains the cosmos in the condition of existence.

By about 80 B.C. the Indian imagination was envisaging time on a truly vast scale, with universes as 'numberless as the sand-grains of the Ganges', each complete with its own space and time conceived in thousands of millions of years, appearing and vanishing like bubbles.[2] Against this vast panorama of phenomena an individual person might seem totally irrelevant, were it not for the cardinal and ancient Upaniṣadic doctrine that such universes, collectively and individually, appear within the absolute, the *brahman* (whose Buddhist counterpart is the *dharmakāya*), only in response to the particularization of each individual self. And neither the universe nor the limited self have any independent presence as object save to a correlative subject. And to the ultimate subject, the *ātman*, all such phenomena are illusions.

This means that there can be no once-for-all genesis, no material 'big bang', for an individual universe. For genesis would imply a unique beginning in time pointing towards a unique end. Folk belief and common experience mistake what can be called logical priority for temporal priority. But to the Indian mind genesis is a continuing function, continuing only as long as it appears to continue. To help intuit the absolute which unfolds its infinity of implicate orders is the main function of art — along with ritual, drama, poetry and philosophy, all of which are in fact inseparable from the arts.

The relationship between the phenomenal and the absolute, which subtends, sustains and explicates it, is indicated in two images of major deities well known in Hindu art — Śiva as dancer, Natarāja or Tandavalakṣanam, and Viṣṇu Anantasāyin asleep on the endless serpent of the ocean of non-being. In both cases the humanoid image represents the reality-level of the absolute; to each absolute the phenomenal stands in the relation of the dance to the higher reality of the Dancer, or of the inner dream to the Sleeper. The cultural task for humankind is to assimilate to Dancer and Sleeper.

The ideas of time and space described produce a kind of inclusive bracketing of all forms of thought, by which temporal succession and spatial extension are taken comprehensively. What I have called the absolute represents the focal meaning. From whatever point reasoning and experience begin, they can only reach coherence by virtue of the wholeness of the absolute which cannot be subject to any of them and to which all the subsidiary components of perception and thought refer.

In the Hindu context the absolute is called the *brahman* which acts as the supreme whole of subsidiary 'wholes' and which ultimately justifies the integrity of all lesser structures.

The great Sanskrit grammarian and theorist of language Bhartṛhari (5th cent. A.D.) explained how the overall meaning of sentence-structures originates with the unity of the *brahman*. The word-components amount to break-downs exfoliated from the whole, each bracketing a specific reach of experience within it, the spread of the whole set conveying something of the scope of the whole. A Japanese scholar[3] has pointed out that the medieval Sanskrit written language developed a strong leaning towards nouns and noun-formations from verb and adjective, and the elimination of most true verbs, which he sees as connected with the Indian urge towards overall unity and taking processes as qualities of permanent states — qualities being forms of relationship as F. H. Bradley has described in *Appearance and Reality*.

The Indian conception of integral time allows any time to be compressed or extended, as in some European fairy tales. This function appears in a story told in a religious text called the Yogavasiṣṭharāmāyana about a divine teacher whose pupil kept demanding that the teacher explain to him the nature of *māyā*, phenomenal illusion. So the teacher sent him to fetch water from a village nearby. There the pupil fell in love with the daughter of the house where he first went to beg water. He married her and lived with her for many years, producing much-loved children. Then, one night while a terrible storm raged, the whole family was swept away terrified in a torrential flood. At the peak of his anguish the pupil 'awoke' to find himself back where he had started, with his teacher asking him gently 'Where is the water, my child?' As well as revealing the nature of illusion, this story also casts an interesting light on the well-known Indian conception of reincarnation.

The linguistic bracketing is paralleled in the languages of Indian art. These are based upon broad, inclusive shapes which correspond with conceptualized reaches of the represented image — thorax, hips, arm, leg etc. Indian sculpture composes its bodies according to established canons of proportion from sets of standard, entirely convex volumes. Concavities only occur where convexities meet. This art seeks always to produce as nearly as possible a totally continuous surface uniting the volumes. This appears as a continuous undulating contour as delighted hand and eye move around the figure. Where breaks are unavoidable to accommodate sharp projections, at least part of the surface maintains its continuity. Draperies usually follow the volumes of the body and only turn concave where they are meant to be floating free.

Traditional painting comprehends and renders intelligible its spaces as well as its solid volumes in terms of enclosed areas of space; bodies are sometimes contained by an undulant contour derived from sculpture, fortified by modelling tone just within the contour where the surface turns away from the eye. The artist uses sets of standard curved lines, knowing how each should run before he makes it. The areas represent shaped progressive subdivisions of ground inwards only from its inclusive format: wall spaces in shrine or palace or, in smaller work, partitions laid out on the sheet of palm-leaf, cloth or paper. The negative shapes remain undefined. Colours are treated similarly as a range of comprehensive types, each colour filling its area of surface virtually unmodulated. Each set of colours laid into the areas generates a particular recognized feeling-tone. Individual colours may also have intentional symbolic meanings, say as representing substances or elements of feelings, the colours of garments or the skins of people from different parts of India.

The metaphors which lie at the bases of the symbols work by pointing at physical correlates which are called on to mean more than they are. The analogy between the correlate and its meaning crosses the regions of the ordinary world, indicating a common form or mode of operation between the physical correlate and the non-physical match. This form is not supposed to be 'objective and verifiable' in ordinary terms, but only recognizable by the human complete with his or her sense-faculties, in the manner of poetic imagery. The linking may work through visual, taste, sound or touch relationships.

The two views of the physical referent were recognized by A. K. Coomaraswamy[4] as *pratyakṣa* (common view) and *parokṣa* (higher view). The *parokṣa* aspect may be shown in art by an image of an object which bypasses the *pratyakṣa* aspect and extracts and emphasizes its formal, affective element. For example, the *parokṣa* aspect of the ordinary *pratyakṣa* opening lotus may be taken as the radiating petal-form subtending elaborate pierced ornament, which illuminates the symbol-metaphor of 'lotus'. Just as the lotus flower appears and opens on its single stalk above the surface of water from its rhizome in the mud of the bottom, so phenomena or deities cross from the invisible beyond into the light of common day.

The clutch of symbols and metaphors shaping Indian artistic symbolism is closely woven together. In any artistic complex where they appear together they reflect significance upon each other. This mutual enhancement is lost if they are isolated and discussed as single symbols with self-contained and consistent references. Each individual art-work is a complex structure of symbols, none of which alone can convey the intended meaning, and some of which may seem incompatible. Nevertheless we are obliged to approach them singly; and this is what generations of scholars have done, including A. K. Coomaraswamy, Paul Mus, F. D. K. Bosch and Mircea Eliade. To analyse subsidiary component elements provides us with an 'armature' for interpreting the focal meaning of the varied combinations and manifestations.

The basic symbols with their metaphors are: the centre, with its levels and circuits; the lotus; the mountain; the generative and fertilizing waters; organic juice as energy; sex and its physical attributes; the inverted tree; descent and ascent through tiers; speech and the alphabet. We can best think of them all as Bhartṛhari did of the words of sentences, as separations within a whole to enable it to be exfoliated.

The centre is the most important symbol of all. It may be as well to indicate why it is the most adequate symbol for any comprehensive whole, since to the Western mind it would be the enclosing circumference. The point is that a circumference sharply demarcates what it encloses from what lies outside its boundary, thus affirming the existence of the latter. The wholes we are discussing are intended to be extensive, not simple exclusive categorized distinctions. A focal generative centre from which they expand without definite limit is thus the strongest symbol for what is meant. Like the centre of a wheel it is the centre of a universe radiating from it and revolving around it in its own plane. It has an implied vertical axis, with top and bottom.

The central mountain of the world, mount Meru, incorporates the centre. Old mythology describes how the corps of gods, pulling together on that great snake called Ananta (endless), whom they had wrapped around the mountain like a rope, used Meru as churning stick (the axis) to churn and solidify the worlds like butter out of the milk of undifferentiated chaos.

Later diagrams describe the space of the world as a circular plane disc laid out around the central Meru and encircled without being shaped by the ocean of undifferentiated Being. The disc may be subdivided into coloured areas laid out in the cardinal directions and interpreted as mythical geography or as fields of substance. Layers of relative density may be ranged one above the other on the axis. The disc of the heavens lies just above the region of the earth. The generative energy of the universe flows in, pure, at the apex of the axis, becoming denser as it percolates downwards radiating at each level.

The dot, either raised in stone or painted at the centre of a diagram, represents the central point where the previously invisible energy of the absolute flows into existence to unfold, like a lotus, the phenomenal world. The Sanskrit word for 'dot', *bindu*, also means 'seed'. Seed and energy are interpreted in the sexual sense. In the central shrine of all Śiva temples this image is referred to by a stone-carved erect phallus. The shrine is a cubic, stone 'womb-house', symbolizing the objectivity of the female earth into which the vitalizing energy of the seed projects.

The central axis is also symbolized, especially in early art of the centuries B.C., by the post, pillar or column. A column with a lotus capital, or with lotuses on its faces, implies a central axis rising from the absolute depth of the generative waters in which the actual lotus roots lie hidden. Many Indian columns have bases shaped like pots — containers for those same waters whose place is not literally under the earth, but beyond it.

The tower of the Hindu temple, fully evolved by about A.D. 1000, is another emblem of the central axis, conceived as a stone-cut image of mount Meru. Around it are slung high invisible cities beyond sense, then the ordinary heavens and below them the common earth. At the summit of the tower a single flat cake-like disc of stone edged with vertical radiating flanges symbolizes the central point where the energy beyond penetrates into the realm of manifestation.

The lower tiers of the shrine-tower symbolize the celestial regions; South Indian temple towers bear ranks of small blind pavilions. At the level of the shrine itself, raised on a high plinth and approached by a staircase, is the main shrine containing the icon of the resident deity, with its antechamber and public hall whose own roofs are worked externally as lesser mountains. The inner ceiling of the shrine is often carved as a lotus opening downwards from its stalk which is thus conceived as running down within the tower. It is often vividly carved and elaborately fretted. This symbolizes the primary appearance of the transcendent deity into its physical icon immediately beneath.

Around the exterior of the temple, at shrine level, are bands of niches containing figures of the divine inhabitants of the heavens: gods proper as well as lesser beings, including musicians and dancers. Among them are the *apsaras*, divine girls of surpassing beauty filled with inexhaustible sexual desire who may reward dead military heroes and wise men with sexual delights far beyond those known on earth. All wear crowns, jewels and splendid clothes to signify their possession of all that the heart can desire. At ground level, at the foot of the temple, there spreads out through space and time the untransfigured and banal world which we poor humans inhabit, responding to our individual experiences, labouring and suffering. In it the temple appears as a centre as yet unassimilated to our inner understanding.

Within the Hindu temple two main functions are carried out before the shrine: the first is worship and the second offering ceremonial gifts to the deity who is supposed to return the offering with interest — a rite of exchange between men and gods. Worship and offering are carried out daily, with special fervour and ritual on special occasions. Normal worship (*pūjā*) consists of presenting before the deity acts and objects which symbolize the human senses: food for taste, perfumes or flowers for smell, fine cloths for touch, bells or music for hearing, lights and dancing for sight. Many large temples used to have a corps of resident musicians and female dancers, earthly representatives of the celestials depicted on the heaven bands, who perform as their divine prototypes do to make the temple a true image of celestial glory.

The innermost icon of the shrine is usually a major sculpture into which the deity has been induced to enter by appropriate ceremonials, just as he or she does when invoked into a temporary painted image in folk ceremonies. Normally the icon is carved in stone or cast in bronze. As a matter of historical fact a rustic emblem of the divine entering the world — a special ancient tree, a stone painted with stripes, a rock face — may have served as the original focus around which a whole temple grew. And many emblems are used to symbolize the divine centre for domestic worship, including a pot, a miniature tree, a snake, a *liṅga* or a small bronze anthropomorphic image of a patron deity.

The exterior surfaces of many temples are carved with multiple vertical and horizontal mouldings, complex rhythmic rebates and lavish foliage decoration. This last symbolizes the sap or juice of transcendent fertilizing energy which flows through the whole fabric of the temple. It radiates its influence into the terrain around, perhaps through an attached system of water-irrigation from a reservoir. The sculptural style in which the bodies of the divine beings are carved on the outer surface shows them inflated like bubbles into total convexity, which suggests that they are illusory, like everything else, and only appear at the meeting place of original energy encountering human desires. The rich and elaborate ornaments they wear also symbolize the divine abundance and wealth that imbue the temple. Kings and queens used to identify with the icons in temples which they built or patronized, claiming divine sanction to rule and provide both water by hydraulic engineering and social control from the sacred centre, whether Hindu or Buddhist.

It is worth mentioning that an important Hindu aesthetic theory was developed on the basis of a fifth century A.D. classical drama text called the Nātyaśāstra, culminating about A.D. 1000. The theory conceived the time-course of the events portrayed in a play or poem leading to its resolution, as paralleling a return to the original centre from which the human world arises, in terms of feeling and symbolic act. In a sense all the Indian arts are concerned with gathering, vivifying and reconstituting creatively 'prior' conditions of human experience. The modes of music, and the prototypes of sculpture and painting, are thought to exist as superb heavenly entities, the task of each artist being to reveal and expose the beauties inherent in the celestial original. Art therefore seeks, so far as possible, to charm the eye, the ear, the hand and the mind; and engage them into the imagery of the whole.

Another principal image of the centre is the tall, domed and peaked Buddhist stūpa or dagoba, a type of monument still very much alive, of which thousands have been built. The earliest (third to second century B.C.) were hillock- or barrow-like humps of earth. Near their summits relics of the body of the Buddha or Buddhist saints — hair, fragments of bone, a tooth — were deposited in a shaft a few feet deep, surrounded by a small square railing. Over this centre was set on a post an honorific umbrella. This became first threefold, then progressively elaborated into a towering superstructure supported by a huge axial pillar embodying the image of the world-centre, to which the Buddha's teaching pointed. Around each stūpa was an enclosure with gates opening on to the four directions of the world, implying that the stūpa was the 'centre'. In southern regions these gates had 'doorsteps' carved as half-lotuses; and a preaching hall in which the Buddhist doctrine was recited by the order of monks to the faithful was aligned with the stūpa. Decorations were either symbolic or conveyed narratives central to Buddhist teaching. The stūpa itself grew gradually taller and taller, until it came to resemble a massive tower based on a spreading plinth containing an undercroft housing Buddha icons.

In its vertical sense the stūpa evolved five principal levels which were interpreted as relative densities of the elementary ingredients of reality. The base symbolized solid earth. The dome symbolized water, the die crowning it air and the conical tiers of original umbrellas fire. A pointed finial symbolized the subtlest form beyond which was only the absolute, the *dharmakāya*. Some Nepalese stūpas are given eyes painted on the die, suggesting that the whole stūpa represents an ultimate or transcendent human identity. The symbolism of the circular centre, with another centre above, and four surrounding regions, became a focal notion in much medieval Indian and Tibetan ritual and meditative practice. An extremely elaborate system of anthropomorphic principles evolved which represent symbolically the regions of human feeling, action, doctrine and experience.

The humanoid Buddha image embodies another complex of ideas based upon the vertical axis. The Buddha — who was a human teacher (*c.* 563 – 483 B.C.) and repudiated absolutely the idea that he was divine — came to be thought of as having three bodies. There was his 'actual' body, the *nirmāṇakāya*, which could be but was rarely represented in art. Since he was held to have become fully identified with the absolute, his 'absolute body', the *dharmakāya*, is by definition unrepresentable. But between the two, a third body, the 'body of glory', the *sambhogakāya*, was capable of representing symbolically the Buddha nature — icons carved in stone, cast in bronze, painted or made in any material according to canonical prescriptions of proportion and layout. Its physical attributes, some going back to ancient astrological theory, symbolized aspects of the true doctrine. The *sambhogakāya* is smooth and rounded, golden in colour. It has, among other characteristics, a bump on the top of the skull, called *uṣṇīṣa*; long arms; webbed finger; lotus marks on palms of the hands and soles of the feet; a twist of hair between eyebrows and breasts. Even when gesturing or walking its total calm is conveyed by physical symmetry.

The *sambhogakāya* is represented in a limited number of canonical postures, performing symbolic gestures. The postures include standing, walking, lying down to die, and sitting cross-legged, erect. The gestures include 'preaching', offering blessings and protection. The seated body also represents the 'meditation' during which the Buddha gained his ultimate insight into the absolute and became identical with the *dharmakāya*.

Meditation is a key notion, a central focus of all Indian religion and art. There are different doctrinal explanations of the nature of meditation, Hindu, Buddhist and Jain, each one being modified by the followers of the other two. Broadly speaking, meditation implies looking intensely within oneself so as to watch and control the movements and urges of the mind and the psycho-physical organism, focusing them on to a centre. Since the personal mind-body compound is held to be an essential correlative to the perceived and experienced world, subject generating object through desire and attachment by the intermediacy of a system of progressive objectification: therefore meditation also focuses and controls the phenomenal world. The consequence of successful meditation is the transcending of physical, fragmented reality into a unified state of uninhibited, undistracted calm; it brings release from the busy hither and thither of wild monkey-like mental activity, the anxious struggle and fantasy which keep most people bound into their ordinary state of misery. The calm of release puts an end to rebirth, to pain and submission to the trammels of time and sequence.

Whereas ordinary people may remain content with the external symbolism of the temple, the erect column of the spine of the meditator is meant actually to become not only his or her centre, but THE centre. There are different kinds of meditative discipline, or yoga, whose followers may disagree in detail. But some, often called Tantric, carry through the identification of the spinal column with the cosmic centre, and with the structure of the temple, by means of a system of symbols and bodily acts based upon the idea of a 'subtle' body within the gross. This guides the processes of such yoga. Before pursuing this further we must first consider the imagery of the Goddess.

From very ancient times, in many regions of the world, the creative activity of nature was connected by an obvious analogy with the generative powers of women. A female figure, a goddess, came to symbolize this activity very early on. In India 'Pṛthivī (the earth), mother of all', was the first of many such symbolic figures. Their sculptured and painted forms convey graphically their female generative attributes for the sake of which they were adored, worshipped and prayed to. This ancient functional female divinity remained interpolated into many stages of the complex we have so far discussed; and her many artistic *personae* represent her various capacities, including the generation of fertility and wealth. In general she is called *śakti* (from the Sanskrit root *śak* = to be able) signifying 'power to act'.

Her importance is great. As *prakṛti* she symbolizes the first stage of the appearance of undifferentiated material actuality everywhere. She translates the absolute into any of the forms it projects. Obviously, as the 'Great Mother' of all that exists, she is the lotus-power that condenses nuclear energy into actual shapes which are, of course, phenomena, illusory in any ultimate sense. But without her no male seed-energy becomes actual. She is the form and colour which the invisible centre projects. Even the centre-dot would be invisible without her. She is the body of the temple, transmitting energy downwards and radiating it outwards. She is the mirror refracting and diffracting the original divine spark. She also is the power of speech and grammar, embodied in the sacred and beautiful letters of the Sanskrit alphabet, who lays out the intelligible structure of the world, the webs of libido and knowledge, of language and the arts by which we express it. She is also the shaper of the human body through which the energy flows via the inner subject to project its differentiated world on to her cloud of basic objectivity (*prakṛti*). She is the creating, sustaining and terminating power of time for bodily beings and forms.

All women personify her and act as her surrogates. To fulfil her roles sculpture and painting depict her holding appropriate implements — a mirror, a musical instrument, a lotus, a sword. Divinely beautiful, like a sixteen-year-old girl, she is a mother with large breasts and capacious womb. But when she is interpreted as an agent of destruction by disease or warfare, she is depicted as ravaged and bloodstained. As personification of death and the cremation ground she is shown black, red-eyed with fangs and a lolling tongue — and called Kālī. As Durgā, personifying the combined energies of all the gods of heaven, she is displayed as beautiful and riding a huge lion. In sum she is Time as active process and appearance; which brings us full circle to where we began — and back to the meditating yogi who is the hero and culmination of Indian culture. For the agency he needs to enlist is, of course, *śakti*'s, whether acknowledged by masculine pride or not.

Every person is an image of the centre, like every temple, if they can only know it. The task of every meditator is to identify with the one centre. The spinal column may become a kind of hollow tube into which flows through the crown of the head — sometimes identified as the main cranial suture or the pineal gland — the divine energy, conceived either as a juice, milk from the udder of a divine cow, or a stream of vibration. The subtle body acts like an inverted tree, passing the juice as its sap along myriad branching channels through the organs of mind and sense out into realization as the world. Some interpretations see no need for *śakti*. Others recognize her essential agency in this whole process.

The yogic/meditative process is described in different terms, including artistic ones. The basic procedure involves gathering to the centre all the energies diffused — and wasted — in projecting the illusory world of suffering. One method may be to condense them into the ancient sacred *mantra*, the syllable 'OM' (*a-u-m*), which the meditator chants repeatedly, beginning the opening vowel low down at a deep pitch, prolonging and passing the vibration up into the nasal sinuses and skull as a fine hum. The passing may be thought of as up a hollow tube in the spine which then becomes active and radiant.

More elaborate meditative imagery envisages levels up the central column of the subtle body, between crotch and crown, represented by lotuses with different numbers of petals. In normal life the original energy is disseminated all the way through to the bottom; the lotuses droop down, and the energy condenses finally into the form of a personal serpent goddess called Kuṇḍalinī which lies sleeping and coiled in the lowest lotus, covering the lower end of the spinal tube with her mouth. The snake is an ancient Indo-European image of human spinal energy. By yogic techniques, some of them sexual, Kuṇḍalinī is made to awaken, straighten, enter the tube and ascend, vitalizing and opening each lotus as she goes, to gather the world-distributing energy dispersed at each level. At the crown of the head she unites her gathered actualizing energies with the invisible (male) originating seed; and the way opens to the beyond, the absolute.

Aids in this process are first chanted syllables, *mantras*, which help in gathering and condensing various dispersed sonic-frequency energies; and second *yantras*, which are diagrams performing an analogous function for dispersed visual energies. The latter are usually painted on a smallish scale (though architectural ones are known from medieval times) and contemplated during ritual worship (*pūjā*) and meditation. They may be inscribed with the letters of mantras and passages of sacred texts, which embody functions of the goddess. And the symbols of all kinds which appear in them are designed to aid in precipitating the original 'mass forms' or 'fields' of experience on the way to total reconstitution. The sense-emblems — lights for sight, bell or music for sound, fabric for touch, food for taste and flowers for smell — can signify the total field of each sense; and serve as focuses for meditation on them.

Altogether, we can see the functions of all India's artistic symbolism as being: to help reverse human experience of genesis, reintegrate the wasteful entropy of time and regain the continuing original whole; all this without denying humanity, but instead awakening the human faculties and responses as fuel for the effort.

NOTES

1 Michael Polanyi, *Meaning*, Chicago, 1975, chap. II and III.

2 Ancient post-Vedic reckoning (e.g. in the Sulva Sūtras) dealt with huge powers of 10 (e.g. 10^{53}), imitated in early Buddhist reckoning of the time-span of the Buddha's reincarnations (e.g. 3×10^{51} years). Many universes are mentioned in the Mahāvastu of the Buddhist Mahāsanghikas, in relation

to the Lokottara doctrine. The phrase quoted comes from the Saddharmapundarika, chap. II. Vast numbers and scales of cosmos were familiar in Hindu myth and philosophy by the fourth century A.D., along with the mathematical concept of infinity.

3 Hajime Nakamura, 'Time in Indian and Japanese Thought', in *The Philosophy of Time*, 1968.

4 A. K. Coomaraswamy, essay 'Paroksha', chap. V of *The Transformation of Nature into Art*, New York, 1934, repr. 1956 (but not included in R. Lipsey's anthology).

3

SYMBOLISM IN THE VEDAS AND ITS CONCEPTUALIZATION

Karel Werner

Indian religious tradition, not surprisingly, claims supramundane origin for its holy scriptures, the Vedas. This view has been duly noted by Western scholars, but it has never been given serious consideration. In fact, it has always been tacitly dismissed by them, basically for two main reasons. First, in the early days of Indian studies most scholars had complete personal faith in Christian revelation and the idea of taking in any way seriously the claim of another tradition to have divine sanction and of trying to explain what that claim might mean outside the context of the faith of the followers of that tradition never really occurred to them.

Second, many scholars have tended to interpret the Vedic tradition from a positivistic standpoint and characterize it as a primitive or archaic stage in the development of Indian religious thought.[1] In that kind of approach the claim virtually all religions, including the Vedic one, make for their origins as stemming from a divine source has no chance of being objectively examined as to its meaning in the context of the history of religions.

However, the progress of academic research in the field of religious studies variously termed 'history of religion(s)', 'comparative religion' or even the 'science of religion' (*Religionswissenschaft*) achieved in the past two or three decades[2] makes such attitudes rather obsolete. Dismissing or ignoring a claim within any religious tradition, like the one made for the Vedas, would perpetuate the implicit conviction of the superiority of the position held by the interpreter, be it one of the uniqueness of the Christian tradition in having the sole right of regarding itself as possessing the divine authority, or one of the positivistic variety which sees such a claim as lacking any possible foundation in reality and as, therefore, basically meaningless from the point of view of epistemology.

However, the academic discipline concerned with the study of religions cannot forever brush aside the insistence of religions, variously expressed, that they have supramundane origin. Surely, it must be a part of the task of scholarship to interpret, within its conceptual framework, even such a claim in a meaningful way.

In India this claim is mostly made in the usual manner: the Vedas are believed to be the product of direct divine revelation. And on the surface it appears, as L. Renou argued,[3] that this revelation has been very much revered but seldom really followed either in spirit or in letter. However, it is now possible and necessary to acknowledge the complexity of the Vedic message which was delivered simultaneously on several levels — addressing ordinary people, educated classes like priests and aristocrats, and also a spiritually minded minority of philosophers, mystics and yogis — through the medium of the language of symbols and myths.[4] This symbolical and mythological idiom of the Vedas requires in our time careful interpretation. The meaning of the symbols and myths has to be deciphered and then they have to be translated into the developed conceptual language of our age. Then our attitude to and understanding of the Vedas may substantially change and we shall see the question of the origin of the Vedas and their destiny in India in a different light from Renou and others.

In applying the hermeneutical principle of multi-level interpretation of the Vedas for the purpose of expressing their messages in the conceptual idiom of our time, it is necessary to ascertain in each case what levels of interpretation can be seen as justified and to decide which level of interpretation one is concerned with. It is essential, at the same time, to avoid mixing or confusing different levels of interpretation.

The aim of this paper is to concentrate on the higher level of interpretation, called by Yāska *ādhyātmika*, which one can term 'spiritual' or, perhaps, mystical, and to demonstrate with a few selected examples that the Vedic mind reached what can be regarded as the highest peak of spiritual achievement, comparable to that of the Upaniṣads and Buddhism or also to that of neo-Platonic and medieval mysticism. In fact one could say that the Vedic achievement was perhaps approximated or reached anew in some subsequent epochs of development of Indian religions, but has hardly ever been surpassed.

First of all the claim that the Vedas are a divine revelation has also to be interpreted on more than one level. On the usual religious level (*ādhidaivika* in Yāska's terminology) it is simply a matter of faith. On the spiritual level of interpretation it represents what the mystics and yogis refer to as personal vision or direct experience of the transcendent. The phrase 'divine revelation' (*śruti*) thus becomes a symbolical expression for what in conceptual language would be called direct perception of the transcendent and is, in fact, often expressed in the Vedic hymns by one single word, *dhīti* (vision).[5]

If this is so, then the Indian tradition never really digressed from the Vedas, but kept renewing or trying to renew the vision of their originators, the seers (*ṛṣis*), through the spiritual endeavours of its religious leaders, yogis and mystics; and kept expressing their experiences in ever new idioms, sometimes remotely echoing the language of the Vedas, sometimes creating new symbolical imagery and mythology and also, of course, struggling to give them conceptual expression in its philosophical systems.

Turning now to the Vedas themselves, I would like to present first an example of a symbolical expression of what, on analysis, appears to represent an underlying spiritual or mystical experience of the transcendent; I find it in the, by Western research, very much underestimated and neglected female deity called Aditi who despite her 'low profile' even in the Vedas themselves is called in them 'the perfect goddess' (RV 2,40,6), 'mother of gods and kings' (RV 1,113,19; 2,27,7) and who is finally said to be 'all that has been and will be born' (RV 1,89,6).

No separate hymn is dedicated to Aditi, but she occurs in many hymns throughout the Vedas praised and adorned with numerous epithets, although never described as having physical features.

A clue to the interpretation of her meaning is her name, already explained by Max Müller as 'not bound' (*a-dita*), 'not limited, absolute, infinite'.[6] As a noun the word means 'unbounding', 'boundlessness' and 'freedom' and is used in the latter sense a few times in the Vedas (RV 1,24,1; 7,51,1).[7] As an adjective it means 'boundless' or 'infinite' and is used about the sky (RV 5,59,8; 10,63,3). To worshippers Aditi is a symbol of freedom from the bondage of sin and guilt (RV 1,24,15; 1,162,22; 7,93,7; 8,56,14) and from suffering (RV 8,18,6).

A further clue to an understanding of Aditi is her motherhood which is not limited to the gods and other beings but is extended to the entire universe in all its dimensions. In other words she stands for the divine source of the whole of manifested reality. And a further, no less important, point is added when she is proclaimed not only father and mother but also son — which means that she represents manifested reality itself as well as its source. The relevant verse (RV 1,89,10) reads as follows:

> Aditi is heaven, Aditi is inner region, Aditi is mother, father and son, Aditi is all gods, Aditi is all human races, Aditi is all that has been born and still is to be born.[8]

This complexity and depth of the nature of Aditi, particularly her double character as both parent and offspring or the source of life as well as life itself, finds expression in various other hymns. Thus although she is the mother of all gods, and particularly of a group of seven or eight gods called after her Ādityas, one of them, Dakṣa, is seen also as her father:

Dakṣa was born of Aditi, Aditi of Dakṣa, for Aditi was born as your daughter, o Dakṣa! (RV 10,72,4 – 5).

She is also found connected with various other mythological images of divine parentage. She is called mother Earth (RV 1,72,9; AV 13,1,38), she is both Heaven and Earth (RV 4,55,1) and is often referred to as cow (RV 1,153,3; 8,90,15; 10,11,1), her milk being *soma*, the sacred drink (RV 9,96,15). She has many epithets such as 'divine and foeless' (RV 7,40,4), 'far-spread and wide-ruling' (RV 8,56,12) and 'luminous and celestial' (RV 1,136,3), some of them clearly pointing to her spiritual significance.

It is indeed quite surprising that previous interpretations of Aditi were so inadequate. Not even Max Müller fully recognized her role in the Vedas at the top level of interpretation and was unable to draw obvious consequences from his own interpretation of her name. He wrote in 1882:

Aditi means *infinitude*, from *dita*, bound, and *a*, not, that is, not bound, not limited, absolute, infinite. Aditi itself is now and then involved in the Veda as the Beyond, as what is beyond the earth and the sky and the sun and the dawn — a most surprising conception in that early period of religious thought.[9]

And in 1891 he commented on her thus:

Aditi, an ancient god or goddess, is in reality the earliest name invented to express the Infinite; not the Infinite as the result of a long process of abstract reasoning, but the visible Infinite, visible, as it were, to the naked eye, the endless expanse beyond the earth, beyond the clouds, beyond the sky. That was called Aditi, the un-bound, the un-bounded; one might almost say, but for fear of misunderstandings, the Absolute, for it is derived from *diti*, bond, and the negative particle, and meant therefore originally what is free from bonds of any kind, whether of space or time, free from physical weakness, free from moral guilt. Such a conception became of necessity a being, a person, a god. To us such a name and such a conception seem decidedly modern, and to find in the Veda Aditi, the Infinite, as the mother of the principal gods, is certainly, at first sight, startling.

And then he proceeded to explain how the 'thoughts of primitive humanity' worked and how 'the poets of the Veda indulged freely in theogonic speculations' and how Aditi, the mother of gods on the one hand and a child of Dakṣa and a subordinate deity on the other, was an outcome of these speculations.[10]

Müller was still misled by the theory of personification of nature phenomena as the sole origin of high gods and ideas in antiquity into overlooking or disregarding the obvious mystical significance of Aditi. The concept of infinity and of the 'beyond', it is true, could not have arisen as a result of abstract reasoning which, we can assume, did not exist at the time, but since the Vedas are primarily records of the religious experience of man at the time of their origin, it is really only a very small step to seeing Aditi as the expression of man's mystical experience of the 'beyond' or of the transcendent in a contemplative vision (*dhīti*) of the ancient seers (*ṛṣis*). Müller, although a 'dreamer', as he was called by Oldenberg, could not take that step, believing as he did that the Vedas were 'neither beautiful, in our sense of the word, nor very profound'.[11] It was the ruling evolutionary view which required that previous ages be looked upon as incapable of profundity.

Those who labelled Müller a 'dreamer' were, naturally, still less favourable to Aditi than he was. Oldenberg wrote: 'Aditi is a personified concept. Her name means "not-bound-ness" (*Nichtgebundenheit*), we may translate it, more simply, as "freedom".'[12]

Oldenberg's preference for ascribing to Vedic authors' minds a high capacity for abstraction (although this was a decidedly later development in the history of thought as Müller already clearly realized) rather than crediting them with deeper religious or spiritual experiences, was continued for quite some time in Indian studies. Thus Macdonell, for example, explained Aditi as a personification of an abstract idea, although in face of her undoubted antiquity, proved by her appearance in all books of the Vedas, he did worry about how to account 'for so early a personification of such an abstract idea', as personification of abstract ideas fitted neatly into the accepted evolutionistic view only if it could be seen as a relatively late development towards the end of the Vedic period. Macdonell explained it finally by inventing an ingenious theory which required him to venture on speculation about the pre-Vedic period:

As mentioned earlier, Aditi, while being the mother of all gods, had a special group of seven or eight sons called after her Ādityas and sometimes simply sons of Aditi (*aditeḥ putrāḥ*). Macdonell suggested that since *aditi* meant also 'freedom' the latter expression simply meant, in pre-Vedic times, that these gods were 'sons of freedom', which was to be taken as a figurative epithet. Freedom then was, according to him, duly personified into a divine mother of gods, Aditi.[13] Keith agreed with this theory and summarized it, rather dogmatically, thus: 'Aditi was conjured up from a phrase meaning sons of freedom or rather perhaps guiltlessness', the last qualifying addition being his little contribution to Macdonell's theory.[14]

This purely conjectural explanation of Aditi is a good example of that shallow and laboured conceptualization of the Vedic imagery which still sometimes haunts the pages of books on the Vedic religion. L. Renou, for example, had comparatively recently still nothing new to say about Aditi and based his view of her on Macdonell and Keith when he summarily and brusquely proclaimed: 'It is undoubtedly a case of a secondary form, owing its subsistence to the word Āditya.'[15]

Jan Gonda, as we might expect, does not subscribe to this outdated theory and comes a little nearer to the transcendental nature of Aditi. He agrees with Oldenberg that she represents and bestows bondage-free existence, but in addition he stresses her nature as 'Great Mother' and the way in which she is identified with mother Earth and her mythological equivalent, the cow, and also with the whole universe. He refers to TS 1,11 where the navel of the earth into which one puts offerings is described as her womb. She stands for him for the ideas of breadth, expanse, boundlessness and freedom and she is also the goddess of *ṛta*, the eternal law.[16] But not even he ventured an interpretation on a deeper level which his researches into the meaning of *dhīti* would have allowed him.

A hint pointing in the right direction has been available since the end of the last century in the work of Paul Deussen, although his conclusions are rather limited and inadequate. He commented on the verse quoted and translated above (RV 1,89,10) by saying that here appeared, still timidly and in a mythological veil, the idea of the unity of the universe and that this was later developed in two other hymns (1,164; 10,129) which represent to him the core of the philosophy of the RV.[17]

This is correct as far as it goes, but the way Deussen formulated his assessments shows how deeply he was influenced by the evolutionistic thinking of his time as applied to ancient forms of religious and philosophical achievements. He saw in human history an evolution of philosophical thinking, progressing from childish, half-conscious and imaginative activity of the human mind to man's rational and conscious appreciation of the *moral* nature of the highest insights of his mind. There was no room, in his outlook, for insights of a *spiritual* kind, which the ancient mind could express only through symbolical and mythological imagery. He missed this whole dimension of Vedic experience, mainly because mythology was to him a corrupt process, a deviation from the evolution of thought towards rationality. And so he failed to see the depth of human experience behind symbols and myths and their illustrative and explanatory significance escaped him completely.

In this respect Deussen did not differ much from all those scholars who in the pursuit of rational explanations of Vedic deities, their meaning and origin, turned a blind eye on their living content — which is their real value as representations of man's communication with reality on a deeper level of experience.

In my view Aditi cannot be understood and explained unless we are prepared to accept that it was mystical or deep spiritual experience which lay behind the verses in which she is described and addressed. To regard her as the personification of a concept as Macdonell and Keith did with the connivance of Renou, does not mean anything to us today, it is an empty phrase. To remain content with summarizing her mythological features and her significance for the worshipper, as Gonda did, is leaving untapped the dimension of depth behind religious symbols and myths to which, after Otto and Jung, interpreters of religion should be open. The scope and a need for a fresh assessment are clear.

Let us, then, summarize the clues to Aditi's meaning which have come to light so far: she represents (1) 'boundlessness', 'infinity' and 'freedom from bondage and suffering'; she is (2) the divine mother, that is the transcendental source of the entire manifested reality, past present and future; and (3) being the son of her own offspring, Dakṣa, she is also the manifested reality itself.

When we examine all these characteristics of hers with our knowledge of the phenomenon of mysticism (as examined in volume one of the present series) we realize that Aditi possesses all the attributes which a mystic feels are there when he achieves union with the absolute or God. We can therefore say that Aditi represents, in the deepest possible sense, the Vedic seers' conscious mystical experience of the unity of man with reality as a whole in all its multidimensional complexity and also with the source of manifested reality when it rested in its pre-manifest latency 'before time began'.

Thus Aditi is not just the visible infinity, but in her aspect of future motherhood prior to giving birth to the world she also represents that infinity and boundlessness which precede the limitations imposed on reality by its manifestation in innumerable shapes and forms as separate things and personalities; these limitations being experienced by mystics as bondage which causes suffering. But being viewed as a goddess, a person, although with elusive features which do not lend themselves to description as in the case of other gods, she does not represent anything like an impersonal precreational chaos or 'gaping void', but indicates that reality, even in its pre-manifest latency, is a conscious structural unity, something for which we have no other concept than that of a person. (And that is, perhaps, why God cannot but be perceived by a religious believer in terms of a personal creator rather than an impersonal creative force.)

Nevertheless, and in spite of what has just been said, the element of vastness, infinity and, from the standpoint of the manifested world of things and beings, voidness that is present in the mystical experience of unification leaves a residual impression of impersonality as an underlying characteristic of the ruling force behind visible reality. (And man, in his descriptions of his encounters with the transcendent has never fully overcome this dichotomy. If the impersonal aspect of the transcendent is emphasized to the exclusion of its personality element, we get a so-called 'atheistic' religion like early Buddhism. But Buddhism has not escaped this dichotomy either, as is shown by the developments in Mahāyāna with its Trikāya doctrine and its cosmic Buddhology.)[18]

So Aditi appears to combine in herself both the impersonal and the personal aspect of the transcendent and, short of a mystical union with her, can be approached on lower levels both by a philosophical mind as the hidden One beyond existence and non-existence, and by the worshipper as a mighty goddess who can grant freedom and relief from suffering.

The motherhood of Aditi symbolizes the mystery of creation and also the experience of the mystic of being an offspring of the infinite, together with the rest of manifested reality. This is not to be understood as merely a kind of creation or emanation of the world from the transcendent 'at the beginning', as it were, but as a constant flow between the unmanifest and the manifest, for Aditi is the mother of everything that has been and also that will be born. This again suggests the origin of Aditi in mystical experience rather than in sole speculation on the origins of the world. A thinking mind, whether a simple or a sophisticated one, can be satisfied with the idea of a first cause from which an independent and continuous line of causes and effects then proceeds further. (An extreme example of this kind of religious rationalistic thought was the European deism of the eighteenth century.) A mystic, on the other hand, experiences his total dependence on the divine, he feels that he owes his sustenance directly to God in every single moment of his life and so does the rest of creation in the past, present and future.

The image of Aditi being father, mother as well as son, in other words, being not only the source of the manifested reality and of all creatures, but at the same time this reality itself and, by implication, every single creature within it, is the expression of the experience of mystical union of the individual mystic with his God or with the divine source, a recognition, arrived at by non-rational or suprarational means, of the essential oneness of the transcendent with the manifest as a whole and with every individual part of it. This oneness is the reason why the world is not chaotic but appears to be ruled by the inherent law of balance (*ṛta*) which is both cosmic (natural law) and individual (moral law). Aditi is the queen of this law (AV 7,6,2; YV — VS 21,5). This image also represents a recognition of the possibility for every part of the manifested reality, for every creature, to find its way back into the hidden oneness, to the freedom of the transcendent, as the prodigal son returns home to his father and mother. This may be difficult to understand conceptually and to express adequately in rational terms (as we can see from the later texts of the Advaita Vedānta system), but the reunion does not take place on the surface of reality with its apparent diversity. It is supposed to happen in depth, in the inner region or dimension of the individual experience where it meets with the hidden inner dimension of the universal. This is expressed symbolically by the navel of the earth which, as Gonda mentioned, is the womb of Aditi, an important hint which shows that the navel of the earth, known also from Greek and other mythologies, is not meant (at least on the *ādhyātmika* level) to represent the middle of this earth on its surface, but is the central point, the point of contiguity, at which the unmanifest or the transcendent and the manifest meet. It is the womb from which the universe and its creatures emerge, but it is also a gate through which one can enter the transcendent when the appropriate offering has been made, i.e. when the superficial sense of separateness has been abandoned.

Here we have perhaps mankind's oldest known peak achievement in its struggle for knowledge of itself and of its place in the order of reality. It is an achievement which, it has to be stressed again, was not a result of conceptual development, of the process of abstraction in a speculative approach, but of mystical quest and experience which transcends the normal cognitive capacity of man in his everyday life. It was undoubtedly the possession of only a few, but it seems to have been their objective to convey some of it to others. The verbal expression of this insight then had necessarily to take the form which was understood and responded to at that time, and that was the form which we now call mythological. In it symbols rather than concepts are the vehicles of communication of uncommon messages. And although not understood fully and consciously, the message of Aditi was certainly absorbed and influenced the way of life of ordinary people, for symbols have the power to transmit their message even if they are not understood or noticed by the superficial mind.[19]

Another mythological illustration from the Vedas of the oneness of the world with its source, of the mystic with God, is the god Varuṇa, the foremost son of Aditi. With his mother he is the lord and guardian of *ṛta*, the law of the manifested universe, both material and spiritual.[20] He represents the manifested cosmos with all its dimensions, including the heavenly ones, which sprang forth from the transcendental source. His name suggests an astonishingly appealing interpretation. The root *vṛ* means 'to cover, envelop, surround, encompass, enclose'. Varuṇa, therefore, means literally 'the encompasser',[21] 'the coverer', 'the enveloper'. A thing exists only by enclosing, 'encompassing' within its surface a section of the infinite and empty universal space. The infinity of space is not thereby abolished and space itself both permeates and surrounds the thing, which is a structure created, we are told nowadays, merely by subatomic particles whirling around in empty space according to precise laws. Similarly one can explain 'mental things'. A person or personality is a structure of dynamic forces which we may call character qualities and which 'whirl around' within the cosmic element of consciousness or 'mentality', the inner or interim dimension of reality (*antarikṣan*, corresponding to the later concept of Mahāyāna Buddhism, *ālaya vijñāna*), slicing out of it the individual consciousness of a person, all that happening according to the cosmic law, *ṛta*.

A further instance of the Vedic assertion of the essential oneness of the individual with the universal, of the manifested reality with its source, is furnished in a hymn (RV 10,64) where the seer in mystical experience recognizes and claims relationship with the gods and expects that Aditi will confirm his brotherhood with them when they all meet with him 'at the central point' (verse 13). The 'central point', on the level of external religious worship meaning sacrificial altar, represents on the level of spiritual experience, like the navel of the earth, the inner point of contiguity where the individual and the universal, the manifest and the transcendent, meet. So when the seer or mystic reaches this heart of reality by the integration of his surface consciousness with the inner region of his own personality, penetrating through all its layers into the centre, he will meet there the forces of cosmic reality (gods) at their source.

It is this mystical or spiritual experience and knowledge that is the central message and meaning of the Vedas and not merely the sacrificial lore of bargaining with the gods or the magic manipulation of the forces of nature to the advantage of the sacrificer. These latter elements, which were always conspicuously present and which, in later Vedic times, became predominant, are only a secondary, albeit more widely acclaimed, aspect of the Vedic message and belong to the lower (*ādhidaivika* and *ādhibhautika*) levels of its interpretation. From the mystical Vedic experience as understood on the spiritual (*ādhyātmika*) level of interpretation, there is then a direct line to all the subsequent peak achievements in Indian spiritual development which were expressed in different idioms in the Upanisads, in early Buddhism, in the Hindu schools, particularly in Patañjali's Yoga system and in Advaita Vedānta, in the schools of Mahāyāna Buddhism and also in some modern presentations such as that of Aurobindo.

Only this mystical layer of the Vedas can justify and explain the high reputation which the Vedas have enjoyed throughout the ages, even when the clue to their full interpretation has been lost. Looking at the Vedas in this way enables us also to appreciate the struggle of Indian religious and philosophical tradition to reiterate and reformulate that which was most valuable in the Vedas and we may therefore conclude, contrary to Renou's view, that the Indian tradition has not strayed away from the message of the Vedas.

Not every reformulation or translation of the idiom of symbols and myths into rational language is an adequate conceptualization of them. Often it can represent the effort of a mind which has not had the spiritual experience underlying the ancient symbols and myths it is struggling to decipher, and which has lost entirely or to a large degree the capacity to take in their message through direct impact (whether consciously or without being fully aware of the fact, in the sense of Freud's observation). In other words, such a mind may not be capable of an emotional let alone a higher spiritual (non-rational) or mystical response to them, so that their impact on it is rather limited and its formulation then will not do full justice to the original message encoded in the symbols and myths.

The process of rationalization and conceptualization of earlier Vedic spiritual achievements had already started in the later Vedic period, and its results are usually seen by scholars as the beginnings of Indian philosophizing and, consequently, as a progressive step and a higher achievement in comparison with the preceding mythical period.

Although the development of conceptual thinking is undoubtedly an important accomplishment in the history of the Indian mind (and of the human mind in general), it does not, in itself, necessarily represent a higher stage in man's understanding of himself and of reality as a whole. On the contrary, the conceptual approach on its own, in its excessive rationalism, is often unable to grasp and express living realities effectively and may, and often does, lead to experiences of alienation. That is one of the reasons why religious and other movements, including political ones, have never entirely renounced the use of symbols, old ones as well as newly created ones, because it is important for them to address people's living emotions directly, even if their impact reaches them only on an unconscious or semi-conscious level.

The process of conceptualization of the early Vedic spiritual message which started during the late Vedic period is a certain sign that the old symbolical imagery was already then wearing out, and it seems that some of the best minds among the Vedic authors of the late period felt the need to reformulate it for themselves and others. And if they had something to say from their own spiritual experience, the language which they naturally applied was one which is much nearer to our own way of thinking, because it proceeds in deliberations rather than in mythological stories, although it still employs some symbols, particularly when the mind faces an unexplored level of experience or an uncommon ground of speculation.

The best example of this late Vedic trend is the celebrated Nāsadīya Sūkta (RV 10,129), often called, rather inaccurately, the Creation Hymn. As can be expected, it is not quite free from symbolic images, but there is no mythological tendency in it. It has been summarized, translated and commented on many times and despite differing opinions on some parts of it, there has been a general consensus that it is an outstanding and unsurpassed specimen of Vedic philosophical endeavour. Its reading and translation are not, on the whole, controversial, so I use here, with some suggested corrections, Macdonell's old rendering:

1. Non-being then existed not nor being:
There was no air,* nor sky** that is beyond it.
What was concealed? Wherein? In whose protection?***
And was there deep unfathomable water?

* *rajas* — also: space
** *vyoman* — also: heaven
*** *śarman* — house, dwelling, shelter, protection

2. Death then existed not nor life immortal;
Of neither night nor day was any token.
By its inherent force the One* breathed windless:
No other thing than that beyond existed.

* *tad ekam* — that one

3. Darkness there was at first by darkness hidden;
Without distinctive marks, this all was water.
That which, becoming, by the void was covered,
That One by force of heat* came into being.

* *tapas* — heat; creative or mystical flame

4. Desire* entered the One in the beginning:
It was the earliest seed, of thought the product.**
The sages searching in their hearts with wisdom,***
Found out the bond of being in non-being.

*	*kāma*	— desire, love
**	*manaso retaḥ*	— mind's seed
***	*manīṣa*	— intelligence, understanding, wisdom

5. Their ray extended light across the darkness:
But was the one above or was it under?
Creative force was there, and fertile power:
Below was energy, above was impulse.

6. Who knows for certain? Who shall here declare it?
Whence was it born, and whence came this creation?
The gods were born after this world's creation:
Then who can know from whence it has arisen?

7. None knoweth whence creation has arisen;
And whether he has or has not produced it:
He who surveys it in the highest heaven,
He only knows, or haply he may know not.[22]

The author of this hymn obviously struggled to express his thoughts and insights in rational and descriptive terms. He used expressions which had symbolical meaning only where concepts just were not available to him and could hardly be created at the time, while meaningful symbols were still ready at hand.

The source of the author's ideas does not seem to have been merely reasoning on the basis of existing Vedic material. Some of his verses make the impression of being based on visionary, mystical or yogic experience put into words which only partly convey the depth of his vision. It can be, however, regarded as certain that the author knew well the preceding Vedic tradition and was fully aware of the depth of its message. His reference to a 'then' when being and non-being did not exist — a mysterious kind of dimension of latency beyond the concepts of being and non-being — might well have been his way of understanding and expressing that aspect of Aditi which represents the precreational infinity before she gave birth to the universe. He found a conceptual designation for this dimension which he, too, understood to be dynamic and purpose-bent (as the infinite symbolized by the goddess who is the Great Mother of creation certainly is), but he hesitated to call it a person and chose a neutral expression 'that one'. That he could not entirely get away from the notion of a highest personal god is shown by his final suggestion that the overseer of the world in the highest heaven might, or might not, be responsible for, or know the mystery of, creation.

Turning to the analysis of the hymn verse by verse, I abstain from summarizing previous comments and interpretations of the hymns, because they deal with it from quite different starting points and have little relevance to the aims of this paper.

The first verse, concerned with the precreational situation when this manifested universe of things and beings was not here, shows the author's understanding of being and non-being as two relative and interdependent notions applicable only within the manifested universe as we know it, including any heavenly or spiritual planes of existence. The question is: was there any kind of latent existence, and if so, what was that mysterious dimension of latency? Was it an entity of a personal character, protecting or sheltering the unmanifest world like a mother her unborn baby (*śarman* has the overtones of close personal sheltering)? The question whether there was unfathomable water points to the conceptually inaccessible state of the unmanifest voidness which yet is a hidden fullness, pregnant with the manifoldness of the later manifested reality. Water is a symbol for this latency of the still unmanifest cosmos (and therefore for chaos in the original Greek sense) as well as for the unconscious mind, as transpires from some passages of post-hymnic texts.

The second verse, stating that there was no life and death, no day and night, virtually says that time, like space, was not yet manifest. But there is no question of there being nothing and so in the absence of manifoldness the expression resorted to by the author was the mysterious entity 'that one', which was unidentifiable yet dynamic (breathing windless) with unharnessed, inherent force. The third verse reveals how this spaceless, timeless, yet dynamic sole absolute, first covered by and hidden in the darkness of undifferentiated but sensitive latency (water) and entrapped in voidness, came into existence by the force of its creative ardour (*tapas*).

'That one' of the second verse and 'that one' of the third verse obviously are not quite one and the same, but represent stages of that one's dynamism, the second stage being 'that one' as the first evolute or manifestation of itself. The latent, unmanifest, but dynamic and powerful 'one' that has no beyond now comes into manifest being because of its inner creative tension. And from here on the hymn deals only with the manifested reality, namely how from being one it proceeded to the stage of duality. This seems to be arrived at in two different ways: (1) by the introduction of two correlative and interdependent concepts of existence and non-existence (an elaboration on the first line of the first stanza) where the duality of being and non-being comes across clearly as the characteristic feature of the manifested reality, and (2) by pointing out the polarity of existence in the fifth verse.

But prior to that the fourth verse brings out the psychological, manifest equivalent of the latent inner flame (*tapas*), of the dynamism by whose force 'the one' emerged from latency into existence. It is desire or love (*kāma*), the foremost mental tendency (*manaso retaḥ*). The author then proceeds to indicate how the knowledge of these things came about: it was by contemplative absorption, by diving into the depth of their hearts with intelligence (*manīṣa*) that the seers discovered the conditionality of being which is limited by non-being, the oldest known formulation of the impermanence and relativity of existence, limited both in space and time.

The fifth verse then introduces the already mentioned ever-present quality of existence, namely polarity, which is reality's inner dynamism, a kind of dialectical tension found on all its levels, physical, biological and also mental as a stimulus to thought and creativity. It might represent even the inherent quality of the dynamism of 'that one' understood by the sages as creative force and fertile power, energy and impulse. From here is then derived the subsequent manifoldness of manifested reality. How this proceeded in detail is of no interest to the author who, as a philosopher, dealt only with first principles.

Having thus finished his metaphysical inquiry into the mystery of the beginning and source of existence, the author pauses in verse six and looks back at the problem again, with a sober mind. And in a truly intellectual and utterly honest fashion he asks: 'Who knows for certain?' The insights which sprang from intuition and the understanding which may have been gained during contemplative absorption seem somehow incomplete or bring no absolutely solid certainty when put into words. And this would be even more so if the hymn were a purely philosophical reconstruction of the ancient mythological message of the seers of old — of their vision of the primordial unmanifest oneness (Aditi) that gave birth to the manifested cosmos (Varuṇa) and to everything in it.

The questions and doubts continue throughout verses six and seven. But the doubts and uncertainties of this philosopher-poet of the late Vedic period about the origin of creation are not expressions of scepticism. He probably also had his vision, his insight, his intuitive understanding. But he also knew his limitations and he equally knew that celestial planes of existence were conditioned parts of the manifested cosmos just as this material world was, and therefore not even the inhabitants of those planes, the gods, could know the mystery of the beginning of it all. So perhaps only he who is the highest one in the universe knows, but perhaps he does not, for was not the vision of the precreational situation (verses one to three) without a personal god? 'That one breathed windless'. And so even the highest god (in post-Vedic tradition known as Brahma and then mostly as *īśvara* (the Lord), possibly belongs to this side of manifestation. The riddle of life is not to be resolved by speculation or by conventional religious ideas taken on faith, but only by suprasensory and suprarational vision. That would appear to be the implication of the hymn.

On the basis of this hymn we can also easily understand the later Buddhist and also Hindu attitudes to the god Brahma as it is reflected in the Pāli Canon (particularly in the D 1,1) and in the Purāṇic cosmology. According to this view Brahma is born in the process of world manifestation at the beginning of a world cycle and directs the creation and presides over the universe for one great world period. At its end he dies and after a period of cosmic rest he or another Brahma is reborn and this is repeated in a ceaseless sequence of periods of world emanation from, and world absorption into, the transcendent.

The Creation hymn is unique in the whole of the Vedas and that is why it has been so often quoted, but it would be wrong to assume that it represents an isolated case produced by a solitary thinker. Sporadic utterances in other hymns show (e.g. RV 1,164; 4,23; 10,2; 10,82; 10,90; 10,121 and elsewhere) that the spirit of philosophical inquiry into the nature of the transcendent and the origin of experienced reality was considerably widespread, although, by its nature, not likely to be reflected in detail in the Vedic collections. But of course the Upaniṣadic philosophy and later philosophical systems, particularly Sāṅkhya and Vedāntic schools are in many respects elaborations of concepts and ideas scattered in the Vedic hymns, some of which are so superbly, albeit succinctly, expressed in this hymn.

The early beginning of the conceptualization of the ancient Vedic spiritual message may have been prompted by the gradually fading understanding of the archaic symbolical language and it may have in turn contributed to the gradual loss of the grasp of the deeper meaning of the Vedas at least on the part of the average person. But the feeling that there was real power behind the Vedas has never faded and it has perpetuated the reverential attitude towards them, affording them a permanent position of authority in the whole of Hindu tradition.

The modern process of conceptualization of the symbolical language of the Vedas started with the philological work of early Indologists concerned with lexicographical tasks and problems of translation. It then continued in the form of attempts to interpret the Vedas and their world view and this was done according to hermeneutical principles derived from the nineteenth century's positivistic and, to some extent, Christian bias, both preventing researchers from appreciating the high achievements of the Vedic mind in its earliest period of creativity. The resulting picture of the Vedic view of the world, life and existence was inadequate and very simplified if not simplistic. Much of it still lingers on in the minds of the older generation of Indologists and occasionally reappears in popular compendia of the history of religions. A need for reassessment is therefore obvious and so it is clear that the process of conceptualization of the Vedic message has not yet been completed and will have to be carried on, within the field of Indian studies. It will have to take into account all the achievements of recent research into history of religions and also attempt the difficult task of philosophical interpretation and analysis wherever applicable.

NOTES

1 Cf. my article 'On Interpreting the Vedas', R 7 (1977), no. 2, pp. 189 – 200.

2 For a discussion of methodological problems in Religious Studies in connection with the 'higher reality' in religions see my article 'The Concept of the Transcendent. Questions of Method in the History of Religions', R 13 (1983), pp. 311 – 22; as to the name of the discipline, cf. particularly note 25 of that article.

3 L. Renou, *The Destiny of the Vedas in India*, Delhi, 1965.

4 For a discussion of a multi-level interpretation of the Vedas see my article referred to in note 1. Its original version was presented at the first Symposium on Indian Religions in Cambridge (20 – 23 March 1975) under the title 'Problems of Interpretation of Indian Religions'. This principle of interpretation, applied to the Vedas already by Yāska (Nirukta 7, 1 – 2) and in modern times by Dayananda, was used also by F. R. Allchin in his paper '*Gāyatrī Mantra* and the Beginnings of Indian Theology' delivered during the same Symposium and never, to my knowledge, published. It was frequently referred to also in the works of M. Eliade (for references see my article quoted in note 1). I further used it in my article 'The Teachings of the Veda and the *ādhyātmika* method of interpretation', *Golden Jubilee Volume*, Vaidika Samsoddhana Mandala (Vedic Research Institute), Poona, 1981, pp. 288 – 95; and also in 'Men, Gods and Powers in the Vedic Outlook', JRAS 1982, no. 1, pp. 14 – 24.

5 Cf. the book dedicated to this concept by Jan Gonda, *The Vision of the Vedic Poets*, The Hague, 1963.

6 F. Max Müller, *The Vedas*, Calcutta, 1956 (a collection of papers from different publications, written between 1865 – 98).

7 Cf. A. A. Macdonell, *Vedic Mythology*, Strassburg, 1897, repr. Delhi, 1974, p. 121.

8 *áditir dyaúr áditir antárikṣam áditir mātā sá pitā sá putráḥ*
víśve devá áditiḥ páñca jánā áditir jātám áditir jánitvam
Text according to T. Aufrecht, *Die Hymnen des Rigveda*, Bonn, 1877. I translate *pañca janā* (lit. 'five races') as 'all races', for that is the meaning which the expression is almost certainly meant to convey, being perhaps an archaic way which survived from the IE stage. Cf. Hittite *pankus* (→ total, united, general, each), stemming from the proto IE **penkʷe* explained by Polomé as indicating the *total* number (originally of fingers of the hand) and only later used exclusively for 'five'. For references see Winfred P. Lehman, 'Linguistic Structure as Diacritic Evidence on Proto-Culture', p. 3 – 5, *Indo-European and Indo-Europeans* (Papers presented at the third IE conference, University of Pennsylvania), ed. George Gardona, etc., Philadelphia, 1970, pp. 1 – 10.

Interestingly, modern classification, including the latest controversial theory of Carleton S. Coon (*The Origin of Races*, 1962), divides humanity also into five main races.

9 Müller, *The Vedas*, p. 116.
10 Müller, *Vedic Hymns*, Oxford, 1891, Part I, pp. 241 – 2 (SBE XXXII).
11 Müller, *The Vedas*, p 95.
12 Hermann Oldenberg, *Die Religion des Veda*, Darmstadt, 1970, pp. 202 – 3 (1st ed. 1894).
13 Macdonell, *Vedic Mythology*, pp. 122 – 3.
14 A. B. Keith, *The Religion and Philosophy of the Veda and Upanishads*, Delhi, 1970, pp. 215 – 17 (1st ed. Harvard, 1925).
15 Renou, *Vedic India*, Calcutta, 1957, p. 61 (French 1947).
16 J. Gonda, *Die Religionen Indiens I, Veda und Älterer Hinduismus*, Stuttgart, 1960, pp. 83 – 4.
17 P. Deussen, *Allgemeine Geschichte der Philosophie I, Allgemeine Einleitung und Philosophie des Veda bis auf die Upanishad's*, Leipzig, 1920, p. 105 (1st ed. 1894).
18 One can speculate further and point out that in our modern civilization this dichotomy is present, too. Science has established the concept of impersonal laws of nature and, since Einstein, seems to be aspiring to formulate a unitary theory of the universe; and yet despite widespread scientific materialism many people, including individual scientists, find a purely scientific outlook unsatisfactory as a philosophy of life and do believe in a personal God. For a long time the two extreme views — the science-based outlook which does not accept anything beyond and above material reality governed by inherent natural laws and the religious faith relying on a personal God-Creator for final answers — were hostile to each other until they reached a certain uneasy mutual tolerance, as religion did not succeed in its past endeavours to subjugate science and the optimistic expectation of scientific materialists that with the progress of science religion would go away has not materialized. Some signs seem to indicate that attitudes are softening to some extent in some quarters, particularly where old certainties have been undermined, as in modern physics, so that a certain openness to non-materialistic philosophical ideas can be seen (Max Planck, Heisenberg) or even willingness to consider mystical vision

as a valid channel of approach to the mysteries of reality is displayed (F. Capra).

19 This has been established by depth psychology as recognized by Mircea Eliade: 'The historian of religions is especially grateful to Freud for proving that images and symbols communicate their ''messages'' even if the conscious mind remains unaware of this fact. The historian is now free to conduct his hermeneutical work upon a symbol without having to ask himself how many individuals in a certain society and at a given historical moment understood all the meanings and implications of that symbol.' Mircea Eliade, *The Quest: History and Meaning in Religion*, Chicago, 1969, p. 21.

20 For references in the RV see Keith and Macdonell, op. cit.

21 See Macdonell, *Vedic Mythology*, p. 28.

22 A. A. Macdonell, *Hymns from the Rigveda*, Calcutta-London (The heritage of India Series; date not given, but surely after 1918). The hymn has been reprinted also in *A Source Book in Indian Philosophy*, ed. S. Radhakrishnan and C. A. Moore, Princeton, 1957.

4

ORIGINS OF FORM AND STRUCTURE IN MONUMENTAL ART

John C. Irwin

My approach to the problem of the origin of form and structure in monumental art, backed by nearly half a century of research and specialized experience in Indian archaeology and art history, is interdisciplinary, following an independent and somewhat unorthodox course. The underlying aim has been to extend discoveries made by Sanskritists in the area of myth and to apply them to problems still unsolved in archaeology and art history. Chief among them are: (1) the archaic meaning of the sacred tumulus which is universal in different forms to all ancient cultures and is variously termed ziggurat, pyramid, barrow, stūpa, etc; (2) the role of the pillar which featured in many archaic cultures as the image of the world's axis (*axis mundi*) under such varied guises as 'victory column', obelisk or 'pillar of triumph' and in reduced form also as a portable standard: the Christian 'Cross' carried in processions or on battlefields belongs here, too.

Theoretically, the basis of my work is the recognition of the fundamental distinction between *cosmology* and *cosmogony*, which has been neglected or blurred in the work of many academics. The term 'cosmology' is better known and concerns the structure of the universe after the so-called 'creation' of the dualistic world, that is the division between heaven and earth, day and night, fire and water, light and darkness, good and evil, male and female, etc. 'Cosmogony', on the other hand, which is primary, deals exclusively with the *genesis* of the cosmos as implied by its Greek terminal *-gonia*, meaning 'birth'.

Evidence has been accumulating in recent decades to suggest that the basic elements of the archaic cosmogony were once widely, if not universally, shared by all archaic cultures known to us, and that it originally infused all primitive religious thought concerned with origins. My own interest is in the role cosmogonic myth served as the principal inspiration in the creation of monumental art.

Contrary to what seems to be widely believed, the ancient world's obsessive concern with cosmogony, or 'how the world began', owed nothing to curiosity or to 'love of story telling': it was an expression of religious *mystery*; and its language was *metaphor*. It was based on a need to get into right relationship with the sacred world as the source of the Cosmic Order on which, as prehistoric man felt, his existence and survival wholly depended. This cosmic order was in turn based on *mythical* or *sacred* time, which was *cyclic* rather than linear; so that the birth, or the recurrent birth or rebirth, of cosmos was felt to be the key to the perpetuation of life on earth. This relation between cyclic time and recurrent birth is manifested, for example, in the annual return of the sun and the seasons enabling the germination of seed.

In India as in ancient Greece and other archaic cultures the cosmogony was expressed as the birth of order out of chaos, the 'formed' out of the 'unformed', the Vedic *sat* out of *asat*.[1] From the point of view of the art historian the process of artistic creation, 'of giving form to', literally '*in*-forming', is closely paralleled by the cosmogonic one in which 'creation' of the world involves the externalization of forces 'already existent' rather than the creation of 'something out of nothing'. This further finds close correspondence in the etymological definition of the word 'evolution' from the Latin *e* plus *volvere*, literally the 'rolling out' or 'unfolding' of what previously existed latently.

In cosmogonic myths the demiurgic act implies that the creator (when there is one) acts as a kind of magnetic force over the pre-existing world of chaos: in this way the undifferentiated powers or entities of the primordial world are forced into the opposite poles of existence which express themselves in the dualities of our universe mentioned earlier.

These ideas are not new, they gradually emerged over several decades of scholarly reflection, yet their implications in the field of aesthetics have remained relatively unexplored. But today enough data have become available to venture some conclusions.

The role of myth in the form and structure of monumental art was already intuitively grasped a century ago by W. R. Lethaby, an Englishman of reserved genius, who wrote before any distinction between cosmology and cosmogony was widely grasped or clearly formulated. During his lifetime he was either mocked or ignored by academics. But recently his key publications have been resurrected and eagerly scanned by the *avant garde* of Western historians of architecture.[2] Lethaby grasped already by 1881 that throughout the whole ancient world the building of sacred monuments had been first and foremost a *rite* by which man sought to identify himself with the source of the cosmic order. For this purpose he placed himself and his monuments at the mythical *centre of the universe*.

This point was known in ancient cultures as the 'navel of the earth' (Greek *omphalos*, Sanskrit *pṛthivi-nabhi*). Its meaning was grossly misunderstood until A. J. Wensinck, professor of Semitic philology at

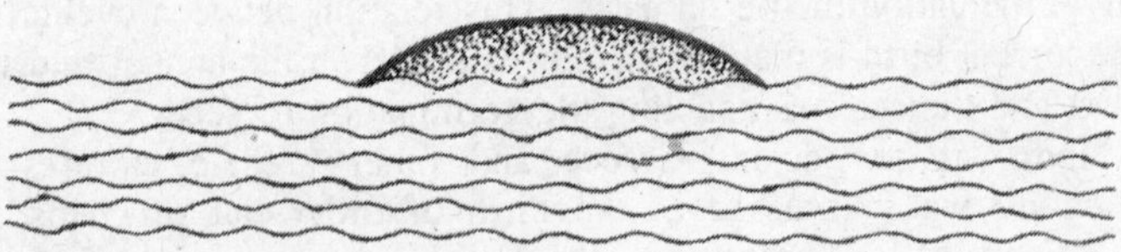

Fig. 1. (a) The Primordial Mound

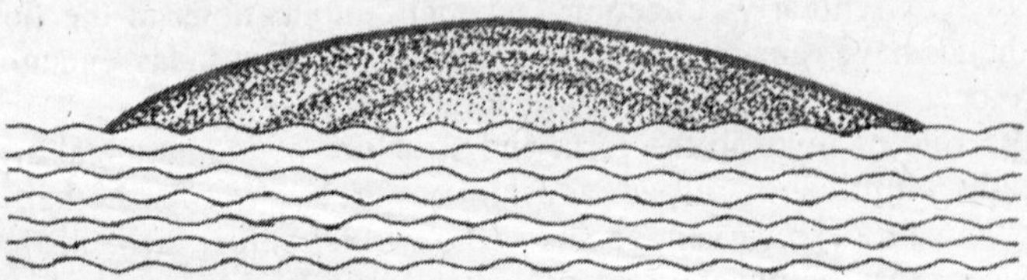

Fig. 1. (b) the 'swelling' of the Mound

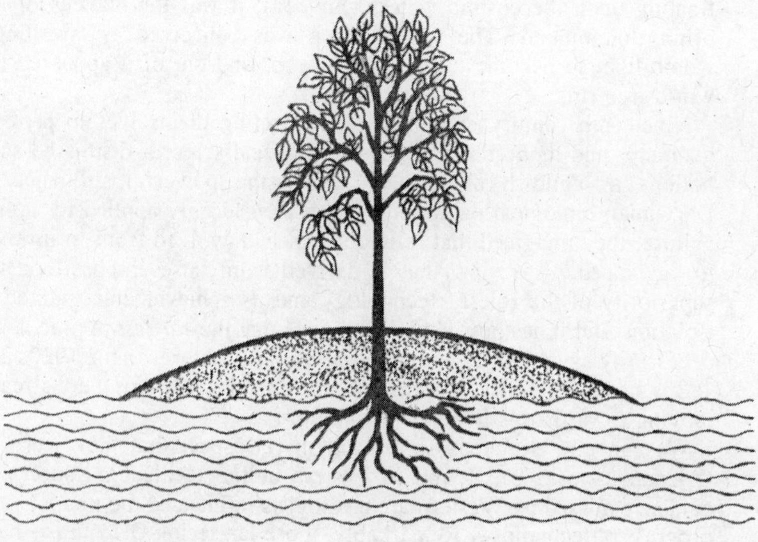

Fig. 2. The Primordial Mound and the World Tree

the University of Leiden, published a seminal monograph proving that, within the context of cosmogony, the meaning of 'navel of the earth' was the same as the meaning of the spot at which heaven and earth had been mythically separated and the world was thus 'born' *in illo tempore*, 'in the beginning'.[3] And since this was conceived as having happened in sacred, i.e. cyclic, time, *repetition* was of its *essence*. Henceforth the building of every sacred shrine was a paradigmatic reiteration of the archetypal 'separation' of heaven and earth, i.e. its 'creation', as it later came to be called in some religious traditions.

In the beginning the *terra firma* was conceived as a clod of mud floating upon the cosmic waters (Fig. 1a); it was the nucleus of the primordial mound. The mound itself was conceived as 'swelling', womb-like, to become our earth (Fig. 1b) and out of it appeared the world tree (Fig. 2).

Nineteenth century evolutionists, restricting themselves to profane geometry and modern principles of empirical science, dismissed such notions as childish or absurd. Under the powerful influence of Darwinian biological evolution, which they loosely applied to human culture, they imagined that religion, too, had evolved from 'primitive' to 'advanced' — a view that is derived from false emphasis on the superiority of the role of technology and its achievements, judged in isolation. But it has now become obvious that the *earliest* in time is not necessarily synonymous with the *simplest* in structure. In the 1920s and 1930s a small minority of archaeologists and art historians were already moving towards this historic recognition.

We can now see it as significant in retrospect that they were all Orientalists who had found in Eastern cultures valuable sources of evidence missed by Western archaeologists influenced too much by the progress of technology. Remarkably, those far-seeing Orientalists have been joined, since Einstein, by one or two physicists with a new orientation. I would include among the Orientalists in question A. M. Hocart who served for some years as Archaeological Commissioner in Ceylon; Paul Mus, the French author of a famous work on Borobudur, later a staff member at the Collège de France; Walter Andrae, the German pioneer of West Asian archaeology; and Carl Hentze, the Belgian Sinologist, still writing in the 1950s.

These scholars were quite unaware of the combined impact their views would later come to exercise. The first Indianist to utilize their work in the context of Indian culture was A. K. Coomaraswamy, the emigré curator of Indian art at the Boston Museum of Fine Arts. He died in 1946 which was the historic year in which F. B. J. Kuiper, professor of Sanskrit at Leiden University, reidentified the archaic cosmogony as embodied in Vedic texts which constitute the oldest and most complete source of cosmogonic myth yet known in the world, still grossly misunderstood by scholars infected with outdated evolutionist thinking.[4]

In the Vedic myth, involving Indra, the demiurgic act of 'creation' is portrayed as Indra's destruction of the demon Vṛtra who held back the waters of life within the primeval mound. At the same moment as Indra pegged the mound with his spear (which became the Cosmic Pillar) and released the waters, heaven and earth were separated, the sky propped up, the sun arose from the cosmic waters and light was born (Fig. 3a); simultaneously, the four directions of space were created (Fig. 3b).

In 1957 further progress was made with the publication of the late Professor Eliade's remarkable essay about the 'centre of the world, the temple and the home' in which he dealt perceptively with what he recognized as the structural correspondence between the domestic, religious and cosmic place-settings variously expressed in religious and monumental architecture.[5] Eliade's ideas were little short of a revelation to me, since they explained for the first time what lay behind the architectural historian's jargon of referring to ancient monuments as 'architectural microcosms', vaguely defined as 'images of the universe'. I now saw them as images of the '*creation*' of the universe in the poetic, mythological or metaphoric sense which means that, referring tc the *cosmogonic* process, they are dynamic rather than passive images. They are processes rather than formulas. It is this dynamic aspect that I have endeavoured to reinforce and apply in my own work.

In the atmosphere of strict specialization, an Egyptologist professes ignorance about Assyriology and vice versa; a specialist on Hellenism will not venture outside the Mediterranean; and all of them will admit that India is a closed book to them. Is it modesty, lack of interest in wider implications of research, or downright lack of imagination? Leading scientists point in the direction of the necessity of interdisciplinary drive where imagination plays an important part. It was Einstein who once warned that 'imagination is more important than knowledge'.[6]

It would be, of course, absurd to think that one can be an expert in everything, but the real point is that, if we are humanists, our basic study is man and his situation in the world. That must be the true perspective of every genuine specialist, in archaeology, art history, history of religions or what-have-you. Thus we each have a responsibility to keep ourselves informed of problems in different fields, parallel or relevant to our own. Otherwise we would be only technicians rather than true scholars.

In pursuing my search for the origins of form and structure in monumental art I have come to recognize that the culture and civilization of India provide a shining incentive to look afresh at our

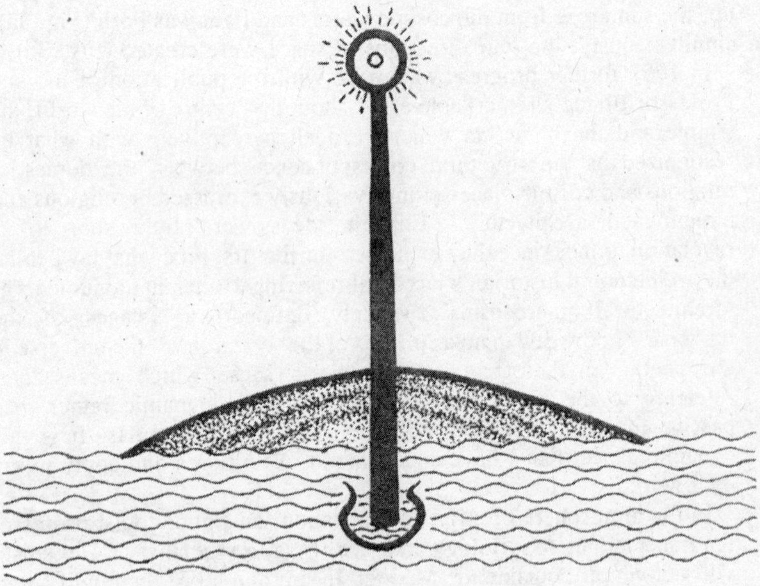

Fig. 3. (a) The Cosmic Pillar, the Waters and the Sun

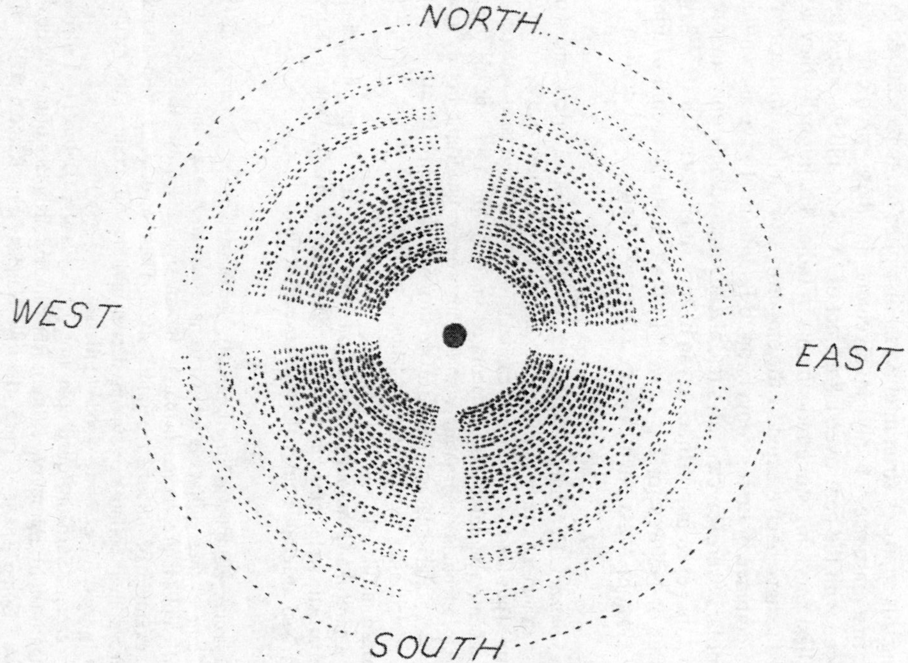

Fig.3 (b) The Four Directions of Space

own Western inheritance from the past. It makes it possible to draw new conclusions about the meaning of this inheritance; and, in turn, to throw new light on the traditional understanding of certain Indian monuments and the ideas that inspired their creation. I am aware that in pursuing this approach strict intellectual discipline has to be adhered to.

The first instance of my involvement in these problems was concerned with the controversial subject of 'Aśokan' pillars which are the earliest surviving stone monuments in India. Traditionally they are believed to have been erected by the emperor Aśoka in the third century B.C. to commemorate his conversion to Buddhism. I have shown that those pillars were erected at sites already sacred not only in pre-Buddhist, but even in pre-Indo-Āryan history. It all started in 1973 with my series of lectures for the Lowell Institute at the Museum of Fine Arts in Boston, Mass., which were later reworked for publication.[7]

Editor's summary: Generally speaking, the so-called 'Aśokan' pillars consist of a plain shaft and a more or less elaborate capital which in turn may have up to four parts. Thus the famous Sārnāth capital has: a bell-shaped basis with petal-like ornament; a circular abacus decorated in relief with four animals (bull, lion, horse, elephant) alternating with chariot wheels; quadruple lions sitting back-to-back; and a large *dharmacakra* surmounting them. In all, sixteen pillars, named after their present locations, are examined in the series and summarized in the list shown in Table 1.

After a careful and thorough examination of their structure, their foundations and their artistic style, supplemented by a comparison with post-Aśokan pillars, Irwin arrived at relative chronology of several of them:

Early group: Rāmpūrvā 2 (bull capital); Sankīsā (elephant); Kosam; Vaiśālī (lion). None of these pillars is known to have had an Aśokan inscription, the bull and elephant are carved in purely Indian style and only the lion is the earliest example of imported heraldic style. Their inadequate foundations, which led to their collapse or sinking deeper into the soil, point to the method previously used for erecting wooden pillars.

Later group: Sārnāth (quadruple lions); Topra (= Delhi 1); Lauriyā-Nandangarh (lion); Rāmpūrvā 1 (lion); Rummindei (birthplace of the Buddha); Gotihawa. Some shafts (Topra, Lauriyā-Nandangarh, Rāmpūrvā 1) are inscribed with Aśoka's edicts. In some cases (Sārnāth, Rummindei, Gotihawa) there is independent evidence that they were erected by Aśoka. The foundations of this group are adequate for their weight.[8]

Irwin examines in the minutest detail the ornamentation of the capitals, and shows conclusively that important elements in them are of older Indian origin. He further argues that the imported features known as 'Perso-Hellenistic' are better understood as West Asian (traceable ultimately to ancient Egypt); they appear on the pillars of the later group. Several pillars of the early group clearly

Table 1. Distribution of 'Aśokan' Pillars

Location	Surviving part	Emblem
1. Allahābād (originally thought to have come from Kosam = Kauśāmbī)	Shaft (re-erected) and fragment of abacus	Unknown (since shown to have been a bull)
2. Bodh Gaya	Shaft (re-erected)	Elephant
3. Delhi no. 1 (originally from Topra)	Shaft (re-erected)	Unknown
4. Delhi no. 2 (originally from Meerut)	Shaft (re-erected)	Unknown
5. Gotihawa (on Nepal border)	Stump of shaft, fragment of 'bell'	Unknown
6. Kosam = Kauśāmbī	Shaft (re-erected)	Unknown
7. Lauriyā-Ararāj	Shaft	Unknown
8. Lauriyā-Nandangarh	Complete *in situ*	Lion
9. Nigālī Sāgar	Two shaft fragments	Unknown
10. Rāmpūrvā no. 1 (capital now in Calcutta Museum)	Shaft & capital, now separated	Lion
11. Rāmpūrvā no. 2 (capital now at Delhi)	Shaft & capital, now separated	Bull
12. Rummindei = Lumbinī (Nepal — near Indian border)	Shaft, fragment of 'bell'	Unknown
13. Sāñcī	Complete, but in fragments	Quadruple lions
14. Saṅkīsā	Capital	Elephant
15. Sārnāth	Capital, incomplete (stump and parts of shattered shaft)	Quadruple lions, fragments of *dharmacakra*
16. Vaiśālī	Complete *in situ*	Lion

appear to be pre-Aśokan, with the possibility of some of them being early Mauryan if not pre-Mauryan. Traces in the foundations (e.g. at Sāñcī) allow the further conclusion that in some cases the stone pillars replaced still earlier wooden ones

In analysing the symbolism of the pillars, Irwin draws on the evidence which he adduces from reliefs depicting 'Pillars of Law' and lion pillars on Buddhist monuments, as well as from pillars erected in irrigation ponds and Brahmanic temple compounds. He finds in them evidence for a much older symbolism of the *axis mundi* founded in the 'cosmic waters' below the earth and reaching up to the sun at its zenith. The key to this symbolism is the archaic myth of creation in which cosmic waters stand for the original chaos and the *axis mundi*, symbolized by a pillar, a tree or a mountain, serves as a prop separating heaven and earth at a point known as the navel of the earth. In India this process of creation was described in the Vedic myth wherein Indra pierced the demon Vṛtra, thereby releasing the waters, separating heaven and earth, propping up heaven and allowing the sun to rise high. As all this happened in mythical time, which is cyclic, the process of creation is symbolically re-enacted annually in connection with the New Year. The same conception can be traced in the ceremonies related to fertility, such as marriage. From here there is a clear link to the phallic symbolism in the Śiva cult.[9]

As a result of his heroic deed Indra became the king of gods. His deed became the paradigm for earthly kings who ruled by Indra's divine right as agents of the cosmic law; this was symbolically commemorated by the annual Indra festival, in which the pillar representing Indra is worshipped in the form of a portable pole or *yaṣṭi*, also carried in battle as Indra's banner.[10] Another instance of the re-enactment of Indra's deed is the Rājasūya which endows the king with extra power by placing him at the centre of the universe which is identical with the navel of the earth. At the moment of consecration, standing upright upon his throne, which is symbolically imagined as at the summit of the Cosmic Pillar, he is also mythically united with the sun at its zenith.

In Buddhism the old symbols acquired new meaning. Their focus is the Buddha's enlightenment under the Bodhi tree, which became the central cosmic event. But the old symbolism was not entirely obliterated; and the artistic quality of Aśokan monuments is not a result of the achievement of one epoch nor a beginning of Indian monumental art inspired by foreign models; rather it represents a culmination of a process based on ancient Indian tradition, although also deeply rooted in an archaic and universally human outlook.

Irwin strengthened his case for pre-Aśokan pillars being associated with Brahmanic cult by examining further the pillar no. 1 (see Table 1), standing at the confluence of the two sacred rivers, Gangā and Yamuna, at the ancient Prayāga, the modern Allahābād.[11] He showed conclusively that the pillar did not originate at Kosam, as formerly claimed, but had always stood at Allahābād/Prayāga (= place of god/place of sacrifice), a centre of a very ancient pillar cult. He further showed that the missing emblem was, in fact, a bull; so that this stone pillar, previously attributed to Aśoka, was actually a Brahmanic bull-pillar of pre-Buddhist origin. The Aśokan edicts inscribed on the shaft were carved as a result of the emperor's specific instruction to publicize his edicts on pillars already standing.

Also worth mentioning in this context is Irwin's investigation of the so-called Lāt Bhairo, located on the northern outskirts of Benares and visited by him in 1980.[12] Lāt Bhairo means the staff of Bhairo or Bhaironāth, the boundary-god of the city, worshipped as hereditary policeman or *kotwāl*, assimilated in Hindu legend to Śiva in his terrifying form (*bhairava*). Originally a full-scale pillar once described as 30 metres high, the pillar now survives only as a stump. It was burnt and felled in communal rioting in 1809, and then encased in protective copper sheeting installed by the District Magistrate; and is even now worshipped by Hindus as a Śiva *liṅga*. Still kept an eye on by the police, it has never been investigated beneath the copper for fear of riots. It cannot therefore be established whether it was founded on a placement stone like Aśoka's pillars or upon less stable foundations as is the case with pre-Aśokan bull- and elephant-pillars. (*End of editor's summary.*)

A pillar which was actually erected by Aśoka himself is no doubt the lion-pillar at Sārnāth, the reputed site of the Buddha's first discourse. My reconstruction (Fig. 4a) shows the pillar as originally intended to be seen, rising straight from the ground, towards its capital of four addorsed lions surmounted by a *cakra* (originally symbolizing the solar wheel). My second illustration (Fig. 4b) shows the structure below ground where the base of the tapering shaft is only rough-hewn; the monument rests upon a foundation slab of stone. Originally sacred pillars had been made from the trunk of a sacred tree, ritually felled, carved and again erected. The tapering form of a sacred tree is preserved in this monolithic pillar of stone. It is, of course, a religious monument and it duplicates both for the 'cosmic pillar' and the 'world tree'

The capital of four addorsed lions (Fig. 4c) evokes 'the four directions' of space. On the abacus are four wheels alternating with four animals: the lion, the bull, the elephant and the horse (of which the bull and the elephant are visible on our sketch). The summit wheel (surviving only in fragments and reconstructed in Fig. 4a) is not just the 'Wheel of Law' of doctrinaire Buddhism, but also a symbol of the sun. Thus the evolution of monumental art from bare structure to the incorporation of emblems and decorations continues to evoke its cosmogonic origins.[13]

Turning to another Buddhist monument, the stūpa, I had classified it as a sacred tumulus mythically evolved from the 'primordial mound'. I showed further the prior importance of the axial pillar found in the stūpa, as of symbolical significance derived from the tree/pillar in the mound.[14] Fig. 5a is a plan of the great stūpa at Sāñcī based upon the original excavation report, and Fig. 5b is an elevation-view. We note that the stūpa is enriched by a processional pathway (*pradakṣiṇapatha*), and the entire sacred area is surrounded by a railing (*vedikā*); there are

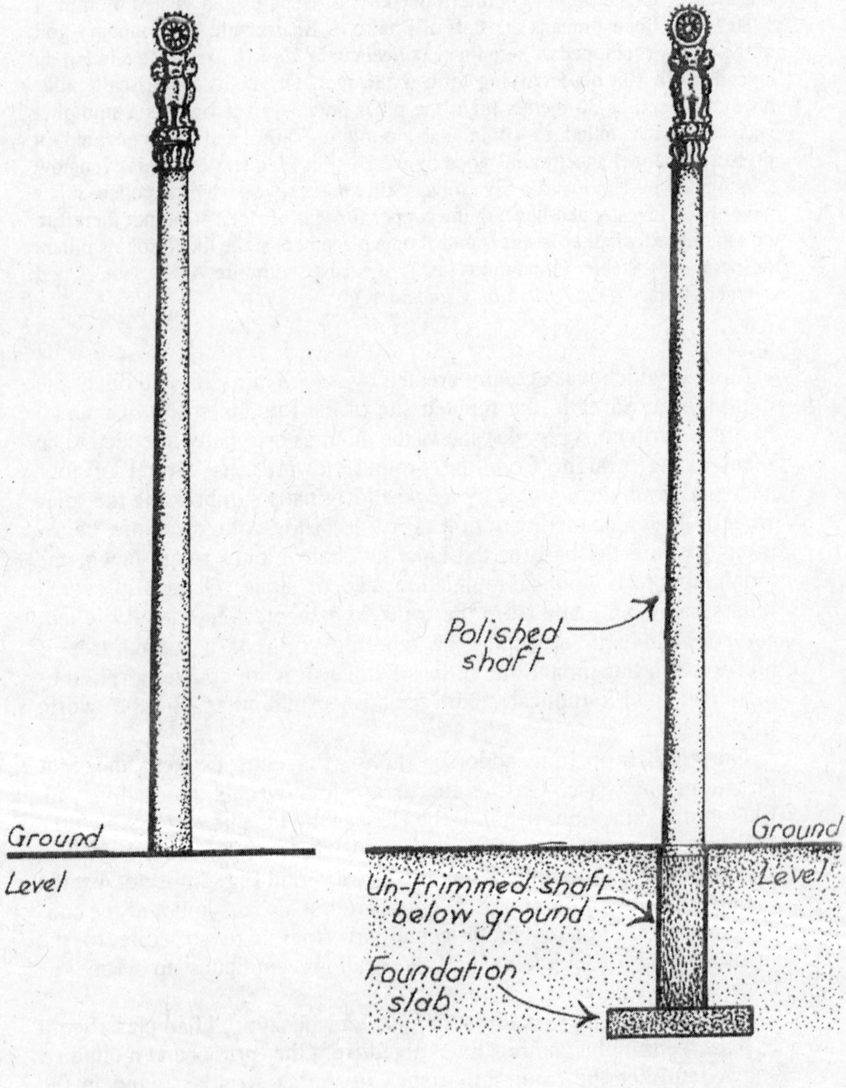

Fig. 4. (a) (left) The Sārnāth Pillar: a reconstruction as it would have originally appeared

(b) (right) The Sārnāth Pillar: the section showing structure below ground

Fig. 4. (c) Detail of the Capital as it survives today

four gateways, placed at the four cardinal points, richly decorated with pictorial sculptures which have formed the basis of our knowledge of the beliefs and legends of early Buddhism. The stūpa itself has been extensively restored, but the fundamental axial pillar is seen emerging at the summit of the dome, here supporting the *chattras* (sacred 'umbrellas' or canopies). The monument has evolved its own sophistication of decoration, but the basic traditions of form and structure are steadfastly fulfilled.

It is seen from the plan (Fig. 5a) that beside the south gate is the site of the pillar erected by Aśoka. The stump of the shaft still survives *in situ* (Fig. 5b) while the lion capital, similar to that of Sārnāth (Fig. 4c), is in the Sāñcī site museum. The excavations and restorations revealed that the stūpa had been enlarged several times, and thus the Aśokan pillar originally stood at a short distance from Aśoka's original stūpa and not in its present cramped position almost touching the railing of the later enlargement of the monument.[15]

Editor's summary: Irwin investigated another ancient pillar monument in connection with the symbolical role which 'the wheel-pillar or *cakra-stambha*, chief emblem of early Buddhist art', acquired in the new doctrine.[16] It is the pillar known locally as Minār-i-Chakri and situated in Afghanistan, 15 km south of Kabul, which he personally inspected in 1979. Its name (the etymology of the Arabic 'minar' suggests 'object that gives light'; 'chakri' is clearly from Sanskrit *cakra*, 'wheel') points to its ancient function as an emblem of the sun, symbolizing the dawn of creation when heaven and earth became separated by the cosmic axis and the sun thus rose from the captivity of the primordial mound. This was represented in the Vedas by *vṛtra*, 'the power of resistance', also referred to as Vṛtra, the primordial demon-serpent.

The worship of the Buddhist wheel pillar, attested on many reliefs, is not explained by its usual association with the phrase of 'the turning of the wheel of the law' (*dharma-cakra-pravartana*) regarded as referring to the Buddha's first sermon in the Deer Park at Sārnāth. Irwin re-examined the textual evidence and concluded that it was also associated with the two earlier events: 'one was the most popular in Buddhist narrative art; the other, central to the whole of Buddhist religion.' The first was the story of the Buddha's victory over the demon Māra and the second his enlightenment, 'the starting point of his career as the Buddha'. They are virtually interchangeable. 'Therefore, in so far as the Wheel-pillar is symbol of anything, it stands for both the Buddha Himself and his Enlightenment!'

The conquest of Māra by every Buddha and his enlightenment occur in each epoch on one and the same spot known as the *bodhimaṇḍa* (mound/throne/altar at the base of the Bodhi tree) which cannot be located in terms of 'profane geography'. This event is, in fact, mythologically identical with the defeat of Vṛtra and the freeing of the sun from the primordial mound in the Vedas, and thus a reiteration and adaptation of the archaic 'creation myth'.[17]

The Buddhist link to the ancient cosmogonical mythology was explored by Irwin in yet another paper in which he focused on the meaning of the legendary first pronouncements of the newly-born Buddha-to-be to the effect that he is chief (*aggo*, meaning in fact 'first' and applicable to time, space and quality), best and eldest in the world (MN III,123; Horner's translation III,168).[18] Irwin stresses that his concern is not with the doctrine, which expresses what is unique in a religion and what differentiates it from other religions, but with cult which, however much it may be specialized in its later manifestations, always has roots in a common archetypal past. By scanning Vedic texts Irwin finds the formula of the first words based on phrases used in the context of the 'beginning', of the birth of Prajāpati and of Indra and Vṛtra as the foremost among gods and *asuras*. By examining symbolical depictions of the great events in the Buddha's life on reliefs of Buddhist monuments he discovers that, besides the three well-known representations of enlightenment by a tree, first sermon by a wheel and the Buddha's death by a stūpa (all of which have been linked by him to cosmogonic symbolism also in his other investigations), there is a relief from the Bharhut stūpa which clearly depicts the archetypal Divine Mother standing on a lotus and lustrated by a pair of celestial elephants. The lotus stems from a 'vase of plenty'. This medallion represents both cosmic and divine birth, while the Buddhists regarded it as portraying Māyā, the mother of the future Buddha. There is only a small step from this to understanding the traditional nativity of the Buddha-to-be in the cosmogonic context, especially with the added depiction of his first steps indicated by lotus flowers; a Kushāna relief in Mathura Museum which shows him standing on a mound while uttering the first words strengthens further the core of Irwin's thesis: 'that all aniconic symbols of the Buddha's presence . . . have their ultimate source in cosmogonic myth, and more especially in the Vedic version of that event, which was Indra's victory over Vṛtra'.

An additional result of Irwin's investigations is his contribution to the solution of the problem why the early representations of the Buddha or even of the Buddha-to-be were aniconic. He points out that until a relatively late period in the development of religious iconography, the cosmic deities were never worshipped in human form, while lower terrestrial deities such as tree-spirits, water-spirits and guardian deities (*yakṣas*, *nāgas* and *bhūtas*) were. Cosmic deities were worshipped as aniconic images such as Mound, Cosmic Tree or Pillar [also as solar disc or wheel, stars etc.]. They did, however, assume human form for earthly visitations and the distinction between the two categories became gradually blurred. In AV (10,7,38) the cosmic pillar (*skaṁbha*) and even the ultimate divine principle (*brahman*) were already being called *yakṣa*. And even the Buddha is occasionally referred to by this term in Buddhist sources. [It is well known that images of *yakṣas* served as models for the earliest known statues of the standing Buddha.] The worship of higher deities under aniconic forms continues even today at 'sacred spots' (*bhavanas* — marked by a tree or stone or mound) outside some Indian villages, although nowadays such spots may also have icons of deities. But the worshipped aniconic representations now as in ancient times are not what we call 'symbols' of the divine, but *actual manifestations of sacred power.* This is clear from the AV 10,7,29 – 30 where it is said that *skaṁbha* is Indra and Indra is *skaṁbha*.

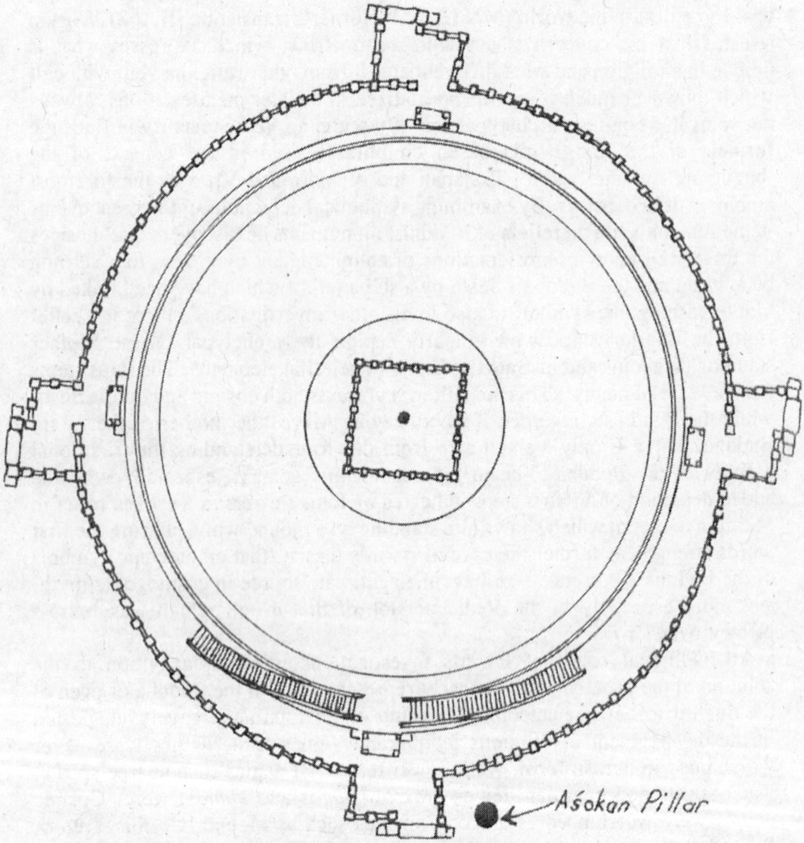

Fig. 5. (a) The Great Stūpa at Sāñci: plan

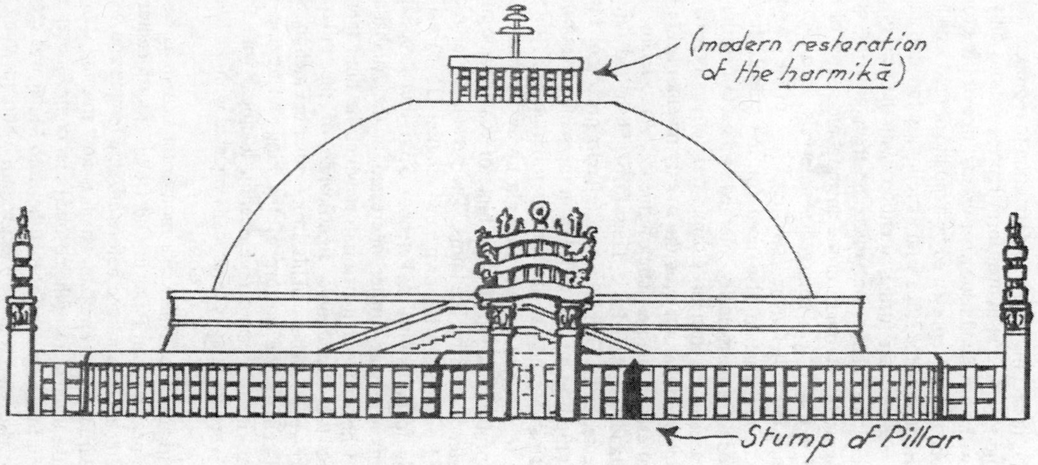

Fig. 5. (b) Elevation viewed from the south, showing the stump of the Aśokan Pillar beside the South Gate

Similarly the primordial mound in its countless cultic forms (tumulus, *caitya*, altar, navelstone, plinth such as the one the newly-born Bodhisattva stands on in a Gandhāran relief now in Musée et Institut d'Ethnographie, Geneva) does not represent but *is*, or is one with, the divine principle of the unmanifest world prior to creation. Thus, we can say, it follows logically from Irwin's presentation, that it was in keeping with an old tradition to represent the Buddha by aniconic forms, and to arrive at human form representations only later.

The question of how the pre-Buddhist *caitya-vṛksas* (tree of life growing out of the cosmogonic mound, often represented by a mound of mud with a pillar or *yūpa* stemming from it) became the stūpa with its reliquary function and a place of Buddhist worship receives here further attention, with the help of the same Gandhāran relief, mentioned above, on which the tree, growing out of the square plinth, is recognizably an image of the cosmogonic source of life. The mound as a place of worship 'was enlarged at intervals, as a pious act, in accordance with cosmogonic belief in the "swelling" . . . of the "womb of the universe" ' (*garbha*, a designation also used for the stūpa). In Buddhist practice, the stūpa used to be periodically enlarged as an act of spiritual merit.

In his search for traces of the ancient 'Cosmic religion' associated with the cult of the pillar Irwin found that not even the strictly revelational religions of Christianity and Islam escaped its persisting influence. As to Islam, this is, of course, fully understandable in India.[19] Thus Firoz Shah had three pillars transported and re-erected in the Delhi region; the Topra pillar (no. 3 in Table 1 above) being placed (1369) in his fort at Delhi in the same relationship to his own mosque, the Jami' Masjid, as the sacred pillar *dhvaja* (often called 'flagstaff') would be to a Hindu temple. Brought up by his widowed Hindu mother, Firoz Shah probably acquired some hints of cosmogonic mythology from her and was later briefed by brahmins. The great Mughal Akbar who broke with Islam and proclaimed his own new religion (1575) had another ancient pillar brought to his capital at Fatehpur Sikri, but it collapsed and shattered to fragments. He was further interested in the Allahābād pillar, discussed above, and he enclosed it in his fort which he built there. Being knowledgeable about the cosmogonic significance of the pillar and its association with the kingship, Akbar had his throne pillar in Fatehpur Sikri built in an image reminiscent of the posture of the king during the Rājasūya ceremony, an annual rite of cosmic regeneration identical with the act of primordial creation, when the king is 'mystically equated with the life force of the universe'.

Irwin further investigated the remarkable monument known as Kutb Minār (A.D. 1192) and the nearby 'Iron Pillar of Old Delhi' (fourth century A.D.). The latter had been erected on a mound before a Viṣṇu temple and would have had the 'sun-bird' Garuda as its emblem which is now missing. Irwin shows that the pillar has all the usual signs of the cosmic pillar commemorating Indra's cosmogonic act. Irwin further maintains that the Kutb Minār was erected with the same cosmogonic associations in the background. 'Qutb' meaning 'axis', he interprets the name as 'axis giving light'. It could not, of course, have had an obvious solar emblem on top, but its cupola, several times renewed after damage by lightning and an earthquake, had a 'sunhole', an ancient solar emblem which survives in the religious architecture of all traditions.

Irwin has applied his theory of the origin of pillar monuments in the ancient universal cosmic religion rooted in the myth of creation, solar worship and fertility cult also to the European monuments such as market crosses and the Celtic wheel crosses. Already in his paper on 'Buddhism and the Cosmic Pillar' he published two pictures of the Bromborough market 'cross'; one being an old drawing (though published only in 1875) from the time when it was still a monument crowned with a sundial and orb without any Cross Ecclesiastical, and the other, a photograph, as it is now after Victorian reconstruction [carried out, ironically enough, in 1874] which replaced the sundial and orb with a gothic-style carved head topped with a cross. He has since formulated his thesis, supported by massive evidence, in his latest paper 'Pillar and Cross'[20] which he himself regards as the most ambitious he has so far attempted. (*End of editor's summary.*)

NOTES

1 Editor's note: In this context it may be opportune to remind ourselves of RV 10,129 (discussed in the editor's article) where the unformed dimension remains outside the concepts of *sat* and *asat* which both belong to the dimension of the 'formed', this side of creation, like all other dualities. The precreational dimension is seen as outside the concepts of 'being' and 'non-being'. The thrust of Irwin's argument is not affected by this discrepancy which is only terminological and occurred already in some of the Vedic texts themselves.

2 W. R. Lethaby, *Architecture, Mysticism and Myth*, London, 1881, repr. by The Architectural Press Ltd., London, 1974, ed. by Godfrey Rubens.

3 A. J. Wensinck, *The Ideas of the Western Semites concerning the Navel of the Earth* (Verhandelingen der Koninklijke Akademie van Wetenschappen te Amsterdam, Afdeeling Letterkunde, n.s. 17, no. 1), Amsterdam, 1916.

4 See F. B. J. Kuiper, *Ancient Indian Cosmogony*, selected essays, ed. with an Introduction by John C. Irwin, New Delhi, 1983 — Professor Kuiper's important work on the cosmogonic significance of Indra in the Vedic texts was developed over several years.

5 Mircea Eliade, 'Centre du Monde, Temple, Maison', *Symbolisme cosmique des Monuments religieux* (L'Instituto Italiano per il Medio ed Estremo Oriente), Rome, 1957.

6 William Blake was driving at the same thing when he wrote in his own language (in *The Last Judgement*): 'The nature of my work is VISIONARY and IMAGINATIVE: it is an endeavour to restore what the ancients called the "Golden Age".'

7 They appeared in four instalments under the title ' "Aśokan" Pillars: a reassessment of the evidence', *The Burlington Magazine*, (London), vol. CXV (November 1973), pp. 706 – 20; vol. CXVI (December 1974), pp. 712 – 27; vol. CXVII (October 1975), pp. 631 – 42; and vol. CXVIII (November 1976), pp. 734 – 53.

8 Irwin returned more thoroughly to the question of dating in his paper 'The True Chronology of Aśokan Pillars', *Artibus Asiae*, vol. XLIV, 4 (Institute of Fine Arts, New York University, 1983), pp. 247 – 65.

9 For further study of this link see Irwin's paper 'The Axis Mundi and the Phallus: Some Unrecognized East-West Parallels', *Folklore Studies in the 20th Century* (proceedings of the centenary conference of the Folklore Society, University College, London, 1978), ed. V. J. Newall, Woodbridge, Suffolk & Totowa, New Jersey, 1980, pp. 250 – 9.

10 Further details in Irwin's paper 'The Heliodorus Pillar: a Fresh Appraisal', *Art and Archaeology Research Papers*, no. 6 (December 1974), pp. 1 – 13; revised as 'The Heliodorus Pillar at Besnagar', *Purātattva*, Bulletin of the Indian Archaeological Society, no. 8 (1975 – 6; issued 1978), pp. 166 – 76.

11 He dealt with it in two papers: 'The Prayāga Bull Pillar: another pre-Aśokan monument', *South Asian Archaeology 1979*, proceedings of the Fifth International Conference of The Association of South Asian Archaeologists in Western Europe, held in the Museum für indische Kunst der Staatlichen Museen Preussischer Kulturbesitz, Berlin 1979; and 'The ancient pillar-cult at Prayāga (Allahabad): its pre-Aśokan origins', JRAS 1983 (no. 2), pp. 253 – 80.

12 'The Lāṭ Bhairo at Benares (Vārāṇasī): Another Pre-Aśokan Monument?', ZDMG, vol. 133, no. 2 (1983), pp. 321 – 52.

13 The full structure and symbolism of the capitals of the 'Aśokan' pillars is discussed in the third instalment of my series quoted in note 7.

14 'The Stūpa and the Cosmic Axis: The Archaeological Evidence', *South Asian Archaeology 1977*, Papers from the Fourth International Conference of South Asian Archaeologists in Europe, Naples (Istituto Universitario Orientale), 1979.

'The Axial Symbolism of the Early Stūpa: An Exegesis', *The Stūpa: its religious, historical and architectural significance*, ed. A. L. Dallapiccola & S. Z-A Lallemant, Wiesbaden (Südostasien Institut, Universität Heidelberg), 1980.

'The Stūpa and the Cosmic Axis (*yūpa-yaṣṭi*)', *Acāryavandana: D. R. Bhandarkar Birth Centenary Volume*, University of Calcutta, 1984.

15 Sir John Marshall & Alfred Foucher, *The Monuments of Sāñchī*, 3 vols., no place and date given (probably Calcutta, 1947). Marshall's account in vol. I, pp. 19 – 20, identified the original brick core as the Aśoka's original stūpa which springs from the same floor-level as the Aśokan pillar near the present south gateway. The pillar itself is discussed in vol. I, pp. 25 – 9 and illustrated in vol. III, pl. 106 – 7.

16 'Buddhism and the Cosmic Pillar', *Orientalia Iosephi Tucci Memoriae Dicata*, ed. G. Gnoli & L. Lanciotti, Rome (Istituto Italiano per il Medio ed Estremo Oreinte), 1987, pp. 635 – 60.

17 The wider context of this myth is discussed in Irwin's paper 'The Sacred Anthill and the Cult of the Primordial Mound', HR, vol. 21, no. 4 (May 1982).

18 'The Mystery of the (Future) Buddha's First Words', *Annali dell' Instituto Orientale di Napoli*, vol. 41 (1981), pp. 622 – 60.

19 References to Islamic associations are scattered in most of Irwin's papers, but the following ones deal with the topic directly: 'Akbar and the Cosmic Pillar', *Facets of Indian Art*, ed. R. W. Skelton et al., London, 1986, pp. 47 – 50 (proceedings of a seminar at V & A in April 1982).

'Islam and the Cosmic Pillar', *Investigating Indian Art* (Veröffentlichungen des Museums für indische Kunst, vol. 8), Berlin, 1987, pp. 133 – 45 (proceedings of a Symposium at that museum in May 1986). Another version of this paper was delivered by Irwin at the 8th International Conference of South Asian Archaeologists at Moesgard, Denmark, in July 1985, the Proceedings published as *South Asian Archaeology 1985*, London 1989.

20 Originally a lecture presented at the British Council in Calcutta in 1987 and published in *RILKO Newsletter* No. 33 (1988), pp. 6 – 24 (RILKO stands for 'Research into Lost Knowledge Organization' of which Irwin is President Emeritus), and it will be included in a small volume of Irwin's essays *Tree and Pillar*, ed. Margaret Hall, RILKO, 1991.

5

VENERATED OBJECTS AND SYMBOLS OF EARLY BUDDHISM

Peter Harvey

As is well known, early Buddhist art did not depict Gotama, or any previous Buddha, in a human form. It must have been partly due to the current Hindu practice which portrayed, in human form, only minor deities such as *yakkhas*, but also to the feeling that the profound nature of a Buddha could not be adequately conveyed by a mere human form. This holds true even for the scenes from his life before enlightenment which may reflect the Lokottaravāda speculations that even as *bodhisatta* he was 'transcendental'. Or it may have been merely an acknowledgement of the immense spiritual power built up by developing the 'perfections' of a *bodhisatta* over many lives.

The major gods of Brahmanism were represented only by symbols and early Buddhist art made also considerable use of them to convey through this aniconic form something of the nature of the Buddha, as in Fig. 1 where the empty space surrounded by worshippers is occupied only by the Buddha's footprints made meaningful by the wheel symbol. The early symbols continued in use even after portrayals of the Buddhas in human form developed from the second century A.D. and were often preferred as better indications of the inexpressible nature of a Buddha.

More important than symbols, though, early Buddhism attached significance to certain venerable objects as reflected in a preamble to a Jātaka story, at J IV,228 (cf. Miln 341), where the Buddha refers to three types of *cetiya* (shrine), clearly in descending order of importance:

1. *Sarīrika-cetiya*: shrines containing physical 'relics' (called *dhātus*, i.e. 'elements') of a Buddha or an *arahant*. They referred primarily to the bones and teeth left after cremation, but copies of such funerary remains and hair or nail clippings of enlightened ones came also to be included.

2. *Pāribhogika-cetiya*: shrines of things used by a Buddha which include alms bowl and robe, their copies, and sites of key events in the Buddha's life which became important places of pilgrimage. The most important objects of this category are the ones emphasized in J IV,228: the tree under which the Buddha attained enlightenment, its saplings and in later tradition even any member of the species Aśvattha (Ficus Religiosa) which became known to Buddhists as the Bodhi or Enlightenment tree.
3. *Uddesika-cetiya*: shrines 'indicating' the nature of a Buddha: first symbols and all kinds of aniconic portrayals of the Buddha images when they developed.

RELICS

Physical relics are seen as the most powerful focus for Buddhist devotion. They act, first, as reminders of a Buddha or saint, their spiritual qualities, their teachings and the fact that they have actually lived on earth. This in turn shows that it is possible for a human being to become a Buddha or a saint. While even copies of relics can act as reminders, they cannot fulfil the second function of relics proper, because these are thought to contain something of the spiritual force and purity of the person they once formed part of. As that person was free of spiritual faults and possessed great energy for good, it is believed that his relics were somehow affected by this. They are therefore seen as radiating a kind of beneficial power. This is probably why ch. 28 of the Bv states: 'The ancients say that the dispersal of the relics of Gotama, the great seer, was out of compassion for living beings.'

Miraculous powers are also attributed to relics, as seen in a story related in Mv XXXI, 97 – 100. When king Duṭṭhāgāmaṇi (161 – 137 B.C.) was enshrining some relics of Gotama in the great stūpa at Anurādhapura, they rose into the air in their casket and then emerged to form the shape of the Buddha. In a similar vein, VA p. 433 says that at the end of the 5000 year period of the Buddhist era all the relics in Sri Lanka will assemble, travel through the air to the foot of the Bodhi tree in India, emit rays of light and then disappear in a flash of light. This is referred to as the *parinibbāna* of the *dhātus*. Relics, then, act both as reminders of Gotama, or some other holy being, and as actual tangible links with them and their spiritual powers. The Mv XXX, 100 says, indeed, that there is equal merit in devotion to the Buddha's relics as there was in devotion to him when he was alive.

Fig. 1

Fig. 2

Fig. 1. Rāhula being presented to his father shown in aniconic representation. Drawing according to a relief from a stūpa railing at Amarāvatī. Cf. D. L. Snellgrove (ed.), *The Image of the Buddha*, Paris & London, 1978, pl. 19, p. 38.

Fig. 2. Relief medallion depicting a *bodhighara* (Mathura, 2nd cent. B.C.). Cf. J. Irwin, 'The Stūpa and the Cosmic Axis', Fig. 27.

BODHI TREES

In pre-Buddhist India there was already a cult of sacred trees such as the Aśvattha. They were often surrounded by a railing and had a mud platform at the base as a place to put offerings to the tree or the minor deity seen as inhabiting it. When worshipped, they were seen as fulfilling wishes and granting fertility.

The Buddha frequently recommended the roots of trees as places for his monks to meditate. He himself, on the eve of his enlightenment, chose to meditate beneath one. This was probably a tree shrine and at night it would have been deserted by villagers in fear of the deity's presence. The awe-inspiring nature of the place would, then, be an aid to develop alertness and self-possession.

According to Vin I,1 – 4 the Buddha stayed near the Bodhi tree for four weeks after his enlightenment. The N extends this period to seven weeks and says that, for the second of these, the Buddha continually contemplated the tree with feelings of deep gratitude for its having sheltered him at his most important time. The Aśvattha tree, then, naturally became a symbol for Gotama's attainment of enlightenment and the state of enlightenment itself.[1]

The original Bodhi tree and its descendants were, like relics, more than symbolic reminders of the Buddha, for they, too, were tangible links with him and his spiritual power. This dimension of power is portrayed in Mv XVIII: when the emperor Aśoka (273 – 232 B.C.) wished to take a cutting of the original tree to send to Sri Lanka, it manifested wonderful powers. A branch severed itself from the tree, floated in the air while it grew roots and later emitted rays of light in six colours.

From the earliest times of Buddhism Bodhi trees seem to have been foci of attention. Devotees would, as in pre-Buddhist tree worship, water them, attach flags to their branches and place offerings on the platform at their base. They would also perform the act of clockwise circumambulation or *padakkhiṇā/pradakṣiṇā*, literally 'keeping to the right'. This action is a common one in the Buddhist tradition; it is also performed round a stūpa and, especially in Tibet, round any sacred object, building or person. Keeping one's right side towards someone is a way of showing respect to them: in the Pāli Canon people are often said to have departed from the Buddha keeping their right side towards him. The precedent for actual circumambulation may have been the Brahmanic practice of the priest walking around the fire-sacrifice offerings or of a bride walking around the domestic hearth at her marriage.[2] All such practices demonstrate that what one walks around is, or should be, the 'centre' of one's life.

Originally Buddhist tree-shrines were, like their predecessors, simply surrounded by a wooden railing (*vedikā*). During Aśoka's time the increasing popularity of the religion led to the development of more elaborate enclosures known as 'Bodhi houses' (*bodhigharas*) as shown in Fig. 2. From their gallery devotees could circumambulate and water the trees without churning up a sea of mud.

BUDDHA-FOOTPRINTS

Another kind of 'utilized' venerable objects are 'footprints' of the Buddha (Buddha-pāda) in the form of depressions in rocks. They act as reminders that the Buddha actually walked on earth and that he left a spiritual 'path' for others to follow; they are also seen as tangible links with him. Whether they were part of the earliest Buddhist cult is unclear, but they were used in aniconic symbolical representations of his presence in the scenes from his life (Fig. 1).

One of the most famous 'footprints' is the depression measuring five and a half by two and three-quarters feet in the rock on top of Mount Siripāda (Adam's Peak) in Sri Lanka. The Chinese Buddhist pilgrim Fa-hsien records having seen it in A.D. 412. The Mv I,77 – 8 (6th cent. A.D.), based on earlier chronicles, refers to the 'footprint' as having been made by the Buddha when he once flew to Sri Lanka by means of his psychic power (*iddhi*).

The symbols of early Buddhism which 'indicate' the nature of the Buddha include depictions of 'utilized' venerable objects, especially Bodhi trees and Buddha-footprints. By at least the second century A.D. large 'prints' of soles of feet were used as cult objects in the art of Amarāvatī and Gandhāra. On them were various symbols such as auspicious svastikas, lotuses and, most frequently, wheels (Fig. 1), a type of mark (*lakkhaṇa*) of a great man said to have been on the body of Gotama from his birth. Later art embellished such feet or footprints with up to 108 auspicious signs such as the sun, moon and Mount Meru,[3] all marvellous things of importance, though lower than the Buddha. Positive copies of the 'real' footprints were also frequently taken and became cult objects.

THE LOTUS

One of the most common and important early Buddhist symbols is the lotus. In India it has always been looked upon as the most beautiful of flowers. Its bursting into blossom above the water made it a symbol for the birth of gods and of the world. In the RV the god Agni is said to have been born from a lotus. In the Brāhmaṇas and Āraṇyakas the lotus was the seat of the creator Prajāpati or the base on which he placed the earth after he had dredged it up from the cosmic ocean. The lotus was particularly associated with the goddess Śrī or Śrī-Lakṣmī, described in a late portion of the RV as 'lotus-born' and holding a lotus in her hand.[4] According to Coomaraswamy she and the lotus represented the earth, the waters (of life) and all the potential and creative energy latent in the waters: 'that wherein/whereon there is or can be manifestation'.[5]

In early aniconic art motifs involving lotuses and Śrī-Lakṣmī were used to depict the birth of Gotama, e.g. in a second century B.C. relief at Bhārhut. Medallions depicting a circle of open lotus petals were particularly common (Fig. 3). As a pan-Indian symbol for birth and creative growth, though, the lotus took on a meaning in Buddhism which went beyond the mere indication of Gotama's physical birth. A passage which frequently recurs in the *suttas* (e.g. S III,140) gives a good indication of the symbolic nuances of the lotus in Buddhism:

> Just as, monks, a lotus, blue, red or white, though born in the water, grown up in the water, when it reaches the surface stands there unsoiled by the water; just so, monks, though born in the world, grown up in the world, having overcome the world, a Tathāgata abides unsoiled by the world.

Just as the beautiful lotus blossom grows up from the mud and water, so one with an enlightened mind develops out of the ranks of ordinary beings, by maturing the spiritual potential latent in all. Like the Bodhi tree the lotus is a symbol drawn from the vegetable kingdom. While both suggest spiritual *growth*, the lotus emphasizes the *potential* for growth, whereas the Bodhi tree indicates the *culmination* of this growth: enlightenment. The lotus as a symbol for spiritual potential is illustrated at M I,169 when the newly-enlightened Buddha surveys the world and sees that some people are ripe for hearing his liberating message while others are less mature. This is likened to the situation of lotuses in a pond where some are thriving below the water, but others have reached its surface or are standing above it unsoiled.

The fact that drops of water roll off a lotus (cf. 'like water off a duck's back') gives this unsoiled flower an added symbolic meaning in Buddhism as a simile for non-attachment. As Mahāmoggallāna says of himself at Thag 1180, 'he is not soiled by conditioned phenomena as a lotus is not soiled by water'. As Miln 375 explains, the 'earnest student of yoga' should be like the lotus in being unsoiled by those who support him, by his disciples, gains, honour, fame or his requisites if a monk. *Nibbāna* is also likened to a lotus in being 'unsoiled by defilements' (Miln 318), since it is beyond attachment, hatred and delusion that worldly beings are involved in.

A third aspect of the lotus' symbolic meaning is, indeed, that the enlightened person, like the lotus standing above the water, has overcome the world (of senses). While arising out of the 'mud' of worldly defilements, he grows beyond them and stands 'above' the world in his non-attachment. As Miln 375 says, the 'earnest student of yoga' must be like the lotus, for 'having overcome and risen above the world, he must stand firm in the supramundane state (*lokuttara-dhamme*)'. Miln 375 also ascribes a further symbolic meaning to the lotus:

> And again, moved by the slightest breeze, the lotus trembles; even so, sire, the yogin, the earnest student of yoga, should exercise restraint among even the slightest defilements, he should abide seeing the peril (in them).

THE VASE OF PLENTY

An early Buddhist symbol of some importance which became one of the eight auspicious symbols in the Sinhalese and Tibetan traditions is the *pūrṇa-ghaṭa* or *pūrṇa-kumbha*, the 'vase of plenty'. It is also an auspicious symbol in Hinduism, probably equivalent to the golden *kumbha* containing *amṛta*, the gods' nectar of immortality, which emerged at the churning of the cosmic ocean.[6]

To decide on the symbolic meanings of *kumbha* in Buddhism we may fruitfully look at uses of the word in *sutta* similes. At S V,48 and A V,337 water pouring out from an upturned *kumbha* is likened to an *ariyan* disciple getting rid of unskilful states, while at Dhp 121 – 2 a *kumbha* being gradually filled by drops of water is likened to a person gradually filling himself with evil or merit. In this way the *kumbha* is generally likened to the personality as a container of bad or good states. A number of passages, though, use a full *kumbha* as a simile for a specifically positive state of being. At A II,104 a person who understands the four *ariyan* truths 'as they really are' is like a full vase (*pūro kumbha*). Miln 414, with Sn 721 – 2, sees one who has perfected his recluseship (an *arahant*, surely) as being like a full *kumbha* which makes no sound when struck: his speech is not boastful, but he teaches *dhamma*. At A I,131 a person of wide wisdom (*puthupañño*) who bears in mind the *dhamma* he has heard is like an upright *kumbha* which accumulates the water poured into it.

The implication of these passages is that the full *kumbha* would be a natural symbol for the personality of someone who is 'full' of

Fig.3.

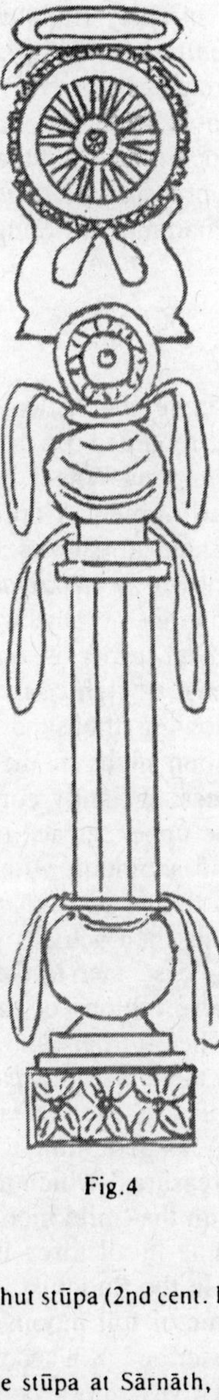

Fig.4

Fig 3. Lotus medallion design from the railing on the Bhārhut stūpa (2nd cent. B.C.; in the Indian Museum Calcutta).

Fig. 4. Composite symbol design from the railing of the stūpa at Sārnāth, early centuries A.D.; from a post-card of the Archaeological Survey of India.

dhamma: a Buddha or a saint. While the Hindu *pūrṇa-ghaṭa* contains *amṛta*, the Buddhist one contains *dhamma*, that which makes life fruitful and brings a person to the *amata* and which in the highest sense (as *nibbāna*) is this 'deathless' state.

In early Buddhist art the 'vase of plenty' was often shown with a lotus or Bodhi tree sprouting from it, so suggesting spiritual growth from the reservoir of *dhamma* which it symbolized. Fig. 4 shows two vases as part of a composite symbol. The upper vase has the disc of an open lotus shown at its lip. Above the lotus is a *triśūla* or trident which represents the *tiratana*: the three 'jewels' or 'treasures' of the Buddha, Dhamma and Sangha.

THE DHAMMA-WHEEL

Above the trident in Fig. 4 is a Dhamma-Wheel (*dhamma-cakka*) surmounted by a parasol, the Indian emblem of sovereignty. The Dhamma-Wheel has been one of the major Buddhist symbols since early times. A crucial key to the understanding of its meaning are the canonical stories of just and compassionate emperors of the past known as *cakkavattis* or 'wheel-turners'. Accounts of these rulers in past ages of the world are found in D II,169 – 98 and III,58 – 79. A wheel-turner is one who rules in accordance with *dhamma*, in the sense of righteousness and moral order. Due to the nature of his rule a glowing thousand-spoked 'divine (*dibba-*) wheel' appears on a full moon night in the sky like a second full moon. Moving above the trees, it finally comes to rest hovering in front of the ruler who is on the upper terrace of his palace. The king does reverence to the wheel and anoints it with water, setting it spinning. He then urges it to roll forth and accompany him in the peaceful conquest of the whole world. This then actually happens. The ruler, his army and the wheel go to the east, then to the south, then to the west and then to the north; in all these regions of the earth other kings accept the overlordship of the 'wheel-turner' and his advice to live ethically. The wheel then returns to the emperor's palace as one of his seven 'treasures' (*ratanas*). Such a list of seven 'treasures', beginning with the wheel, occurs also in the RV as pertaining to Agni or Soma-Rudra; the Mhb I,18 also lists seven 'treasures' which appear at the churning of the cosmic ocean, starting with the 'mild moon of 1000 rays'; five of the seven 'treasures' are the same in all three lists if the moon disc is counted as a wheel.

In the Buddhist legend the wheel, although appearing initially at the time of full moon, is certainly different from the actual moon, as it is described as a second moon. It stays in the emperor's palace as long as he lives ruling compassionately. Shortly before his death it starts to sink down from its established place, and disappears seven days after the ageing emperor renounces the world (D III,59). The wheel is thus portrayed as a kind of apparition seen by both the emperor and his people, which is a sign that a compassionate ruler is still on his throne. The key aspect of its meaning is that it symbolizes the emperor's just rule radiating outwards to all the lands of the earth. Buddhaghosa explains that on the outer side of the wheel's rim are 100 parasols, each accompanied by two spear-heads. These symbolize the emperor's power of peaceful conquest, while the parasols as emblems of royalty represent all the kings of the earth who come willingly to accept the righteous rule of the emperor (DA II,617ff).

A 'wheel-turner' emperor and a Buddha are seen as parallel figures. Both are said to be born with the 'thirty-two marks of a great man' on their body, including a wheel mark on the soles of both feet (D III,142 – 79). On death their bodies should be interred in a stūpa. A Buddha is a great religious leader teaching virtue and compassion and a wheel-turner is a great political leader ruling with virtue and compassion. A Buddha reveres *dhamma* in the sense of righteousness and moral order. A Buddha, then, can be seen as a kind of spiritual wheel-turning emperor. Indeed, at Thag 824 he refers to himself as a *dhamma-rāja*, i.e. Dhamma-sovereign. This notion of the Buddha's spiritual sovereignty came to be expressed by crowned Buddha images which had developed in India by the twelfth century.

It is in the Buddha's first sermon, 'The Setting in Motion of the Dhamma-Wheel' (*dhamma-cakka-pavattana-sutta*) that the notion of the 'Dhamma-Wheel' is rooted. It is further used in S I,191 where the Buddha says to Sāriputta:

> Just as the eldest son of a wheel-turner sovereign rolls on aright the wheel set rolling by his father, even so do you, Sāriputta, roll on aright the supreme Dhamma-Wheel set rolling by me.

In the first sermon the Dhamma-Wheel does not roll until the first member of the Buddha's audience gains insight into his teachings, so attaining the *dhamma-cakkhu*, or Dhamma-eye', thus becoming a stream-enterer. At this the gods are said to have cried out:

> The supreme Dhamma-Wheel rolled thus by the Lord in the deer park at Sārnāth cannot be rolled back by . . . anyone in the world.

The setting in motion of the Dhamma-Wheel, then, clearly refers not only to the Buddha's act of giving *dhamma* in the sense of 'teachings', but also to transmitting it in the sense of spiritual experience and realization. By this act the Buddha inaugurated the 'rule' or influence of *dhamma* — the teachings, the spiritual path and their realizations which culminate in *nibbāna*; this act is clearly paralleled to the wheel-turner emperor's inauguration of an earthly empire.

The 'treasure-wheel' and the Dhamma-Wheel are said, not surprisingly, to look exactly alike. For practical purposes each is depicted with less than 1000 spokes and 100 parasols (Fig. 5). In time the spear-heads disappeared and the parasols degenerated into residual bumps.

In its simplest sense the Dhamma-Wheel represents the transmission of *dhamma* in the first sermon. From this it naturally came to symbolize the Buddha as teacher, the Dhamma as teaching, and the power of both to transform people's lives. The two are, of course, intimately related. The Buddha affirmed that 'who sees *dhamma* sees me, who sees me sees *dhamma*' (S III,120): such 'seeing' *dhamma* is done when the 'Dhamma-eye' arises in a person. The Buddha also said that he was *dhamma-bhūta*, he had 'become *dhamma*' (D III,84): he had fully practised the *dhamma* as spiritual path and had attained *dhamma* in the sense of the path's goal, *nibbāna*. As he fully embodied *dhamma* in this way, he was fully able to give *dhamma* in the sense of teachings.

As with most symbols the meaning of the Dhamma-Wheel, in symbolizing the Buddha and the Dhamma, is multivalent. In RV V,1,164 the sun is likened to a revolving wheel, 'the immortal wheel which nothing stops, on which all existence depends'. Buddhaghosa actually likens the spokes of the Dhamma-Wheel to the sun's rays and the hub to a full moon. It seems appropriate, then, to see the radiating spokes of the Dhamma-Wheel as suggesting that, like the sun, the Buddha shed the warmth of his compassion and the light of his wisdom on all who came to him.

In the RV the solar deity Mitra is said to be the 'eye of the world'; that is, the sun both illuminates and watches over the world. Certain Dhamma-Wheels (Fig. 6) are certainly reminiscent of an eye in their appearance and can thus be seen as symbolizing the spiritual vision of the Buddha at whose death certain followers said (D II,158), 'the eye has disappeared in the world'! The eye-like nature of the Dhamma-Wheel also suggests that it first 'turned' when a disciple of the Buddha first gained the 'Dhamma-eye'. In all this there may well be a pun on *cakka*, wheel, and *cakkhu*, eye.

In the RV the wheel is a possession of the god Varuṇa, the 'universal monarch' (*sam-rāj*) and lord of *ṛta*, cosmic order. The wheel is also a symbol of the regular course of things, and thus of cosmic order, in that the one wheel of the sun's chariot is said to have

Fig. 5

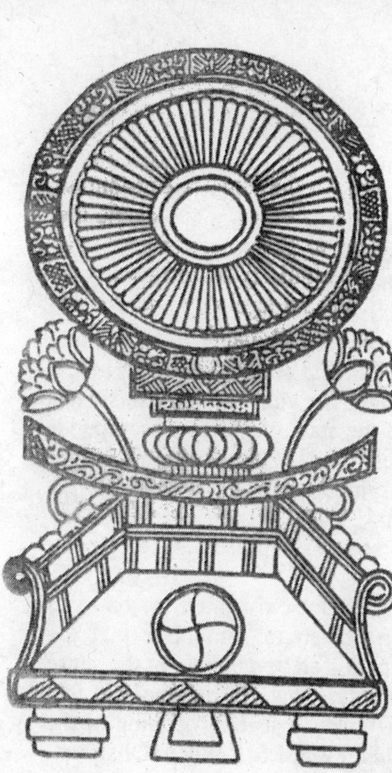

Fig 6

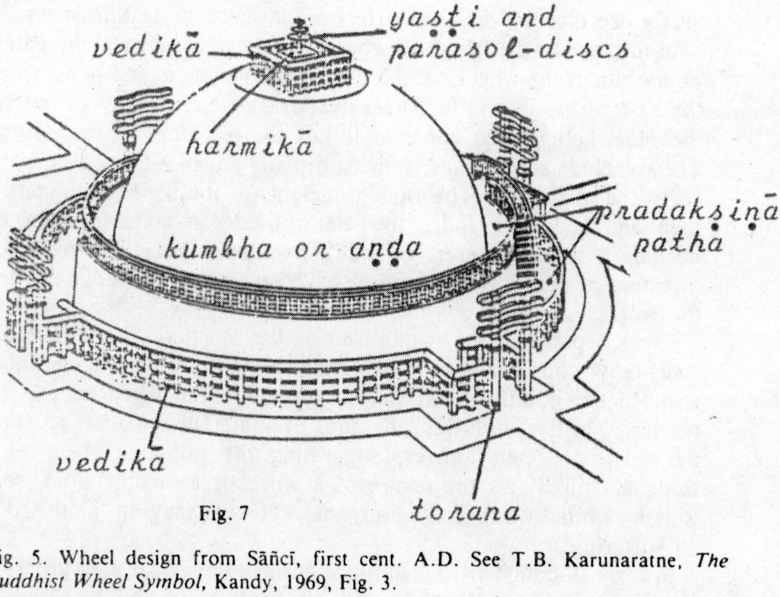

Fig. 7

Fig. 5. Wheel design from Sāñcī, first cent. A.D. See T.B. Karunaratne, *The Buddhist Wheel Symbol,* Kandy, 1969, Fig. 3.

Fig 6. Aniconic portrayal of the Buddha giving his first sermon. The design is from a relief on a slab originally encasing a stūpa at Nāgārjunakonda, 3rd cent. A.D. Now in Nāgārjunakonda Archaeological Museum.

Fig. 7. The great stūpa at Sāñcī. Adapted from A. Volwahsen, *Living Architecture – India,* London, 1969, p. 91.

twelve, five or 360 spokes, corresponding to the number of months, seasons or days in the year.[7] In the Buddhist 'wheel-turner' legend the emperor's rule according to *dhamma* leads to peace and order in his realm. It thus seems appropriate to take the regularly spaced spokes of the Dhamma-Wheel as symbolizing the spiritual harmony and mental integration produced in one who practises the *dhamma*.

In the BU 2,5,15 all gods, worlds and beings are said to be held together in the soul like spokes in the hub and felly of a wheel; in CU 7,15,1 all is said to be fastened on *prāṇa*, the vital breath, like spokes in a hub. In the 'wheel-turner' legend the state of the empire depends on the emperor. The Dhamma-Wheel, then, with its spokes firmly planted in the hub can be seen to symbolize that the Buddha, by discovering and teaching *dhamma*, firmly established its practice in the world. The radiating spokes can be seen as representing the many aspects of the path taught by the Buddha.

The spokes of the Dhamma-Wheel are not only fixed in, but also converge on, the hub. This might be taken to symbolize that the factors of the *dhamma* in the sense of path lead to *dhamma* in the sense of *nibbāna*. In this respect it is worth noting that the Buddha said that his 'setting in motion of the Dhamma-Wheel' was the 'opening of the doors' to the 'deathless', i.e. *nibbāna* (Vin I,6). When Dhamma-Wheels were placed above the gateways to stūpas, it may have been to symbolize that the *dhamma* offers an entrance to deathlessness.

In the case of the 'treasure-wheel' of the 'wheel-turner' the parasols on the rim of the wheel stand for kings who come to accept his rule. In the case of the Dhamma-Wheel the parasols can be seen to represent the great beings who come to follow the teachings of the *dhamma*. These include some kings, some spiritually advanced teachers of other sects and also gods. The Buddha taught for the benefit of 'gods and men' and Sakka, i.e. Indra, the ruler of the Vedic gods, is said to have become a stream-enterer (D II,288), while Brahma, the overlord or 'creator' of the world, is said to have requested the Buddha to teach the world.

Other aspects of the symbolism of the Dhamma-Wheel are more speculative, but still quite likely. As the centre of a spinning wheel is still, so the Buddha's mind was ever still, even when he was busy teaching. In line with this, the hubs of some Dhamma-Wheels are in the form of open lotuses, suggesting the non-attachment of the Buddha's mind. As the centre of a wheel is an empty hole, so the Buddha's mind was empty of any idea of an unchanging 'I', the root of all suffering.

In early Buddhist art, Dhamma-Wheels often appear atop pillars, the most famous example being that at Sārnāth erected by Aśoka. It probably symbolized the universal power of both the Buddha and

Aśoka, who sought to be a 'wheel-turner'. As the legendary wheel remains firm in the ruler's palace while he rules but starts to sink down when he is near death, it appears most appropriate to place it high up on a pillar, to symbolize the health of imperial rule or of the sovereignty of the *dhamma*. In the Sārnāth pillar the wheel was supported by four back-to-back lions, reminiscent of the 'lion's roar' of the Buddha's teaching, supported by a base on which were carved four small wheels and between them a lion, an elephant, a bull and a horse. From Vedic times these four animals had represented the four regions of the world spreading out from Mount Meru at the centre of the flat disc of the earth. These animals could therefore symbolize the aspiration that the *dhamma* would come to influence the whole world, just as the 'wheel-turner' had ruled the four continents of the earth. As his wheel remained in his palace, at the centre of his realm, it could, symbolically, be seen to rest on Mount Meru. In this case the pillar which supports the wheel can be seen to symbolize Mount Meru, the centre or axis of the earth. This would be appropriate as the *dhamma* should be the 'centre' of a person's life.

The pillar was itself one of the early Buddhist symbols as seen, for example, in the composite symbol in Fig. 4. In Brahmanism the sun was seen to have a chariot whose two wheels touched heaven and earth, respectively, with the axle, or axle-tree (*akṣa*), acting as the world pillar, equivalent to Mount Meru. As the Dhamma-Wheel has certain connections with the sun and Mount Meru, the pillar could suggest the *dhamma* as the central point of orientation in a person's life. Other aspects of its meaning will be explored below.

ANICONIC 'BODIES' OF THE BUDDHA

In early Buddhist art symbols were often combined to form aniconic 'bodies' of the Buddha, so paving the way for the development of images of him in human form, as in Fig. 6 where a Dhamma-Wheel stands for the Buddha's head, a short pillar or column for his body and a throne, again suggestive of the Buddha's sovereignty, for his legs. In Fig. 1 a column fringed by flames also represents the body of the Buddha. Such flaming columns no doubt were intended to recall the story of the Buddha's conversion of three fire-worshipping ascetics by overcoming, with his psychic power (*iddhi*), two venomous snakes by returning their heat and flames with his own (Vin I,24 – 5). Flaming columns may also recall the 'wonder of the pairs' at Sāvatthī where the Buddha is said to have risen into the air with a mass of fire coming from the upper part of his body and a mass of water from the lower part (DhpA III,204 – 5 and Ps I,125). Again, flaming columns may symbolize the spiritual energy of the Buddha, later symbolized by flames arising from the crown of the head of Buddha images. As expressed at Dhp 387, 'all day and night the Buddha shines in glory'.

THE STŪPA

The final and perhaps most important symbol of early Buddhism is the stūpa or '(relic) mound'. From pre-Buddhist times, in India and elsewhere, the remains of kings and heroes were interred in burial mounds (tumuli), out of both respect for and fear of the dead. Those in ancient India were low, circular mounds of earth, kept in place by a ring of boulders which also served to mark off a mound as a sacred area.

According to the account in the Mahāparinibbāna Sutta (D II,141–3) when the Buddha was asked what was to be done with his remains after death, he seems to have brought to mind this ancient tradition. He explained that his body should be treated like that of a 'wheel-turner' emperor: after wrapping it in many layers of cloth and placing it within two iron vessels, it should be cremated; the relics should then be placed in a stūpa 'where four roads meet'. The relics of a disciple (*sāvaka*) of a Tathāgata should be treated likewise. At the stūpa of either a person's heart (*citta*) could be gladdened and calmed at the thought of its significance.

After the Buddha's cremation his relics (*sarīras*) are said to have been divided into eight portions and each was placed in a stūpa. The pot (*kumbha*) in which the relics were collected and the ashes of the cremation fire were dealt with in the same way (D II,166).

One of the things which Aśoka did in his efforts to spread Buddhism was to open up these original ten stūpas and distribute their relics in a thousand new stūpas throughout India. Thereby the stūpa was greatly popularized. Though the development of the Buddha image provided another focus for devotion to the Buddha, stūpas remain popular to this day, especially in Theravāda countries. They have gone through a long development in form and symbolism, but this paper will concentrate on their early significance.

As foci of devotion stūpas are primarily of importance due to their contents. These may be reputed relics of Gotama Buddha, a previous Buddha, an *arahant* or another saint, or copies of such relics. They may also be objects 'utilized' by such holy beings, images symbolizing them or texts seen as the 'relics' of the 'Dhamma-body' of Gotama Buddha.

In the most straightforward sense the stūpa acts as a symbol of the Buddha's *parinibbāna*: his passing into *nibbāna* at death. In the aniconic art of early Buddhism reliefs of a Bodhi tree, Dhamma-Wheel and stūpa were used to represent the three key events of the Buddha's life: enlightenment, first sermon and *parinibbāna*. In a wider sense these three symbols represent, of course, the Buddha's nature as the Enlightened One, as the teacher of a universal message and as passed into *nibbāna*.

However, the stūpa is more than a symbol of the *parinibbāna*. It is a complete symbol-system incorporating many of the other symbols discussed above, making it a symbol of the *dhamma* and of the enlightened state of a Buddha.

Some authors such as Irwin,[8] Coomaraswamy (note 5) and, to some extent, Govinda[9] have seen a largely pre-Buddhist, Vedic meaning in the stūpa's symbolism. I wish to bring out its *Buddhist* meaning, drawing on certain evidence cited by Irwin in support of *his* interpretation and on the work of such scholars as G. Roth.[10]

THE SYMBOLISM OF THE STŪPA'S COMPONENTS

The best preserved of the early Indian stūpas is the great stūpa at Sāñcī, Central India. First built by Aśoka, it was later enlarged and embellished, up to the first century A.D. Its diagrammatic representation in Fig. 7 gives a clear indication of the various parts of an early stūpa.

The four gateways (*toraṇas*) of this stūpa were built between the first centuries B.C. and A.D. to replace previous wooden ones. Their presence puts the stūpa, symbolically, at the place where four roads meet as specified in the Mahāparinibbāna Sutta. This is probably to indicate the openness and universality of the Buddhist teaching which invites all to come and try its path, and also to radiate loving-kindness to beings in all four directions.

In a later development of the stūpa in North India the orientation to the four directions was often expressed by means of a square, terraced base, sometimes with staircases on each side in place of the early gateways. At Sāñcī these gateways are covered with carved reliefs of the career of Gotama as *bodhisatta* and also, using aniconic symbols, of his final life as a Buddha. Symbols also represent previous Buddhas. In this way the gates convey Buddhist teachings and the life of the Buddhas to those who enter the precincts of the stūpa.

Encircling the Sāñcī stūpa, connecting its gateways, is a stone railing (*vedikā*), originally made of wood. It encloses and marks off the site dedicated to the stūpa and a path for circumambulating it as the main act of devotion at a stūpa.

From the main circumambulatory path at Sāñcī a devotee can mount some stairs to a second one also enclosed by a *vedikā*. This second path runs round the top of the low cylindrical drum of the stūpa base. The Dv refers to this as the *medhi* (platform), while some modern Sinhalese sources refer to it as the *āsana*, the throne. This structure serves to elevate the main body of the stūpa and so put it in a place of honour. In later stūpas it was multiplied into a series of terraces to raise the stūpa dome to a yet more honorific height. These terraces were probably what developed into the multiple roofs of the East Asian form of the stūpa, often known in the West as a pagoda.

The most obvious component of the stūpa is the solid dome, resting on the base. Its function is to house the precious relics within (the Burmese say that the presence of relics gives a stūpa a 'heart'). The relics are kept in a relic-chamber, usually somewhere on the central axis of the dome. They are often found to rest in a golden container placed within a silver, then bronze, then earthenware ones. The casing of the stūpa dome seems therefore to be seen as the outermost and least valuable container of the relics. Indeed, the usual term for the dome of a stūpa, both in Sinhalese tradition and in two first century A.D. Sanskrit texts translated from their Tibetan versions by G. Roth in his article, is *kumbha* (pot). The Sanskrit Mahāparinirvāṇa Sūtra also reports the Buddha as saying that his relics should be placed in a golden *kumbha*, while the Pāli Mahāparinibbāna Sutta says that the Buddha's relics were collected in a *kumbha* before being divided up. Again, *kumbha* is used as a word for an urn in which the bones of a dead person are collected, in the Brahmanical Āśvalāyana Gṛhya Sūtra.[11] These facts reinforce the idea of the stūpa dome being seen as the outermost container of the relics.

The dome of the stūpa is a *kumbha* not only as a 'relic pot', but also because of symbolic connotations of the word itself. At S II,83 it is said that the process of death of an *arahant*, during which feelings 'grow cold' and only relics (*sarīras*) remain, is like the cooling off of a *kumbha* taken from an oven with *kapallāni* remaining. Woodward translates it as 'sherds', but the PTS Dictionary gives 'a bowl in the form of a skull . . . an earthenware pan used to carry ashes'. The implication would seem to be that a (cold) *kumbha* is itself like the relics of a saint; certainly Dhp 40 sees the body (*kāya*) as like a *kumbha* (in its fragility, says the commentary). Thus the stūpa dome is a container of the relics and also an analogical representative of the relics.

The stūpa dome as a *kumbha* links it to the symbolism of the 'vase of plenty', described above; indeed 'vase of plenty' designs were among those on the dome of the great stūpa at Amarāvatī.[12] These associations would make the stūpa dome, like the vase of plenty, into a symbol for the personality of someone who is 'full' of *dhamma*: a Buddha or a saint. This symbolism neatly dove-tails with another indication of the dome's meaning. As stūpas developed, they sometimes came to have interior strengthening walls radiating from the centre (Fig. 8). The stūpa dome being circular, the impression is strongly given of the Dhamma-Wheel symbol. As the latter is partly a symbol of universal spiritual sovereignty, this aligns with the significance of the stūpa's openness to the four directions.

The stūpa dome, then, is not only a container of the Buddha's relics and their power, but symbolizes also both the state of the Buddha and the *dhamma* he encompassed. The dome is also known in Dv (3rd cent. A.D.) as *aṇḍa* (egg). This must mean that, just as an egg contains the potential for growth, so the stūpa dome contains relics which are sometimes known as *bījas* (seeds). By devotion to the stūpa and its relics a person's spiritual life may grow and be fruitful. This connotation is a neat parallel to that of the dome as a 'vase of plenty'.

Another connection with spiritual growth is provided by the association of the stūpa dome with the lotus. Domes are often decorated with lotus designs and their circular plans resemble the circle of an open lotus flower (cf. Fig. 3). In addition, the Burmese see the shape of the stūpa (whose bulk is its dome) as that of a lotus bud, with the name of its components recalling the idea of a flower bud with its young leaves folded in adoration.[13] We see, then, that a further Buddhist symbol is included in the stūpa as a symbol-system.

Not only are the Dhamma-Wheel and lotus symbols incorporated within the stūpa, but the other key symbol, the Bodhi tree, can be seen to have found a place in this symbol-system as well. On top of Sāñcī stūpa can be seen a *yaṣṭi* (pole) with three discs on it (Fig. 7). These discs represent ceremonial parasols, the ancient Indian emblems of royalty. Large ceremonial parasols are still used in Southeast Asia, for example to hold over a man about to be ordained, i.e. over someone in a role parallel to that of *prince* Siddhattha. In Tibetan Buddhism such parasols are held over the Dalai Lama on important occasions. By placing parasols on a stūpa, there is expressed the idea of the spiritual sovereignty of the Buddha and his teachings (also expressed by the Dhamma-Wheel symbol). In accordance with this interpretation of a stūpa's pole and discs, we see that king Duṭṭhāgāmaṇi of Sri Lanka (2nd cent. B.C.), when he had finished the great stūpa at Anaurādha-pura, placed his royal parasol on it, conferring on it sovereignty over Sri Lanka for seven days (Mv XXXI,90 & 111); he later replaced his parasol with a wood or stone copy.

While there are three honorific parasol-discs at Sāñcī, on later stūpas these generally increased in number, so as to increase the inferred honour.[14] Sometimes they came to fuse into a spire as seen in the

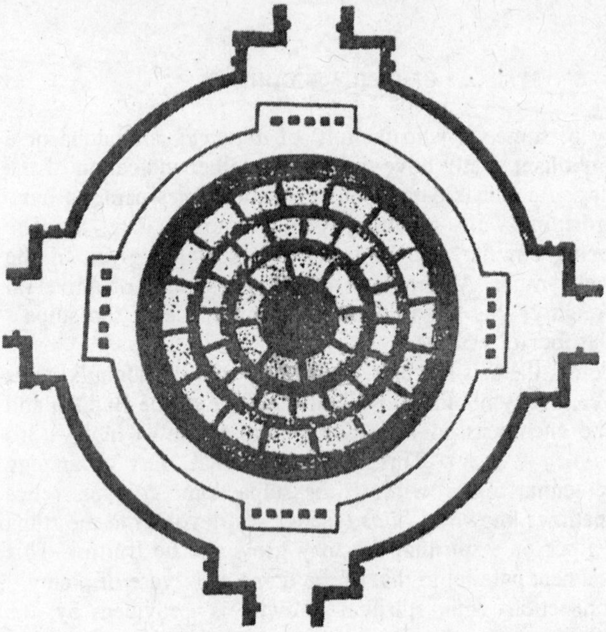

Fig.8

Fig.9

Fig. 8. Plan of the 3rd cent. A.D. Nāgārjunakonda stūpa. From G. Combaz, 'L'Évolution du Stūpa en Asie. Étude d'Architecture Bouddhique', *Mélanges Chinois et Bouddhiques*, Bruxelles, 1933, vol. 12. (1932–3), pp. 163–306, Fig. 71.

Fig. 9. The great stūpa at Anurādhapura, 2nd cent. B.C., 54 metres high.

present superstructure of the great stūpa at Anurādhapura (Fig. 9). Another phase in the development of a spire can be seen in the 14–16th century Shwe Dagōn stūpa in Rangoon (Fig. 10). Here the dome is bell-shaped and has come to merge with the spire to form one flowing outline. Because the spire no longer really conveys the impression of a series of parasol-discs, a separate large metal parasol is placed at its summit.

The use of the parasol as an emblem of royalty probably derives from the ancient custom of a ruler sitting under the shade of a sacred tree, at the centre of a community, to administer justice. The shading tree thus became an insignia of sovereignty. When the ruler moved about, it came to be represented by a parasol. The parasols on a stūpa, then, while being an emblem of sovereignty, *also* connote a sacred tree. Indeed, a second century B.C. relief from Amarāvatī depicts a stūpa which, in place of the *yaṣṭi* and parasol discs, has a tree with parasol-shaped leaves (Fig. 11).

Of course, the Buddhist sacred tree is the Bodhi tree, so the *yaṣṭi* and parasols on a stūpa must symbolically represent this, itself a potent, Buddhist symbol. This idea is reinforced by the fact that, in Burma, free-standing parasols are sometimes worshipped as Bodhi tree symbols, and the metal parasols on stūpas sometimes have small brass Bodhi leaves hanging from them. That the *yaṣṭi* and parasol-discs represent a Bodhi tree is also supported when we examine the structure immediately below them on a stūpa. Fig. 7 shows that at Sāñcī this is a cubical stone surrounded by another *vedikā* (railing). Now these features are reminiscent of those at early Bodhi tree shrines which had an altar-seat at their base and a railing to surround their sacred enclosure. As the style of the stūpa developed, moreover, the cubical stone structure expanded in size and came to incorporate the *vedikā* in the form of a carved relief on its surface (Fig. 9). The important point to note is that Bodhi tree shrines developed into more complex forms (see Fig. 2); as this happened, the superstructure of stūpas mirrored this development (Fig. 12). This is clear evidence that the superstructure of a stūpa was symbolically equated with a Bodhi tree and its shrine.

The structure underneath the royal/Bodhi tree symbol came to be known, e.g. in the Dv, as *harmikā* ('top enclosure'). This was the name for a cool summer chamber on the roof of a building. This connection need not contradict the idea of the structure as a symbolic Bodhi tree shrine, for both a cool 'top enclosure' and a Bodhi tree can symbolize the enlightened mind: the chamber suggests its 'coolness' and the tree suggests its enlightened nature.

While all the components of the stūpa seem now to have been discussed, there remains one of crucial importance: the axial pillar

Fig.10

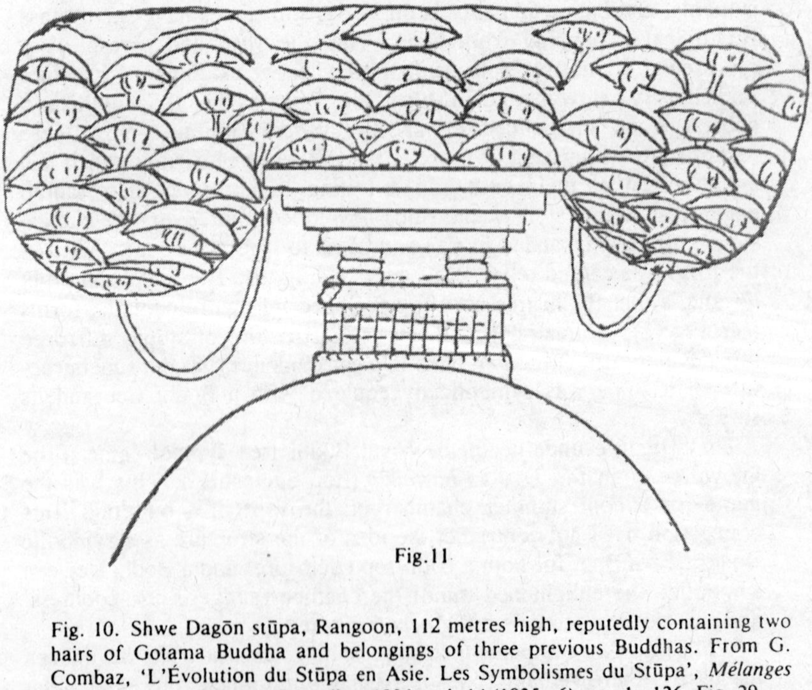

Fig.11

Fig. 10. Shwe Dagōn stūpa, Rangoon, 112 metres high, reputedly containing two hairs of Gotama Buddha and belongings of three previous Buddhas. From G. Combaz, 'L'Évolution du Stūpa en Asie. Les Symbolismes du Stūpa', *Mélanges Chinois et Bouddhiques*, Bruxelles, 1936, vol. 14 (1935–6), pp. 1–126, Fig. 29.

Fig. 11 Relief of a stūpa superstructure on a drum slab, 2nd cent. B.C. Amarāvatī. Drawn from a photograph in J. Irwin, op. cit., Fig. 24

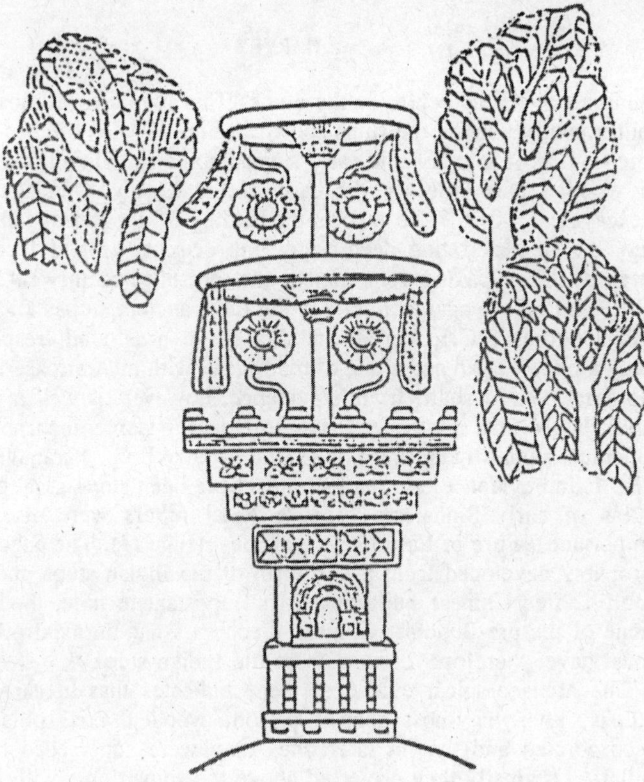

Fig.12

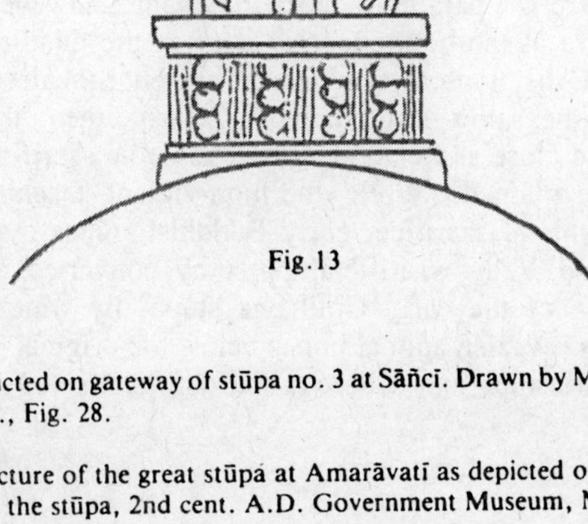

Fig.13

Fig. 12. Stūpa depicted on gateway of stūpa no. 3 at Sāñcī. Drawn by Margaret Hall, as in Irwin, op. cit., Fig. 28.

Fig. 13. Superstructure of the great stūpa at Amarāvatī as depicted on a relief slab originally encasing the stūpa, 2nd cent. A.D. Government Museum, Madras.

running down the centre of the dome. This is hidden in most stūpas, but it can be seen in the stūpa shown in Fig. 13. J. Irwin has reported the finding of axis holes in early stūpas, some containing fragments of a wooden axis pole. In the case of the Lauriya-Nandagarh stūpa (excavated 1904 – 5) he reports the finding of a waterlogged wooden axis-stump penetrating deep below the original ground level. Irwin regards this stūpa as a very ancient one, pre-third century B.C., but S. P. Gupta argues against this.[15] In the most ancient stūpas known (4 – 5th centuries B.C.), Vaiśālī and Piprahwa, are found, respectively, only a pile of earth and a pile of mud faced with mud bricks. They had no axial pole or shaft. Irwin's evidence, however, is well marshalled and shows that a wooden axis pole had become incorporated in Buddhist stūpas by the third or second century B.C.; Paranavitana has also found evidence of what can only have been stone axial pillars in ruins of early Sinhalese stūpas.[16] Axial pillars were also a very important feature of East Asian 'pagodas' (Fig. 14). The pagoda form probably developed from a late form of the Indian stūpa and certain multi-roofed Chinese buildings. It is important to note, though, that none of the pre-Buddhist Chinese precursors had an axial pillar: this must have, therefore, derived from the Indian stūpa.[17]

The archaeological evidence, then, indicates that in early Indian stūpas, after the most ancient period, wooden axial pillars were incorporated and that in later ones they were superseded by stone pillars. Originally they projected above the stūpa dome with the *yaṣṭi* and parasols as separated items, as in the case of the Amarāvatī stūpa (dating from Aśokan times — Fig. 13). When, however, the domes of stūpas came to be enlarged, the axes became completely buried within and the *yaṣṭis* were fixed on top of them as if being their extensions.

One manuscript of the Dv refers to a *yūpa-yaṣṭi* being implanted in the summit of an enlarged stūpa.[18] This, and other references, shows that one term for the axial pillar of a stūpa was *yūpa*. Somewhat surprisingly, this was the term for the wooden post where, in Vedic religion, an animal would be tethered before it was sacrificed to the gods. There is a parallel in more than name, however. The Vedic *yūpa* was square at the bottom, octangular in the middle and round at the top, while the stone axial pillars of ancient Sinhalese stūpas are found to be of the same basic shape.[19] Clearly, then, the axial pillars of stūpas had close associations with the Vedic sacrificial post. How can this be explained? While the non-violent teachings of Buddhism rejected animal sacrifice, early Buddhist stūpas may well have been built round Vedic sacrificial posts by converted brahmins. Indeed, excavation of the early Gotihawa stūpa, by which Aśoka placed a pillar, has revealed animal bones below the original ground level at the base of the stūpa axis where a wooden post stood. The most ancient stūpas lack signs of any axial pillar, probably because Buddhism was not sufficiently well established in the fifth and fourth centuries B.C. for the conversion of a Brahmanic site to have been acceptable. With the increasing popularity of Buddhism it would have come to be acceptable for stūpas to be built around existing Vedic *yūpas*. These already marked sacred spots of sorts: building stūpas on these spots showed that they were now taken over by the new religion. In such early stūpas the original wooden Vedic *yūpa* was probably retained to form the stūpa axis, but later on a stone *yūpa* would have been erected to mark the sacred spot which would be the centre of a new stūpa.

The axial *yūpa* of a stūpa surely had a further symbolic function. To explore this fully it is also necessary to note an alternative name for the stūpa axis. Paranavitana has reported that the monks of Sri Lanka (in the 1940s) gave the traditional term for the stūpa axis as Inda-khīla (Sanskrit: Indra-kīla), i.e. Indra's stake.[20] But the monks did not know the reason for the name. Irwin has argued that both the terms — *yūpa* and Indra-kīla — show the stūpa axis to symbolize the *axis mundi*: the world pillar or world tree of Vedic mythology.[21] I shall summarise Irwin's arguments below before going on to my own preferred interpretation.

Firstly, he argues that the Vedic sacrificial *yūpa* was itself a substitute for the axial world tree, as demonstrated by the way it is addressed in Brahmanic texts and the fact that the tree sections of the *yūpa* (square, octagonal and round) are regarded as representing, respectively, the earth, the atmosphere and the heavens.[22] Secondly, Irwin noted that 'Indra's stake' is the designation, in the Vedas, for the stake with which Indra pegged the primeval mound to the bottom of the cosmic ocean on which it floated, thus giving our world stability.[23] Thirdly, he argues that this stake is mythologically synonymous with the Vedic world axis.[24] He refers to a Vedic cosmogonic myth in which Indra, with his *vajra*, slays the obstructing dragon Vṛtra so as to release the waters of fertility and life locked up in the primeval mound, floating on the cosmic ocean. At the same time Indra props up the atmosphere and heavens with the world axis or tree (which seems equivalent to his *vajra*) and pegs the mound to the ocean bottom, as above. The world axis and Indra's stake can therefore be seen as merging into one.[25] Fourthly, Irwin cites certain archaeological evidence which *might* suggest that Buddhist stūpa builders actually conceived of the above Vedic myth.[26] Some of this evidence is as follows:

(i) a reliquary from the great stūpa at Anurādhapura has a *yūpa* obtruding from its top and sprouting leaves as if it were a tree (as shown in Fig. 15);

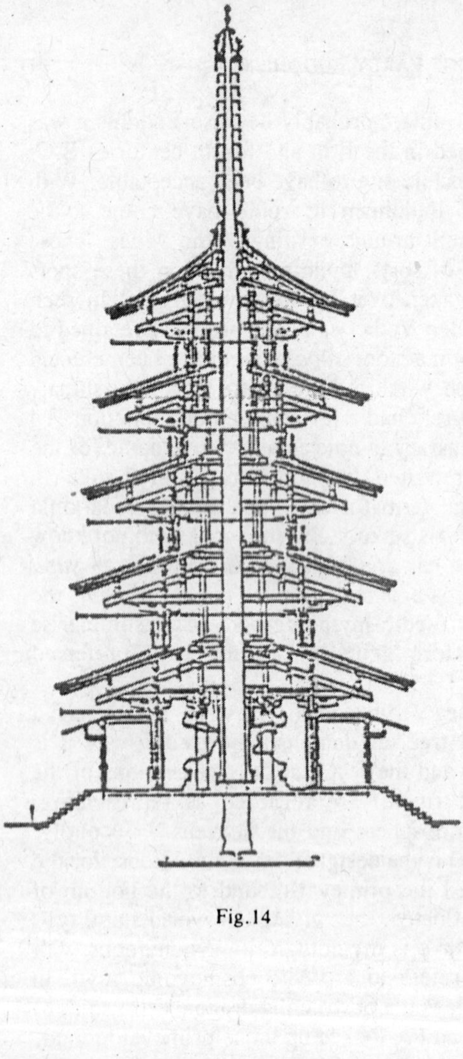

Fig.14

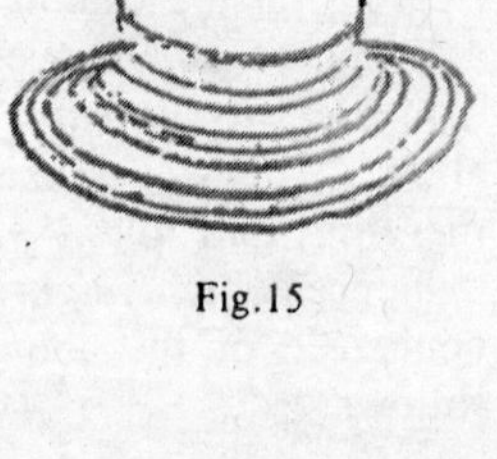

Fig.15

Fig. 14. Cross-section of Hōryūji Pagoda, Nara, 7th cent. A.D. From D. Seckel, 'Stūpa Elements Surviving in East Asian Pagodas', A.L. Dallapiccola, op. cit. (note 8).

Fig. 15. Gold reliquary in the form of a stūpa. From Ruvanvāli stūpa, Anurādhapura, attributed to the first cent. B.C. From Irwin, op. cit., Fig. 23.

(ii) the description of the relic chamber of the above stūpa at Mv XXX,63ff refers to a huge golden Bodhi tree standing at the centre of the stūpa as if the tree were the stūpa axis;[27]
(iii) the circumambulatory paths of some early stūpas were paved with azure-blue glass tiles or glazed tiles decorated with water-symbols, suggesting perhaps that the stūpa dome symbolically rests on the cosmic ocean, as did the primeval mound of Vedic myth.[28]

Irwin therefore sees the stūpa as an *image of the creation of the universe* (the archetype of regeneration), with the stūpa axis founded on the waters and rising through the earth, atmosphere and heavens so as to unite them and form a communicating link between them.[29]

I do not want to rule out Irwin's interpretation, but I feel that there are more 'Buddhist' ones closer to hand: after all, the Bodhi tree and water-born lotus are well-established Buddhist symbols. Moreover, Irwin himself thinks that while the above Vedic myth affected stūpa construction and the meaning of the axis, the Vedic significance came to be mostly forgotten as the old meaning was adapted for the new and increasingly dominant doctrinal scheme.

Inasmuch as the stūpa axis seems to have originated as a Vedic sacrificial post, it can surely have taken on a symbolic meaning from this association. To see what it was we have, firstly, to examine what the Buddhist equivalent of 'sacrifice' was. At D I,144ff it is said that the Buddha was once asked by a brahmin about the best form of 'sacrifice'. Instead of describing some bloody Brahmanic ritual, he answers by talking about giving alms-food and support to monks, brahmins and the poor, about living a virtuous life, being self-controlled, practising *samatha* and *vipassanā* meditations and attaining *nibbāna*. He describes each such stage of the Buddhist path as a kind of 'sacrifice', with the attainment of its goal being the highest and best kind. Again, at D III,76 it is said that a *yūpa* is the place where a future wheel-turner will distribute goods to all, renounce his royal life to become a monk under Metteya Buddha and go on to become an *arahant*. Therefore, what was once a sacrificial post could naturally come to symbolize, in the new religion of Buddhism, its path and goal, i.e. the *dhamma*, and all the sacrifices involved in their practice. Indeed, at Miln 21 – 2 it is said that the monk Nagasena is engaged in

> pointing out the way of *dhamma*, carrying the torch of *dhamma*, bearing aloft the *yūpa of dhamma*, offering the gift of *dhamma*, sounding the drum of *dhamma*, roaring the lion's roar, thundering out Indra's thunder and thoroughly satisfying the whole world by thundering out sweet utterances and wrapping them round with the lightning flashes of superb knowledge, filling

them with the waters of compassion and the great cloud of the deathlessness of *dhamma* . . .

This passage certainly shows that Buddhism could draw on Vedic symbolism, but also that such symbolism is fully buddhicized when used. *Yūpa* is used as a metaphor for the *dhamma*: the Buddhist teaching, its path and goal; and Indra's releasing of the cosmic waters is a metaphor for a great teacher's compassionate bestowal of that which brings deathlessness.

When we look at the other term for the stūpa axis, 'Indra's stake', we also see that this came to have a clear Buddhist meaning. Firstly, we see that from the Vedic myth about Indra's stabilizing stake, Indra-kīla came to be a term for the huge pillars standing firmly in the ground at the entrance to ancient Indian and Sinhalese cities; they were used to secure the heavy gates when they stood open. It also became a term for the gateposts of houses and, indeed, for anything which was stable and firmly rooted and which secured the safety of something. While it might be thought that the stūpa axis was called Indra-kīla because it structurally stabilized the stūpa, this does not seem to have been the case architecturally.[30] It is more likely that the axis was an 'Indra's stake' in a purely symbolic sense, standing for the Dhamma, the stable centre for a Buddhist's life which secures his safety in life's troubles and also acts as a 'gateway' to a better life and, ultimately, to deathlessness. The use of 'Indra's stake' in metaphors in the *suttas* indicates that, in particular, the term symbolizes that aspect of the *dhamma* which is the unshakeable state of mind of *arahants* and other *ariyan* persons. At S V,444 one who understands the four *ariyan* truths and has sure and well-founded knowledge is like an unshakeable Inda-khīla, while at Sn 229 we read:

As an Inda-khīla resting in the earth would be unshakeable by the four winds, of such a kind I say is the good man who, having understood the *ariyan* truths, sees them [clearly]. This splendid jewel is the Sangha; by this truth may there be well-being.

Dhp 95 uses the metaphor specifically of an *arahant*:

Like the earth, he does not resent; a balanced and well-disciplined person is like an Inda-khīla.

This is probably also the case at Thag 663:

But those who in the midst of pain and happiness have overcome the seam-stress (craving), stand like an Inda-khīla; they are neither elated nor cast down.

Referring to the stūpa axis as 'Indra's stake', then would seem to imply that the axis was seen as symbolizing the unshakeable state of an *ariyan* person's *dhamma*-filled mind.[31] Such symbolism harmonizes with that of the axis as a *yūpa* and also with that of the dome as a *kumbha* representing the personality of someone full of *dhamma*.

A final aspect of the symbolism of the stūpa axis is that it was seen to represent Mount Meru, the huge axial world mountain of Hindu and Buddhist mythology, with the circular plan of the stūpa dome representing the circle of the earth. That the stūpa was seen in this way even in Theravāda lands can be seen from several pieces of evidence. Firstly, the huge Bodhi tree which Mv XXX,63ff describes as being in the relic chamber of the great stūpa at Anurādhapura is said to have a canopy over it on which are depicted the sun, moon and stars — all said to revolve round Meru. Around the trees are placed statues of the Four Great Kings, the gods said to guard the slopes of Meru, while the relic chamber walls are said to have painted on them zig-zag shaped walls — such walls are used, at least in the Tibetan tradition, to portray the rings of mountains on the disc of the earth. Secondly, the *harmikā* of ancient Sinhalese stūpas sometimes has the sun on the east face and the moon on the west face. Thirdly, in late Sinhalese texts the term for the drum at the base of the stūpa spire (Fig. 9) is *devatā koṭuva*, enclosure of the deities. This corresponds to the idea that the lower gods dwell on Meru, with Indra's palace at the summit.[32]

I would see the significance of the Meru symbolism as being that the stūpa axis and dome represent the world of gods and men; the implication of this will be brought out below.

THE SYMBOLISM OF THE STŪPA AS A WHOLE

So far I have dealt with various symbolic meanings of the components of the stūpa. The dome, container of the precious relics, can be seen to represent a pot full of Dhamma, a Dhamma-Wheel, a lotus flower or the circle of the earth. The stūpa axis, as a *yūpa*, symbolized the *dhamma* (teaching, path and realizations) and all its 'sacrifices' and, as Inda-khīla, the great stability of the *dhamma* and the unshakeable nature of the mind full of *dhamma*; it also represents Mount Meru, home of gods. On top of the stūpa dome is a cool 'top enclosure' and a *yaṣṭi* complete with honorific parasol discs equivalent to a Bodhi tree, the symbol of a Buddha's enlightenment and his enlightened mind (Fig. 16).

While a stūpa is worthy of devotion due to the relics it contains, it also serves to inspire, because the symbols of its separate components unite together to make an overall spiritual statement. The whole

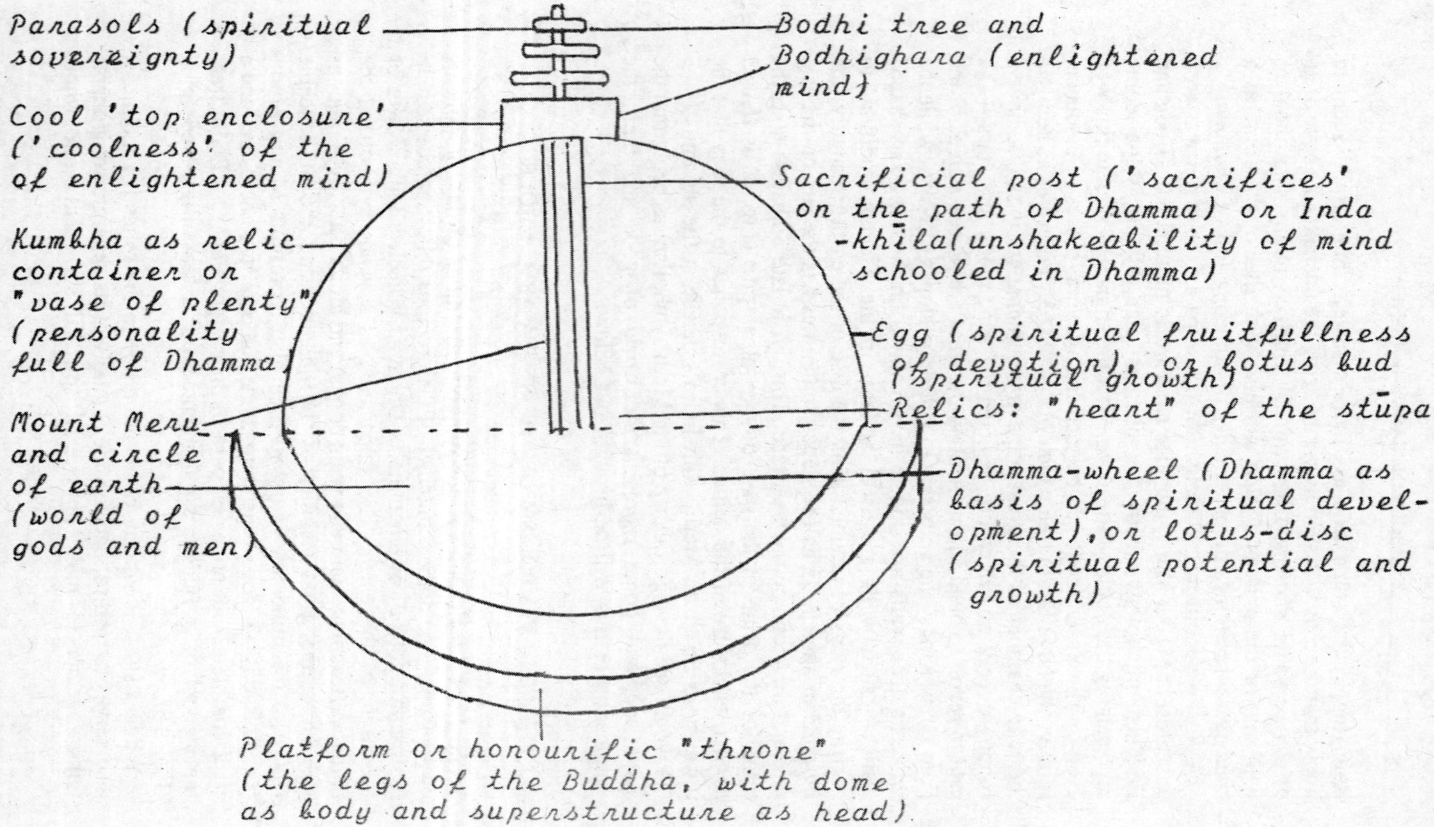

Fig. 16. Diagram of cross-section and partial plan of a stūpa, showing component symbols, with their meanings in brackets

symbolizes the enlightened mind of a Buddha standing out above the world of gods and humans. The symbolism shows that the enlightened mind arises from within the world by a process of spiritual growth on a firm basis of the practice of the *dhamma* which is also the path leading out of the world of humans and gods to enlightenment. A personality full of such *dhamma* is worthy of reverence and has an unshakeable mind. In brief, we can say that the stūpa symbolizes the *dhamma* and the transformations it brings in one who practises it, culminating in enlightenment. It is not surprising, then, that at an early date the various layers of the stūpa's structure were explicitly seen as symbolizing also specific aspects of the *dhamma* and of a Buddha's nature. G. Roth has translated two ancient Sanskrit texts (from their Tibetan versions, see note 10): 'Caitya-vibhāga-vinayabhāva Sūtra', fragments of an unknown Vinaya (from the first cent. A.D.), and 'Stūpa-lakṣana-kārikā-vivecana' of the Lokottaravāda Vinaya (2nd cent. A.D.). They see the stūpa as symbolizing the 'Dharma-body' in the sense of the 37 'requisites of enlightenment' (*bodhipakṣiyadharmas*) and certain other spiritual qualities. Fig. 17 gives the scheme of symbolic correspondences as outlined in the first of these texts. Each layer of the stūpa's structure represents a group of spiritual qualities cultivated on the path, while the spire represents the powers of a Tathāgata.[33]

Another interesting passage quoted by Roth is from 'Kṣudraka-vastu' (of the first century A.D. Mūlasarvāstivāda Vinaya). It also links the stūpa with *bodhipakṣiyadharmas* and deals with the death of Śāriputra at which Ānanda — who has Śāriputra's relics — evinces dismay to the Buddha. The Buddha consoles him by asking him if Śāriputra has taken with him the aggregates of virtue, meditation, wisdom, liberation or knowledge and vision of liberation and whether he has taken away that which is the substance of the Buddha's enlightened perception, namely the four applications of mindfulness; whereupon the *bodhipakṣiyadharmas* are enumerated. This means that, while in physical sense Śāriputra is gone and only his relics remain, the *dharmas* cultivated by him, i.e. the Dharma-body, remain, too. With such passages in mind it would have been very natural for Buddhists to look on the stūpa not only as a container of physical relics of a Buddha or saint, but also as symbolizing the essential *dharma*-qualities which such a person embodied and which still exist inviting others to embody them.

In the Pāli passage on the death of Sāriputta (S IV,161 – 3) the *bodhipakkhiyadhammas* are not specifically mentioned, though Ānanda says that he will bear in mind the strength-giving *dhamma* of Sāriputta, and the Buddha recommends to him, even after his own *parinibbāna*, to abide with himself and the *dhamma* as refuge. This is

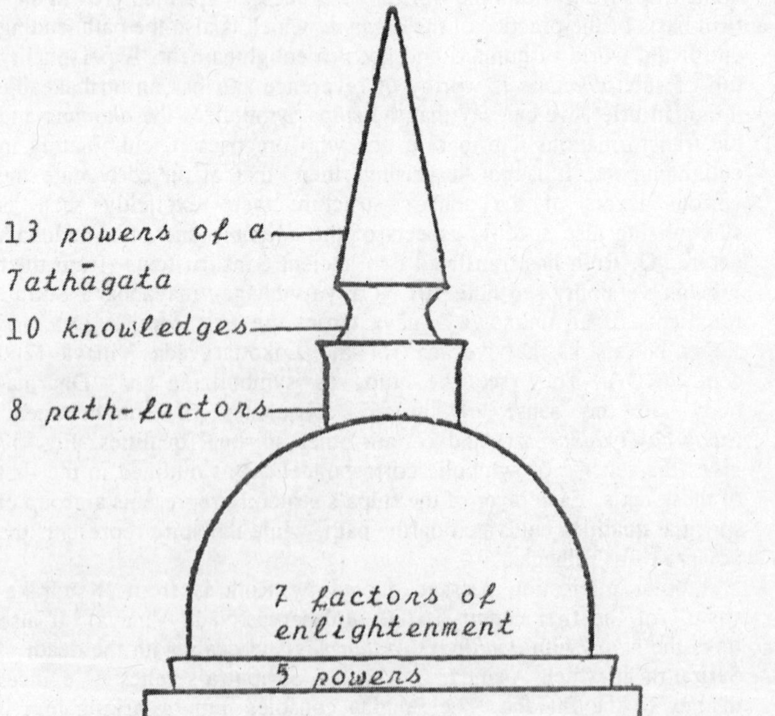

Fig. 17. Stūpa diagram showing correspondences to the 37 *bodhipakṣiyadharmas*. Adapted from Lama Anargarika Govinda, *The Psycho-cosmic Symbolism of the Buddhist Stupa*, Emeryville, 1976, Fig. 13.

to be done by way of the four foundations of mindfulness, the first set of *dhammas* in the list of the 37 *bodhipakkhiyadhammas*. In two Pāli passages on the death of the Buddha, however, there is reference to the *bodhipakkhiyadhammas* (though not by this name). At D II,120 the Buddha lists the 37 *dhammas* as those known and taught by him, which his disciples should master, meditate on and spread abroad so that the holy life will last long and there shall be good and happiness for many. He then refers to his *parinibbāna* as being in three months' time and exhorts his monks just as he does on his death-bed: 'All conditioned phenomena are subject to decay; perfect yourselves with diligence.'

At M II,243 – 5 Ānanda asks the Buddha to ensure that when he dies there will be no unseemly disputes among his disciples or harm to the many folk, as he has heard there have been at the death of Mahāvīra, the Jain leader. In reply the Buddha rhetorically asks Ānanda whether any of his monks differ over what he has taught out of his higher knowledge, i.e. the 37 *bodhipakkhiyadhammas*. He goes on to imply that these comprise the essential path and practice. If disputes arise after his death they will be on matters of Vinaya and of trifling importance.

These passages all emphasize the idea that, even though a Buddha or *arahant* dies, there still remains the essence of the path he taught and realized, in the form of the 37 *bodhipakkhiyadhammas*, and that bearing these in mind and practising them will be of great benefit to people. After the Buddha's *parinibbāna*, while physical relics were important, the *dhamma* is more so, as the Buddha emphasized to Vakkali when he said, 'He who sees the *dhamma* sees me, he who sees me sees the *dhamma*' (S III, 120). It is not surprising, then, that the stūpa, the primary focus of early Buddhist devotion, should not only contain the relics of the Buddha or a saint, but should also symbolize the *dhamma* or the Buddha in the form of his Dhamma-body. Such a symbolic equation of the stūpa with the Buddha is, in fact, reflected in early Vinayas in which, where a stūpa is seen as having its own property (land and offerings), it is sometimes seen as 'the property of the stūpa' and sometimes as the 'property of the Buddha'.

As a final point, I would like to try to tie together the functions of the stūpa as a reliquary with that as a Buddha-symbol, so as to show how the stūpa may be seen to depict both the Buddha's physical and spiritual personality. The classical stūpa contains relics of the Buddha, i.e. some of the 'great elements' (*mahābhūtas*) which composed his body, and should be placed 'where four roads meet' (D II,142). Even ignoring the fact that the stūpa dome came to be known as a *kumbha*, a common metaphor for the personality, these facts suggest that the stūpa may originally have been intended as a model of the enlightened personality. This can be seen from a passage at S IV,194 – 5. Here, a simile is given in which a town stands for the *kāya* (the body, or perhaps the personality other than *viññāna*, the consciousness) and the lord of the town standing for consciousness sits 'in the midst in a square (where four roads meet which represents the 'four great elements') and receives 'a message of truth', i.e. *nibbāna*. As the classical stūpa contains the 'four great elements' of the Buddha and stands at the meeting of four roads, its dome can be seen to represent his *kāya* (Dhp 40 sees the *kāya* as like a *kumbha*), the relics represent the essentials of his body, and the central *yaṣṭi* and parasol-discs (and later the axis, too) represent his consciousness which has received the 'message' of *nibbāna* and been transformed by it. Moreover, as the base of the stūpa is sometimes known as 'throne', and as the throne was used in aniconic 'bodies' of the Buddha, the base, dome and superstructure of the stūpa can be seen to represent the legs, body and head of the sitting Buddha. That such an idea was present in early Buddhist art is indicated by a second century A.D. relief from Amarāvatī which shows the three key events of the Buddha's life. In it the Buddha is shown at his enlightenment by a throne, the Bodhi-trunk and a circle of branches and leaves of the Bodhi tree; at his first sermon by a throne, a pillar and a Dhamma-Wheel; and at his *parinibbāna* by a stūpa with a large base.

I hope to have elucidated, in this paper, the meaning of the most important venerated objects and symbols of early Buddhism. In the case of the stūpa I have tried to show that even prior to its complex symbolism in the Vajrayāna tradition it had developed from simple beginnings into a system of interlocking and mutually supporting symbols which represented the *dhamma* and the enlightened personality embodying the culmination of the practice of the *dhamma*.

NOTES

1 While the Aśvattha tree was the species of tree under which Gotama is said to have become enlightened, D II,2 – 8 states that the six previous Buddhas were each enlightened under different species of tree.

2 ERE III, p. 657.

3 See Buddhaghosa's description at DA II,445.

4 H. Zimmer, *Myths and Symbols of Indian Art and Civilisation*, New York, 1946, p. 91.

5 Ananda Coomaraswamy, *Elements of Buddhist Iconography*, Cambridge, Mass., 1935, repr. Delhi, 1972, pp. 22 & 18.

6 B. Walker, *Hindu World*, London, 1968, vol. II, p. 132.

7 Coomaraswamy, op. cit. p. 25.

8 John Irwin, 'The Stūpa and the Cosmic Axis — The Archaeological Evidence', *South Asian Archaeology 1977* (papers from the Fourth

International Conference of South Asian Archaeologists in Western Europe), Naples (Istituto Universitario Orientale Seminaro di Studi Asiatici), 1979, pp. 799 – 845; and 'The Axial Symbolism of the Early Stūpa — An Exegesis', A. L. Dallapiccola (ed.), *The Stūpa — Its Religious, Historical and Archaeological Significance*, Wiesbaden, 1980, pp. 12 – 38.

9 Lama Anagarika Govinda, *The Psycho-Cosmic Symbolism of the Buddhist Stūpa*, Emeryville, Calif., 1979.

10 Gustav Roth, 'The Symbolism of the Buddhist Stūpa', A. L. Dallapiccola (ed.), op. cit. (note 8). Repr. in *Indian Studies: Selected papers*, by Gustav Roth (Bibliotheca Indo-Buddhica 32), ed. H. Bechert and Petra Kieffer-Pülz, Delhi, 1986, pp.25 – 77.

11 Cf. Monier-Williams' Sanskrit-English Dictionary.

12 D. Mitra, *Buddhist Monuments*, Calcutta, 1971, p. 204.

13 S. Yoe, *The Burman, his Life and Notions*, London, 1910, pp. 158 – 9.

14 G. Roth, op. cit., p. 184, points out that in the Mūlassarvāstivāda Vinaya 'Kṣudraka-vastu' it is said that a Tathāgata's stūpa should have thirteen parasol-discs, that of *arahants* four, that of non-returners three, that of once-returners two and that of stream-enterers one.

15 S. P. Gupta, *The Roots of Indian Art*, Delhi, 1980, pp. 246 – 69.

16 A. Paranavitana, *The Stūpa in Ceylon — Memoirs of the Archaeological Survey of Ceylon*, vol. 5, Colombo, 1946.

17 L. Ledderose, 'Chinese Prototypes of the Pagoda', A. L. Dallapiccola, op. cit., p. 239.

18 Dv, ed. by C. B. Cowell and R. Neil, Cambridge UP, 1884, p. 244.

19 Irwin, 'The Axial Symbolism . . .', p. 21. Cf. the pillar in Fig. 4 which appears to be octagonal.

20 Paranavitana, *The Stūpa in Ceylon* . . . p. 38.

21 Cf. note 8.

22 Irwin, 'The Axial Symbolism . . .', pp. 14 & 28.

23 Ibid. pp. 22 – 3.

24 Irwin, 'The Stūpa and the Cosmic Axis . . .', p. 826.

25 They can also be seen as equivalent to Indra's *vajra* as shown in Āpastamba Śrautasūtra VII,10,3 (as cited by A. Gail, 'Cosmic Symbolism of the Spire of the Ceylon Dagoba', Dallapiccola, op. cit., p. 260) where it is stated that when the Vedic *yūpa* is raised, it is said: 'Rend open the earth, split the heaven-cloud, give us rain water . . .'

26 Irwin, 'The Stūpa and the Cosmic Axis . . .', p. 836.

27 Irwin, 'The Axial Symbolism . . .', pp. 18.

28 Irwin, 'The Stūpa and the Cosmic Axis . . .', p. 831 – 2.

29 Ibid., p. 826. G. Fussman, 'Symbolism of the Buddhist Stūpa', JIABS, vol. 9, no. 2 (1986), pp. 37 – 53, provides a critique of Irwin's interpretation.

30 Irwin, 'The Axial Symbolism . . .', pp. 21.

31 Given that 'Indra's stake' is closely associated and probably mythologically synonymous with Indra's thunderbolt sceptre (*vajra* — see note 25), it is also significant that at A I,124 an *arahant* is described as having a *citta*

like a *vajira*, a term which may mean 'diamond', but which is equivalent to Sanskrit *vajra*.

32 M. Spiro, *Buddhism and Society*, London, 1971, p. 203 reports that in contemporary Burma the stūpa is often seen as representing Meru with the three worlds (*kāma, rūpa* and *arūpa*) represented by the plinth and two parts of the dome, with the spire representing the Buddha.

33 The diagram does not depict the rains canopy (*varṣa-sthātī*) said to symbolize the Buddha's 'great compassion'. The details of the symbolism in the second text differ slightly and it further sees the ground as symbolizing *śīla*, and the first platform as symbolizing *dāna*.

6

PREDESTINY AND EVIL IN HINDU MYTH: AN INQUIRY INTO THE SYMBOLISM OF THE VENA-PṚTHU LEGEND

Jeanine Miller

The legend of Vena-Pṛthu, mentioned in the Manu Smṛti, is related in the Mhb and the Purāṇas and can be traced back, in the form of Pṛthī Vainya, to the AV (8,10), to the ŚB (5,3,5,4) and to the TB where it is referred to several times, and finally to the RV. This shows that it was known, at least in its broad outlines, for a very long time. Certainly the legend must be based on certain historical facts which subsequently became confused, embroidered upon and mixed up with other unrelated facts. But whether historically true or not, its sociological, psychological and ethical implications are of fundamental importance and reveal some of the basics of ancient Indian civilization.

Like all legends and myths, the story has many levels of meaning:

1. The story is concerned with the foundation and justification of social organization.

(a) It tells the origin not only of kingship, but of the divine rights of kings, as descendants of godly kings. It also speaks of what the relationship between kings and people should be: of the duties of kings who are the fosterers of civilization; and of the rights of subjects to demand protection from their kings, and the provision of the bare necessities of existence; as well as of their right to depose kings, whatever their origin, should they prove inadequate or tyrannical.

(b) The story also provides a justification for the maintenance of the classes and thus of the structure of Hindu social order. In this each class, and also each group and each individual, has its specific task to perform; the overall harmony depends upon each one following his particular path, vocation or calling, i.e. *dharma*.

2. From the cosmological point of view the story is concerned with the rebuilding of a world after a period of disruption, destruction or stagnation; and with the teaching of the arts of civilization to child-like humanity by their more enlightened rulers.

3. Its ethical core concerns the problem of good and evil which involves not merely the individual but the whole of society. It addresses the great question of sin, *karma* and the transference of merit and demerit; and thus has direct bearing on the understanding of Hindu social structure.
4. Viewed from a psychological standpoint the story shows two heroes symbolizing two extreme facets of the human personality. On its negative side this personality slides down towards complete disintegration through overweening ambition, ruthlessness and selfishness; on its positive side it strives towards wholeness which leads to reintegration and individuation. This is the process of human maturing from the wild aggressive savage who knows no laws, submits to no one and understands nothing, to the tame, civilized man who lives by law and understands that to live truly is to benefit others.

The present inquiry will concern itself more especially with the last two standpoints and only indirectly with the others in so far as they are bound up with the problems investigated.

The story in its details is obviously not meant to be taken literally. It is symbolic of certain great truths with which the human mind has tried to grapple ever since thought began, as indeed are all myths and legends. The richness of the material is evident and is peculiar to the manifoldness of myths and legends whose multi-level meaning is their essential value and contribution to human lore. In the present instance the story pertains rather to legend than to myth, although the gods do play a preponderant role, but the main heroes are essentially human beings even though one, Pṛthu, is considered a part emanation of Viṣṇu. In myths the focus is on the gods which the human mind projects on the screen of the cosmos in the guise of heroes performing heroic actions, fashioning the cosmos, warring against the forces of opposition, chaos and stagnation and always gaining victory — like Indra in the Vedas, the great heroic god of epic stature. In legends all these daring exploits are ascribed to heroes, demigods, but fundamentally human beings. This is the core of the Vena-Pṛthu story; it deals with the essential human condition: with human frailty and greatness, with man's predicament and his capacity to rise above it, or indeed to sink beneath it, and to achieve greatness through humility or self-destruction through ambition. The gods also play their part here, but only as symbols of forces beyond human control.

PART ONE: VENA

The story unfolds naturally as one proceeds with the examining of the problem it poses. So only a few introductory facts will suffice here.

Vena was born to queen Sunīthā and king Aṅga and has turned out thoroughly evil. His father tries time and again to correct him but to no avail. Vena is bent on evil and thinks of nothing but to impose his perverted will on others even to the point of killing. Finally his father walks out of his kingdom in disgust and disappears for ever. His courtiers scour the whole country but cannot find him. The sage-priests feel obliged, rather than leave the kingdom without a ruler, to consecrate his heir, Vena, as rightful king.

Generally speaking, names in myths and allegories have a meaning that gives a clue to the overall quality of the person. Sunīthā is the daughter of Mṛtyu which means 'death'. Aṅga means 'limb' and this draws our attention to the physical body and stresses the masculine, physical and active (rajasic) side of the person. According to VyP and VP, Aṅga himself is the son of Uru, meaning 'thigh', which further emphasizes the outer and the physical and hence a lower aspect. In the Mhb version Vena's father is the son of Anaṅga, the opposite of Aṅga, i.e. the bodyless one. This name refers to the myth of Kāma, the god of love and desire, whose body was shrivelled up by one glance from Śiva's third eye as he was trying to divert his attention away from his austerities. Thus we have in Vena's paternal ancestry two specific emphases, the body or flesh doomed to corruption, and desire, the source of that corruption.

Sunīthā is the very opposite of Aṅga, given to him to offset his one-sidedness. Her name implies giving or receiving good guidance. She is not at all evil.[1] But her parentage does pose a problem. Her father, Death, represents the very negation of physicality and is also often considered evil. In philosophical terms she would, as his daughter, symbolize the *tamas guṇa*, the static aspect of matter, the lethargic, as the opposite of the vital, the *rajas guṇa*.

In Indian mythology death is usually related to evil.[2] It is understandable that premature and violent death is deemed evil, because it is closely related to punishment for evil doing, not only in Hindu but in all religious traditions of the world. Often lust and death are identified. Cf. BU 1,3,10:

> One should not go to foreign people, one should not go to the end of the world, lest he fall in with evil, with death.

Falling in with evil, bad company and a bad way of life, he would meet with premature death. If death is the culmination of a well-spent life, however, it is natural and may be seen as a well-earned release.

The decrease in the span of human life in each of the four ages of Hindu cosmology was taken as a sign of the waning of *dharma*. As human life becomes more and more a prey to evil and men become more and more enmeshed in matter, the span of life is cut short to prevent a further accretion of evil.

Prajāpati[3] is said to have once fought with Death and the gods are related to have 'struck' and 'thrust it off', thereby reaching heaven, the abode of immortal light (JUB 2,10,1 – 22). In the Vedas and the Brāhmaṇas the wish is for a full span of active life and even for immortality. A sudden death is seen as nefarious even in the Purāṇas. But there is an ambivalence about the idea of immortality. In MtsP (4,30 – 2; and also in LP 1,70,314 – 17) Brahma rebukes Śiva for creating a race of immortals and asks him to create beings 'subject to death', because those 'free from death would not perform prescribed rituals'. It is here taken for granted that the threat of death compels creatures to be virtuous and to offer those sacrifices which in the later part of Vedic civilization were deemed necessary to the gods to keep them immortal. Death as a deterrent among humans is useful to the gods.

So on the mother's side of Vena's parentage the emphasis is on negativity and the dark abyss of death in its most negative meaning and on the father's side on excessive physicality, on the outward-bound psyche that ignores the pull of its depths. The offspring of the union of these two, excessive *rajas* and excessive *tamas*, is Vena, anxiety, desire, the unsatisfied one who, having taken after his grandfather, was obsessed with death, playing the roie of a hunter and killing animals uselessly, and violently strangling children of his own age. His ego-centricity uses outer objects, i.e. other living creatures, to satisfy his own malevolent cravings regardless of the moral implications. VP states that Vena 'inherited the evil propensities of his maternal grandfather'[4] — thereby again identifying death with evil; death here means the negation of every quality.

The union of *rajas* and *tamas* in this particular case emphasizes the worst aspect of both. Besides his infliction from the maternal side with the characteristic of negating everything that is considered worthwhile, Vena's paternal inheritance of excessive masculinity manifests itself in him as rajasic *ahaṅkāra* or self-assertive 'I-am-ness' which is devoid of any feeling for others and leads him to usurp for himself the fruit of the sacrifice with the intention of making himself immortal on the physical level. This is an example of egotism in its most violent form: inflicting death on others while being unwilling to die oneself. He would not, of course, face up to death in its inner meaning, the negation of *ahaṅkāra*. The last thing Vena was capable of was dying to oneself.

BP (IV,13,25 ff.) again emphasizing the evil aspect of death and Vena's baleful heredity, makes a further point of great importance:

> Vena took after his maternal grandfather, Death, who was born of a portion of *adharma*, and so Vena was devoid of *dharma*.

Thus Vena's destiny is sealed from his very conception. Because of his baleful ancestry he cannot be righteous and is predestined to act in a way contrary to accepted norms. He always chooses to behave in opposition to *dharma*; in fact, he has no power or capacity to choose. *Dharma* is defined by MaiU 4,3 as the 'pursuit of the duties of the stage of life to which each one belongs; this is the rule for one's own duty'. And Bowker defines it thus:

> Very roughly, the idea of living according to the pattern of life appropriate to one's own level of attainment and position in society is what is meant by *dharma*.[5]

Vena's *dharma* as head or king is to uphold the order of the society such as it is, to pay tribute to the gods through the priesthood and to be an example of righteousness to his people, all of which he failed to do. Straight after his inauguration as monarch 'he caused it to be proclaimed everywhere that no worship should be performed, no oblations offered, no gifts bestowed on the brahmins' (VP 1,13,12 – 14).

The first step on the path of self-inflation and self-destruction was thus taken. When the sage-priests remonstrated with him, declaring that such a course of action was unthinkable, he declared that the sacrifice should be offered to him as the one responsible for the welfare of all and as the sustainer of the people, and that he should be therefore worshipped as the lord of all. The sages then pointed out that for the preservation of his kingdom and his life they should be permitted to worship Hari, 'the Lord of all sacrifice' with solemn rites; 'a portion of the fruit' thereof would revert to him.[6]

> Viṣṇu, the god of oblations, being propitiated with sacrifice by us, will grant you, O king, all your desires. Those princes have all their wishes gratified in whose realms Hari, the lord of sacrifice, is adored with sacrificial rites (VP 1,13,17 – 19).

This is a reminder to Vena of the meaning of the sacrifice: an offering to the deity as a result of which the deity sends its blessing on men. It is also a statement of the function of priesthood. But the conceited Vena asks: 'Who is superior to me? Who besides me is entitled to worship?' He remains adamant and claims that all the gods 'are present in the person of a king; the essence of a sovereign is all that is divine'; therefore the brahmins must obey his new decree. But they plead further and emphasize this time the *dharma*:

> Give command, great king, that *dharma* may suffer no decrease. All this world is but a transmutation of oblations; and if devotion be suppressed, the world is at an end (VP 1,13,25).

In these few words is contained the essence of the philosophy of the sacrifice: the perpetual give and take, offering up and receiving, that forms the web of universal life and hence the very structure of the cosmos.[7]

Vena is obviously confronted with a choice of conduct and a stern warning. The sages' last admonition goes beyond the implications dictated by the social structure with its distinction of classes and their specific functions, but embraces the whole world in its stress on the *dharma* and its fulfilment in the context of man's relation to duty. The king should be the first to demonstrate true *dharma* in his conduct, decrees and worship.

But devoid of *dharma* from his very birth and therefore incapable of relating to what is righteous and of acting accordingly, Vena is predetermined to take the path of *adharma*. When confronted with the sages' warning and given a kind of ultimatum to take the path of *dharma*, he flatly refuses and gets himself more and more enmeshed in sin. He sinks deeper and deeper into his inflated egohood, sees nothing except himself and his own self-aggrandisement, and understands nothing of the seriousness of the situation brought about by his rash actions and their disastrous consequences, both for himself and for those who depend on him as their sovereign. It is a complete psychological blindness. Sweeping aside all reason, intelligence and even common sense, Vena falls headlong into the abyss of his own negativity.

It is said that the sages will destroy him 'who had first been destroyed by his impiety towards God' either through blades of grass consecrated by prayers (VP 1,13,29) or through the power of sound (BP 4,14,34). These are symbols of powers and processes going on within the psyche. The implication is that the worship Vena arrogates to himself turns against him and destroys him. Total self-inflation, self-aggrandisement and delusions of grandeur end in megalomania, i.e. madness. Whether he is in the end also killed or not is beside the point. In one version of the story his body is magically preserved by his mother, in others his death is brought about by the churning of his limbs. The real point is the fact that Vena is killed psychologically — through the power of his own actions.

Western interpreters sometimes make light of Vena's sin. Thus Dumézil sees his action only as directed against brahmins; his sin lies in the resulting destruction of the class structure:

> Vena, moved by pride, opposed himself to the Brahmans . . . He wanted to prevent these from sacrificing and to reserve for himself alone . . . the monopoly of the ritual, thereby destroying the function of the Brahmans as a social class. The core of his sin consisted in destroying the fundamental structure of society: its division into specific classes. This is confirmed in Manu (IX,67) who says: 'This eminent royal sage who once ruled the entire earth caused a confusion of the castes (*varṇa*), his intellect being destroyed by lust.'[8]

In Western eyes Vena's sin is not terrible and would not deserve the death penalty. But if considered psychologically as a deterioration of the personality through lack of moral judgement and over-inflation, the 'death', whether it refers symbolically to madness or to actual dying, is the inevitable consequence. The main point is that, to the ancient Hindus, the sin of Vena was against *dharma* pure and simple whatever it might imply, even if it is just mixing the classes, usurping the prerogatives of the brahmins or even raising oneself to the level of a god. Having failed in his *dharma* as king, Vena's sin was both 'personal and traditional', to use O'Flaherty's words. Psychologically, making oneself into a god is an overweening ambition which disregards all common sense and cannot but result in madness and is thus self-destructive.

Vena had to pay the penalty for going against *dharma* despite the fact that, being intrinsically devoid of *dharma*, he was incapable by his very heredity of acting otherwise. We are reminded in this connection of the story of the Kauravas in Mhb where this same firmly entrenched belief of the Hindus finds expression in the lofty figure of Gandhārī, the wife of the blind king Dhṛtarāṣṭra and mother of the one hundred sons of whom the eldest, Duryodhana, is also an embodiment of *adharma*. Gandhārī rebukes Duryodhana for his evil conduct time and again, particularly during the battle when he comes to her for her blessing; she warns him that in the end righteousness always inevitably triumphs and he, not being righteous, cannot expect to win. In both the

Vena and the Duryodhana episode the two protagonists allow themselves to become inflated with their own conceit and plunge into the abyss of evil, ignoring stern warnings of disaster as the sure consequence of *adharma*.

A question springs to mind: if anyone born of *dharma* can act in a way contrary to *dharma*, would this not be worse than the sin of someone born of *adharma* who cannot but act, because of this predetermination, in a way contrary to *dharma*? Does not the hereditary affliction mitigate, at least to some extent, the evil ascribed to his action, and so his guilt and his punishment? The Purāṇas are silent on this issue.

Vena's sin of going against *dharma* has as its consequence violent, premature death. Panikkar remarks:

> It is a universal belief that misfortune is a consequence of sin and thus that pain-suffering is always pain-punishment and so pain-purification. It all rests on the myth of pain. Since there is no pain without suffering, the implication is grave; suffering seems to be the ultimate structure of the world, because it is through this suffering that the afflicted order seems to be restored.[9]

The consequence can be changed only by changing one's attitude. The choice is there, no matter whether the hardship is a 'karmic' consequence or a 'punishment'. This comes across also from the New Testament (Luke 13,4 – 5). When his disciples asked Christ whether certain Galileans were such great sinners that they were murdered (clearly, this is another instance of the equation of violent death with sin or evil), he answers with another question:

> Or those eighteen upon whom the tower of Siloam fell and slew them, think ye that they were sinners above all men that dwell in Jerusalem? I tell you: nay, but except ye turn your mind completely (*metanoia*), ye shall all likewise perish.

The implication is clear: wrong outlook and the wrong way of living stemming from it bring about violent events; unless one changes one's attitude to life, one will bring on oneself evil — whether it be punishment in the shape of a violent death or some other catastrophe.

In the Vena episode the emphasis is on 'evil conduct' as a direct effect of evil heredity. That is *predestiny*. If we ask why Vena inherited only the negative side of his parents, the Hindu tradition will answer that this is because he must have behaved in the past in such a way as to bring this evil *karma* on himself. As one sows, so one reaps. Radhakrishnan puts it thus:

> The law of *karma* is not external to the individual. The judge is not without but within. The law by which virtue brings its triumph and ill-doing its retribution is the unfolding of the law of our being.[10]

O'Flaherty comments:

> The myth is about what happened to Vena (his evil), not about what he did (his sin), for in India the significant evil is what happens to one, not what one does. The myth seeks to explain inexplicable causes by describing visible effects.[11]

But surely, the two — what *happens* as a result of what one *does* — are inextricably linked. Vena's wrong attitude which brings about his sudden death may be taken for granted in some of the Purāṇas, but this does not alter the fact that, although the story may be about the outcome of his sin, without such sin there would be no such outcome. The inexplicable causes, furthermore, are bound up with man's previous actions, hence with *karma*. Man makes or mars his own life according to his deeds, for he is aware of what he does and therefore bears full responsibility. O'Flaherty further states:

> Vena's mistake was in not acting to change his fate. The Vena myth presents an extremely detailed description of the effect of his sin, but (with one notable exception) a very vague idea of the cause; for the myth functions on two levels one of which assumes the cause (cosmic predestination), the other of which tentatively introduces a totally different cause (Vena's own inability to oppose fate). (Ibid.)

She does admit, though, that 'in spite of *karma*, the individual can choose to accept his fate or to challenge it'. In Vena's case his own predetermined nature prevented him from seeing clearly and, consequently, from changing his attitude. This is the crucial point.

But the death of Vena is not the end of the problem of evil. From the wreck of his personality emerge two offshoots, a wicked (the tamasic element) and a good son (the rajasic element tinged with *sattva*). Thus the embodiment of evil gives birth to both good and evil.

The story goes that after the death of Vena the sages soon beheld a great cloud of dust arise and spread everywhere on the horizon. They discovered that this cloud was raised 'by troops of clustering robbers hastening to fall upon their prey' (VP 1,13,30 – 1). From the social standpoint, a kingdom without a ruler soon falls prey to anarchy and chaos. Expressed psychologically, the forcible eradication or repression of excessive egoistic inflation is no cure; the destruction of the ego would only serve to let loose all the dark, disruptive forces of the unconscious, normally held in check by the ego whether it is megalomanic or not. In the myth the cloud of dust and the thieves rushing to rob people portray the chaotic state of a kingdom without a central ruler which symbolizes the personality that has lost its central anchorage, the ego-centredness, and fallen prey to disorder, chaos and madness.

Seeing the threat, the sages decide to churn the body of Vena to produce an offspring and thereby reinstate order in the kingdom by means of a new legitimate ruler who must be an issue from the previous monarch in spite of the evil which was attached to him. The whole episode is thus symbolical of the idea of new life born from the ashes of the old. In some versions the sages first rub Vena's thigh, in others his left hand, as if it were a 'firestick', but always it is the inauspicious side. Out of it arises a black, hideous being, described in the VP as 'of the complexion of a charred stake, with flattened features'; from the right arm or hand is born a bright, auspicious being. In BP (4,15,3) both arms are churned and a male and a female appear. The sages recognize them as part manifestations of Viṣṇu and Lakṣmī who are inseparable.

Some have seen in this churning a symbol of exorcism which implies the complete purification of the previous state as a preliminary to the birth of a suitable heir. The churning corresponds to the twirling of the wooden stick in the 'matrix' of a wooden base, the ancient Indian way of producing sacrificial fire. Thus Vena becomes symbolic of sexual polarity which produces offspring. Out of the process Pṛthu is born and arises 'resplendent in person as if the blazing deity of fire had been manifested'.

In all the descriptions of the birth of Pṛthu there is a marked difference in the function of the right and left limb. The respective auspicious and inauspicious meaning of the two is prevalent among all ancient peoples all over the world. Evidence to that effect was collected by Hertz who writes about the meaning of the words right and left:

> The former is used to express the ideas of physical strength and 'dexterity', of intellectual 'rectitude' and good judgment, of 'uprightness' and moral integrity . . . while the word 'left' evokes most of the ideas contrary to these . . . The left is the hand of perjury, treachery and fraud . . . The power of the left hand is always somewhat occult and illegitimate; it inspires terror and repulsion. Its movements are suspect . . . The exclusive preponderance of the right and a

repugnance for requiring anything of the left are the marks of a soul unusually associated with the divine and immune to what is profane or impure.[12]

Out of Vena's left thigh was born Niṣāda who, although repugnant, was not killed. He was recognized as unsuitable to rule and told to sit down, *niṣīda*, hence his name. He was to become the ancestor of barbarous races such as the inhabitants of Vindhya mountains, who were said to be sinful by nature and are described in the VP as 'characterized by exterior tokens of depravity'. The seed of evil extracted from Vena became the seed of an evil generation.

The two offspring symbolize the separation of good and evil born from the same source. The situation then is no longer ambivalent but clear cut. Psychologically Niṣāda may symbolize a sick aspect of the personality, possibly a neurosis, that, like an abscess, contributes, in detaching itself from the whole, to the healing process of the person who is then able to produce a good aspect. Then also, the fact that good does come even out of Vena in the form of Pṛthu might signify that Vena was not completely bad after all, the good side of his ancestry was still there, albeit inoperative. Or it might mean that Pṛthu is born out of the evil Vena as an act of grace on the part of Viṣṇu for the sake of mankind; that would indicate that the grace of God operates however evil a human being may be. The Purāṇas do not concern themselves with such subtle points.

In the myth the good Pṛthu could be born only after evil had been extracted from Vena through Niṣāda:

> By this means the wickedness of Vena was expelled; those Niṣādas being born of his sins and carrying them away . . . (VP 1,13,37).
>
> When Niṣādas and other evil barbarians were born from the Vena's body, the sages knew that the king's sins were gone. When Pṛthu was born from Vena's body, the king became spotless and righteous again and his sin was obliterated, the sin derived from his grandfather Death (PP 2,27,19 ff.).

We are faced here with the problem of the removal of sin, of the transfer of merit or demerit, first through the churning of Vena's limbs, then through the action of the son. One son represents all the impurities inherited from his father which determine him in a similar way to his father — or should we look at him only as a symbol to account for certain tribes outside the pale of Brahmanism? But not even this black dwarf can fully release his father despite willy nilly taking on himself all his sins. Only his good son can accomplish this by performing the prescribed rites. Would he be symbolic of a complete change of attitude followed by good action?

Later Purāṇas (e.g. SP 7,1,336 and GP 6,4 – 8) change the story. Vena has to pay for his sins personally. The sage Narada tells Pṛthu that Vena has been reborn among the barbarians afflicted with consumption and leprosy. So the evil king not only gives birth to a progeny of barbarians from his left side, but is himself reborn as one of them, afflicted, in addition, with the worst of diseases. This is evil karmic result indeed. Motivated by filial piety, Pṛthu seeks out his father, brings him to a Śiva's shrine but is warned by Vāyu against desecrating the holy place. Birds tell him of another holy spot, Goṣpada, with footprints of Nandinī, the daughter of the magic cow. There his father's guilt can be washed away without desecrating the holy spot.[13]

The release of a soul and the negation of sin through purifying rites may not be the right way of atoning for karmic debts from the philosophical point of view, but it is in accordance with the traditional Brahmanic insistence on the performance of rites by the son at the death of his father in order to secure heaven for him. Moreover, the idea of the transference of merit and demerit is also still prevalent today. The VmP (27,1 – 23), however, requires more: Śiva intervenes and tells Vena that after dwelling in his presence for a while he would be reborn as the demon Andhaka and that only after further purifications he would in another birth become Bhṛgin, the leader of Śiva's hosts.

Psychologically, we might say that what is evil in a person will come out in one way or another. This is symbolized in the Vena legend by the birth of the evil son; but the whole nature was contaminated and has to be purified and so the good son performs the purifying rites. Even then, the guilty person still has to live, suffer and expiate before becoming whole again.

There are two highly important philosophical implications in the story: one is the doctrine of the sins of fathers being visited on children (well known from the Bible) and the other is its corollary, the solidarity of all life; we are all bound to one another and the behaviour of everyone affects in ways known and unknown everyone else. The son, whether he is good or evil, suffers for his father's misconduct, even if only through anxiety over his whereabouts and future. The good son gives it expression through his effort to release his father to heaven, thus acting in accordance with the solidarity of life. The sin of one is the sin of all; the same is true of well-being. A further example will be considered later.

One problem brought out by the first part of the legend is the problem of suffering consequent upon evil doing. Why should suffering be the only means of expiation? No satisfying answer seems forthcoming. Panikkar asks:

What is the meaning of suffering? Why do we suffer? The myth of the fall seeks only to explicate this cosmic scandal and at the same time safeguard the prestige of God. In the Indian tradition, the law of karma asserts the normality of suffering, since here pain is always 'consequence' and never 'original'; Buddhism likewise begins with the central fact of sorrow . . . The essential question is not to know who has the right to inflict pain, but to understand why punishment exists at all. The first response, already a demythicized answer, speaks of the medicinal character of pain, but clearly, this is not satisfying. Experience alone shows, and psychology confirms, that pain has today largely lost its purifying value. Even if punishment still retained its medicinal character, the question would not be resolved, one could yet ask why it is necessary to make someone suffer in order to purify him . . . The moment you ask why you must 'suffer' . . . you no longer accept pain on its own; the purifying efficacy of pain shrinks in direct proportion to its demythicization. In short, pain without the myth loses its raison d'être and becomes intolerable. The myth ceases to be effective as soon as you question pain as a purifying process . . .[14]

In the Indian context existence is, in its innermost essence, a 'unity'. As expressed by Bowker:

All that is an aspect or manifestation of Being itself, Brahman. To break down that unity is to introduce tension and conflict and strife.[15]

The world of duality which is our everyday world is inevitably one of tension, of swaying from one opposite to another, from joy to grief, from fear to self-assurance, from cruelty to mercy, from stupidity to intelligence, etc. To a mind completely identified with the world of duality, which it equates with Reality, there can be no solution to the problem of evil. But the very 'identification' holds the key to the solution. At the core of all *being* is *bliss* as testified by the Upaniṣads and all the mystics of all religious traditions who experienced the core of being as *oneness*. It is the centre-point from which individual streams of life emerge and to which they converge; in it there is 'coincidence' of opposites and the state of wholeness. It is expressed by the famous Upaniṣadic equation: *that thou art*. The ṛṣis of AV (4,1,1) expressed it thus:

The *brahman* that of old first manifested from the luminous borderline, the seer has uncovered; its loftiest station, fathomless, he has uncovered as the womb of the manifest and the unmanifest.

To identify oneself with the world of transient realities, of opposites, of mine and thine, and of separativeness means to turn one's back to the world of Reality and oneness, to subject oneself to the tyranny of extremes and, thereby, to bring about suffering resulting from the loss, collapse or failure of what one relies on for satisfaction. Nothing that is divided, fragmented or apart can be ultimately satisfying. To be 'attached' to anything that is doomed to come to an end is automatically to court sorrow. Hence humanity suffers far more than the animal world. But as is clear from Vena's case, suffering is also a result of wrong activities and of the perpetuation of wrong attitudes which preclude the inception of a new orientation and the possibility of one's opening oneself to an altogether new life. However, to view suffering as a mere 'punishment' is a human, albeit natural, distortion of the inexorable law: as you sow so you reap. As Wayman puts it:

> Our own wrong actions become the 'policeman' (in psychological terms, the "super-ego" or punitive self) that drags us away to retribution.[16]

Unjustifiable suffering such as that resulting from man-imposed sanctions, e.g. the over-rigidity of the caste system, is due to misapplication, distortion and abuse of the natural categories inherent in human society and is therefore not a 'punishment', but an inevitable consequence of a long-standing abuse. Some are born with intellectual gifts, some with artistic talents, others with a bent for craftsmanship, others with muscle power; that they should accordingly band together for solidarity, protection etc. and form castes (somewhat like our trade unions) is only natural. Says Vivekananda:

> Caste is a natural order. I can perform one duty in social life and you another; you can govern a country and I can mend a pair of shoes, but there is no reason why you are greater than I, for can you mend my shoes? Can I govern the country?[17]

It is, of course, going against nature and opening the door wide to suffering if such natural groupings ossify into rigid categories without any possibility of natural communication, sharing etc.

Suffering, like everything else in the 'divine economy', has its useful part to play, for more often than not man is brought back to his senses, i.e. performs the 'appropriate action', through being buffeted by thc 'slings and arrows of outrageous fortune'. This is the redemptive quality of suffering, but only those who can see its inner meaning as well as beyond it can fully accept it. The ultimate truth which in Indian tradition is the bliss of pure being (*sat-cit-ānanda*) will never be found within the world of opposites.[18] It can be achieved through a life of 'appropriate action' (*dharma*) which to the Hindu is also the foundation of all truths.

Can we take it that Vena symbolizes mankind in its corrupt state, as fallen into matter which is the 'tempting serpent' leading to disaster, making man into the offspring of death (which also symbolizes corruption), but still capable of redemption — of producing a better race personified in Pṛthu, born through 'divine grace', who redeems his fallen parent? Then it would be a living myth with a universal message.

PART TWO: PṚTHU

Pṛthu, the 'first anointed king' (ŚB 5,3,5,4) and the *ādirāja* of the Purāṇas, chooses to act righteously immediately on being born and is eager to take advice from sages. We might think that there is little merit in it since he is an emanation or part-emanation of Viṣṇu and therefore cannot act otherwise than in accordance with *dharma*, being thus equally predestined, though in an opposite way, as Vena. His illustrious fate is symbolized by Viṣṇu's sign on his hand, a *cakra*.

The advent of Pṛthu breaks the chain of the evil causality. An act of divine grace thus redresses the chaos and restores law and order through a righteous king. In Mhb[19] Pṛthu is consecrated king by the gods, sages and brahmins. The Earth, Ocean and Mountains bring him their homage and wealth. In VP 1,13,44 the great father Brahma, all other gods and 'all things animate and inanimate assembled and performed the ceremony of consecrating the son of Vena'. Indra grants him inexhaustible riches and distributes them according to the principles of *dharma*, *kāma* and *artha* which are also the goals of the three castes.[20] This may also be an indirect way of saying that he reinstated the classes mixed by his predecessor and thereby earned the approval and respect of the priesthood.

Pṛthu, the king whom Dumézil describes as 'designated by the gods, recognized by the sages and accepted by the masses'[21] is highly praised at his consecration by the two panegyrists who were born simultaneously with the sacrifice performed for Pṛthu's birth. These praises spur him on to conform to the ideals thus celebrated in advance. They also attract the attention of his starving subjects who forthwith approach him with the request to restore to them the means of subsistence previously taken away from them. It is his *dharma* to provide for their needs as the appointee of God. This is the Hindu idea of kingship which Vena completely failed to implement.

Blaming Earth for the dearth of nourishment from which his subjects were suffering, Pṛthu seizes his bow and arrows and marches in great wrath to assail the Earth who, under the guise of a cow, flees from his wrath through all the spheres, including the region of Brahma. 'But wherever went the supporter of living things, there she beheld Vainya with uplifted weapons.' In a dialogue the Earth Cow asks, trembling with terror: if you destroy me, how will you support yourself and all created beings? Pṛthu assumes the role of the Supreme Lord and declares that he will support his people by the efficacy of his own 'yoga' (VP 1,13,76). The Earth makes obeisance to him as the Supreme Lord and respectfully suggests the means of drawing from her the milk that would feed the many creatures. Let him give her the calf that will permit her to secrete milk and let him level the ground so that the vegetation may spread about. Pṛthu grants life to the Earth and is henceforth known as her Father, she as Pṛthivī.

So Pṛthu with his arrows levels the mountains, defines the boundaries of villages and towns, causes highways to be made for commerce, teaches his people the rudiments of agriculture and civilization.[22] Therefore the 'heroic son of Vena . . . from conciliating the affections of the people was the first ruler to whom the title of *rājā* was ascribed' (VP 1,13,93).

He brings for the milking Manu Svayabhuva and uses as a milk pail his own hands. As milk he receives herbs and plants. This is a signal for all the creatures of the world to come for the milking, including demons, snakes, trees, mountains. However different and incompatible the classes and species of creatures may be, life is one and the need of nourishment is equally one and the same for all; coming one species after another to the wonder cow, each brings its specific representative in guise of the calf and they all receive according to their nature: (see Table 1)

The symbolic significance of the milker, the calf and the milk pail brought by each class of creatures is of pertinent interest to the whole array of this magnificent panorama of the Earth Cow nourishing her creatures. It first shows the nourishing aspect of the universe or Mother Nature feeding her children irrespective of what worth they may have in human eyes; all are entitled to sustenance, receive it and transmute it in accordance with their own nature. The milker is representative of the category of beings for whom he is chosen. The milk pail, or the means whereby the nourishment is received, is the working tool by which each class performs its particular work and achieves the purpose of its being; it is, as it were, its handiwork and is of less and less precious substance down the scale of being. The milk received as the essence of food is symbolic of the essential characteristic of the class of beings which receive it. The snakes receive poison, the demons blood, the seers piety, the *asuras* illusion, *gandharvas* perfume, men crops and medicinal herbs. It is of the

Table 1

Recipient	milker	calf	milk pail	milk
devas	Savitṛ or Mitra	Indra	a golden cup	*svaha*
asuras	Dvimurdha or Artvya	Virocana	an iron cup	*māyā*
men	Pṛthu	Manu	his hands	crops, herbs
ṛṣis	Bṛhaspati	*soma*	metres (Vedas)	piety
pitṛs	Antaka (time-son of Mṛtyu)	Yama	silver cup	*svadha*
gandharvas	Viśvaruci	Citraratha	lotus leaf	perfume
snakes	Dhṛtarāṣṭra	Takṣaka	gourd	poison
rākṣasas	Rājatanabha	Sumāli	human skull	blood

nature of the seers to be pious, of snakes to poison etc. With men the symbolism is not so obvious. Is it a hint that the plant kingdom was considered to have a specific link with man and that it was meant as his food *par excellence*?

Turning to the 'milk pail', the palms of hands symbolize humility, the willingness to toil, the acceptance of menial work and the dignity of any labour; the gold cup of the gods stands perhaps for the 'chalice' of perfect consciousness with which they view the universe; the lotus leaf of the *gandharvas* is an expression of Nature's delicate achievements in beauty. In the case of men, their hands, their work, their toil express their greatness. They cannot survive without work, but as tillers of the soil, they are co-partners with nature.

In the Purāṇic accounts Pṛthu is the leader of the hosts and indirectly the benefactor of all creatures, because in rendering the earth fertile, he enables all to be nourished according to their need. He has thus found the right means of appropriating and putting to right use the various riches locked up in Nature, paying due respect to her own categories. All of them are necessary and have their part to play in the divine equilibrium and he wins the reverence of all of them.

In a similar vein in the well-known myth of the churning of the ocean, a churning which is interpreted at one level as a sacrificial rite, all the goods of the universe previously contained in the ocean that emerged during the churning were appropriated by the gods and antigods. The ocean of matter, in other contexts called *prakṛti*, from which creatures take their nourishment, is often symbolized in the Purāṇas by the Cow of plenty, an idea which goes back to AV where the cow is named not Earth but Virāj.[23] In the Puruṣa hymn (RV 10,90) Virāj is said to be born from Puruṣa and Puruṣa from Virāj. The name Virāj is in Dumézil's opinion a confirmation of his theory that the cow represents sovereign power in which is vested kingly authority as well as natural riches.

The Earth Cow as a mythological entity seems to be a culmination of a long process in which several originally differing, albeit allied, elements became fused and somewhat transformed, finishing up as the idea of the Cow of plenty which is in the Purāṇas represented by Pṛthivī. This need not necessarily refer to our planet Earth, but to matter, the matrix of all existence, or to Nature, the formative, nourishing aspect of the cosmos.

In the RV the cow or the cosmic buffalo, mother of the universe, is identified with *vāc* (word, *logos*; in Sanskrit of feminine gender) which has been 'meted out' in four sections, three transcendent, the fourth one manifested. Her basic element is 'the imperishable', the sacred syllable (*akṣara*), the eternal word *par excellence*, which manifests at the dawn of creation. In the unmanifest 'she has a thousand syllables';

> The buffalo cow lowed as she fashioned the flowing waters; she who has a thousand syllables in the supreme abode, became one-footed, two-footed, three-footed, four-footed, eight-footed, etc. (RV 1,164,41).
>
> Vāc has been measured out in four sections which inspired Brahmins' know. Three deposited in secret remain inactive. The fourth only belongs to human speech (RV 1,164,45).

The 'mathematical progression' is symbolic of the gradual process of manifestation.

> When in the abode of the Celestial Cow the first of dawns shone forth, the eternal word (*akṣara*) manifested (RV 3,55,1).

Vāc is the melodious cow who milked forth nourishment for all. She is also of mystic speech and a permutation of Aditi who admits: 'Weak-minded mortals have turned to me, the arouser of speech and vision, as to a cow' (RV 8,101,16).

The waters of space, a symbol for primordial or pre-cosmic matter, have a basic attribute: *sound*. Sound as it passes through them stirs them and thus fashions the universe. In philosophical texts these cosmic waters are called *ākāśa*, not quite adequately translated as 'space' or 'ether'; it should also imply the presence of the notion of primordial matter (conveyed by the image of cosmic waters).

The connection between *ākāśa* and the word or speech as creative force comes across also from JUB 1,23,1 – 2: 'In the beginning was *ākāśa* . . . This *ākāśa* is the word, for from *ākāśa* speaks the word.'[24]

Prajāpati pressed this word and from the sap that streamed forth the worlds were shaped (JUB 1,23,3). In the Upaniṣads *ākāśa* is said to be woven warp and woof upon the word (BU 3,8,8 – 10). Hence the word or sound must be an expression, a correlation or an attribute of *ākāśa*.

To us the main point of interest is that all the feminine deities — Vāc, Aditi, Prakṛti, Pṛthivī — are permutations of the same idea, of that subtle essence, the noumenal matter, out of which all things are brought forth, which nourishes them all and through which they all evolve. The creative or formative sound or word resounds from it and each class of beings feeds on it and weaves its own specific essence from it, thus receiving from it all it needs. All this is symbolized by the image of the Cow of plenty.

This comes across also in the verse used in the ritual of Agnicayana: 'Harm not the cow, Aditi, Virāj' (VS 13,43).[25] Virāj is also the name of a Vedic metre which associates it further with the creative power of sound. In AV Virāj symbolizes also nature's cycles of activity and rest, fruitfulness and aridity, birth and death. The Purāṇic Pṛthivī has her prototype in AV 8,10 where, without being pursued, she scours the universe of her own accord. She approaches successively each category of beings (trees, ancestors, gods, men, etc.), offers herself for milking, is killed in turn by each and resurrects after a year, a month, a fortnight, a day, respectively.

Psychologically the Earth Cow obviously represents the unconscious, i.e. that from which surface consciousness feeds. The fact that Pṛthu is able to conquer that which alone can feed all aspects of being shows him as the personified 'complex of the egoic self-consciousness' which has come to terms with the 'feminine unconscious' from where it receives the essential energies which bring back life to the many fragments of the personality that until now have been in a state of distraction and starved of inner sustenance.[26]

The pursuit of the cow from world to world would imply gradual penetration into all levels of the unconscious, from the lowest to the highest — since the Brahma world is referred to — on the part of the conscious ego-complex which thus gains control over it and the capacity to release from it specific energies previously pent up within the unconscious. The episode with the arrow poised is an image symbolizing the fertilization of the feminine unconscious by the masculine consciousness when the latter has been freed, possibly by one-pointed concentration for which this image stands in the Upaniṣads (cf. MuU 2,2,3 – 4).

After the successful ending of his encounter with the Earth Cow, Pṛthu consecrates himself by performing one hundred *aśvamedhas* as a token of his conquest of chaos and his restoration of prosperity to his kingdom. (This last episode, concerned with his relation to Indra, is not related in VP and VyP.) This ambitious project hints, psychologically, at an insidious danger: psychic inflation, a boosting up of the ego as had been seen in Vena's case, with disastrous results. For Pṛthu as a demi-god the problem should be more subtle, but as the story proceeds his divinity is lost sight of and his humanity, with its inherent weaknesses, becomes more and more apparent.

It is not enough for Pṛthu to relate himself successfully to the Earth goddess (Nature), i.e. his unconscious. He has to come to terms with Indra, the king of the gods, who symbolizes the conscious drive, the mental power which controls the senses (*indryas*). He aspires to the status of Indra for whom the one hundred *aśvamedha* rite was the exclusive prerogative. Was he entitled to perform this sacrifice? The story treats us to a most baffling and somewhat absurd and infantile sequence of behaviour on the part of Indra, whose jealousy is aroused when he realizes Pṛthu's intention. Twice he intervenes at the final sacrifice and steals the horse. Twice Pṛthu's son pursues him, snatches the animal but fails to catch Indra who first transforms himself into a mendicant covered with ashes, posing as a liberated *sannyāsi*, and the second time brandishing a skull and Śiva's club to the discomfiture of Pṛthu's son, each time disappearing into his heaven at the crucial moment; thus playing hide and seek and behaving like a trickster sent out to try out Pṛthu through his son, who may be seen to represent an immature aspect of Pṛthu himself.

Indra is a complex figure and suffered a degradation from his high position in the RV to a low status in the Purāṇas:

1. In the RV he is the conqueror of that obstacle which prevents the waters of life from flowing freely and the sun of enlightenment from being raised on high for all to see. He makes cosmos out of chaos; with the aid of the sun he makes pathways where before was darkness (6,21,3ab); he separates heaven from earth and makes wider the intermediate region, thus creating an orderly world with definite demarcations. He also gives freedom to ('makes space for') the gods (3,34,7) and for man he finds the 'way to fulfilment through conflict' (10,49,9). The expression 'space-maker' has meaning on more levels than one. All these accomplishments are the work of the mind, the liberating consciousness as it illuminates the darkness of the

unconscious, asserts itself, claims its freedom of action and creates its own universe. The conscious mind thus asserts itself against the forces of chaos and darkness of the previously untamed unconscious.[27]
2. In the myth recounted in CU (8,7,12 ff.), where Indra and Virocana resort to Prajāpati to find out the meaning of the self (*ātman*), Indra is the genuine seeker of truth, i.e. the inquiring mind bent on the quest for enlightenment. He is shown to be the assiduous pupil, not afraid to ply his teacher with pertinent questions, showing shrewd insight, discrimination, sincerity. He is ready to take the leap into the higher realms of pure consciousness and to find truth.
3. In the Sunaḥśepa legend Indra represents the extreme of individualism, the individual bent on liberating himself by his own efforts. In Panikkar's words 'Indra is always a god who strikes' — not necessarily with his thunderbolt, but as in the Pṛthu and Sunaḥśepa legends, by his unexpected intervention. He is always the strong, brave fighter for freedom.[28]

As the ruler of the senses (*indriyas*) Indra may represent in the Purānas the sensory and thinking aspects of human nature at the expense of the aspect of feeling and intuition which appears completely repressed in him (to use Jung's division of types into sensation-thinking and feeling-intuition). This makes understandable the rather colourless quality of his consort Sacī and also the sudden eruption of the repressed side in him. The episode of his intrusions at Pṛthu's sacrifice is such an irrational outburst. It shows the fragility of the conscious mind in a personality that has not yet achieved integration; it shows itself at the mercy of disruptive factors of the repressed unconscious and stands powerless against them.

Pṛthu's son fails to get rid of Indra, but Pṛthu, by now aware of what has been going on, seizes his bow and arrow in extreme anger in order to slay Indra. At this the priests are the first to intervene, themselves wishing to kill Indra. Then Brahma himself appears and gives all to understand that such an action would lead only to self-destruction.[29] Psychologically Indra represents here Pṛthu's own conscious personality still precariously balanced but nevertheless vital for his achievement of wholeness. A reconciliation is brought about between Pṛthu and Indra on the initiative of Pṛthu when he shows humility and magnanimity, the latter being a quality which belongs to Indra as well who is thereby deeply touched and apologizes to Pṛthu there and then.

The last uncompleted sacrifice stands as a mute witness to human imperfection. Once again man cannot arrogate to himself the status of the gods, but Pṛthu, unlike Vena, is human and intelligent enough to realize this and to accept the human condition. In due course he gives over the reins of the kingdom to his descendant and wanders off into the forest as a *sannyāsi* — entering the fourth stage of life as prescribed by Hindu tradition. He then practises all sorts of extreme austerities (BP 4,23,1 ff.).

CONCLUSION

We have here two parallel situations in the two legends. The second one shows considerable improvement against the first one: In Vena there was incapacity, through wrong predestiny, to come to terms with the human predicament by one who was its very embodiment; hence evil begetting evil in the endless chain of causation which could be stopped only through the 'grace' of 'God'. In the case of Pṛthu the human predicament is accepted by one who, although a part emanation of 'God' (Viṣṇu), is yet human enough to have fallen into the temptation of challenging the gods' superiority or prerogative, but is godly enough to desist in his attempt at the last moment, and to make his peace with the gods and remain human. This would imply that as a human one cannot rely only on oneself; the intervention, or the grace, of 'God' is needed for humans to achieve integration, i.e. true humanhood. But there remains the question of the role of suffering. Panikkar says:

> There must be something cutting very deep into Man and the World if perfection, destiny, joy, plenitude, divinization (small matter what name we prefer) can be attained solely on a path of suffering, by way of the cross.[30]

As shown in this particular legend, it may just be a matter of full acceptance by man of the human predicament of dependence and limitation.

NOTES

Quotations from Purāṇas: VP according to Wilson's translation (Calcutta, 1894); PP according to Wendy O'Flaherty, *The Origins of Evil in Hindu Mythology*, Delhi, 1976

1 A. C. Bhaktivedanta Prabhupada (*Śrīmad Bhāgavatam*, New York, 1976) dismisses her as evil because of her parentage which shows a superficial judgement. He then contradicts himself in a passage where he refers to her as a 'faithful wife' which, in Hindu terms, is the greatest compliment one can pay to a married woman in her role as wife.

2 'Māra has built up an evil connotation in Buddhist literature, while Yama is "King of the Law" (*dharmarāja*), a model of justice.' 'It is clear enough that there are two strains of Yama: (1) a divine Yama of solar nature — the prototype of immortality; (2) a fearful Yama, personification of the evil in man and of his inevitable death . . .' Alex Wayman, 'Studies in Yama and Māra', IIJ III (1959), pp. 55 and 131.

In the Vedas the wish is frequently expressed for long life on earth (RV 10,97,16: 'Free me from Yama's fetter'; RV 7,52,12: 'Like the cucumber from the stem, even so may I be released from death, not from immortality'; cf. AV 3,31. See my book, *The Vedas: Harmony, Meditation and Fulfilment*, London, 1974, chap. on Vedic eschatology. Cf. also ŚB 8,4,2,1 – 2; 10,4,3,1 – 9; 10,4,4,1 – 3; 10,6,5,1 – 7; TS 2,1,4,3 – 4; BU 1,5,23.

See also O'Flaherty, op. cit., chap. on 'The Birth of Death'.

3 Cf. ŚB 10,1,3,1 – 2: 'Above the [mortal] beings [Prajāpati] created death as their consumer. Now one half of that Prajāpati was mortal, the other half immortal; with that part of him which was mortal he was afraid of death.' Cf. also the Puruṣa of RV 10,90, three quarters of whom are in heaven and one quarter on earth.

4 According to Bhaktivedanta Prabhupada's comments to *Śrīmad Bhāgavatam* 'Generally the daughter receives the qualifications of her father and the son acquires those of the mother . . . So the child born of king Aṅga became the follower of his maternal grandfather . . . If the maternal family is very corrupt or sinful, the child, even though born of a good father, becomes a victim of the maternal family.' BP (= *Śrīmad Bhāgavatam*) IV,2,574; also IV,3,849.

5 John Bowker, *Problems of Suffering in Religions of the World*, Cambridge UP, 1970, p. 196. Cf. also p. 217: 'Appropriate action is a vital element in Hinduism. It means acting according to the pattern of life that belongs to one's present circumstances, concerned with the action only, and not with the fruits or rewards that might accrue from it.'

6 The ancient Indians believed that man was born with four debts to pay: (1) to the gods by way of offering sacrifice as a means of co-operating with them for the sustaining of the world, (2) to the *ṛṣis* by way of acquiring wisdom through the study of the Vedas, their legacy, (3) to the ancestors (*pitṛs*) by prolonging life through begetting children, thereby keeping up the link between the ancestors and descendants, and (4) to humanity, involving civic and social duties and good manners, hospitality, morality etc.

7 See my book *The Vision of Cosmic Order*, London, 1985, part IV, '*Ṛta* as the Sacrifice'.

8 Georges Dumézil, *Servius et la fortune*, Paris, 1943, pp. 59 – 60 (adapted from the French original by me). The BandP (tr. and annot. by Ganesh Vasudeo Tagare, 1983) makes it explicit: 'That king brought to a standstill (prohibited) holy rites and devout practice. Transgressing the (injunction of the) Vedas and scriptures he became engaged in sinful activities.'

O'Flaherty asks: 'What did Vena do? The sins attributed to him are traditional (he mixed the castes, he cheated the priests) but not personal.

The flaw is sought first in genetic inadequacies (his mother was the child of death) and then in the first event, the first mistake. This obsession emerges also from the myth of the loss of the Golden Age where again there is "no first mistake"; man is doomed before he commits his sin of lust or hunger.' See *Origins*, p. 363.

Dumézil says further (p. 60): 'Purāṇic tradition tended to make Vena's sin banal, to make it the typical sin of proud kings . . .' There is no doubt that Vena appears doomed or predestined to evil from the first. See also Bṛhaddharma 3,13,1 – 60; 3,14,1 – 45.

9 Raimundo Panikkar, *Myth, Faith and Hermeneutics*, New York, 1979, p. 67.

10 S. Radhakrishnan, *The Principal Upaniṣads*, London, 1953, p. 114.

11 *Origins*, pp. 363 – 4.

12 Robert Hertz, *Death and the Right Hand*, London, 1960, pp. 90 and 105.

13 For a full investigation see O'Flaherty's *Origins*, p. 321 ff.

14 Panikkar, op. cit., pp. 67 – 8.

15 Bowker, op. cit., p. 211.

16 Wayman, op. cit.. IIJ III, p. 54.

17 Vivekananda, *The Complete Works*, Almora, 1924 – 32, vol. III, p. 245.

18 Cf. BU 4,3,21: 'He is not affected by good, he is not affected by evil, for then he has passed beyond all sorrows of the heart.' And at 4,4,19: 'In *brahman* there is no diversity. He who sees diversity goes from death to death.'

19 See Dumézil, op. cit., p. 39.

20 The Hindu's broad outlook made him envisage four main goals in life, corresponding to four stages of life. They are summed up as (1) *dharma* or appropriate action, virtue, the maintaining of the moral law or righteous conduct, the regulating factor in life which overrides all other pursuits and has to be followed throughout iife; (2) *artha*, the pursuit of material gain involving acquisition of wealth and knowledge; (3) *kāma*, pleasure or fulfilment of desire; the last two goals involve social obligations and discipline and are suitable to youth and the prime of life, provided they do not exceed the bounds of propriety; without them existence would be colourless and void of interest; finally, when all has been experienced, enjoyed and assimilated, it is the turn of (4) *mokṣa*, the supreme aspiration to liberation from the trammels of existence and rebirth, which involves renunciation and abstinence and is the culmination of a well-spent life.

21 Op. cit., p. 63.

22 Ronald Huntington, taking his stand from the psychological viewpoint, makes the following valuable comments which throw further light on the whole Pṛthu legend: 'The task assigned to Pṛthu is cast in the traditional heroic mould. He must take upon himself the work of a re-creation of the universe, an ordering of chaos parallel to that primal creation which took place in the eternal beginning. He is to be the agent of birth . . . i.e. again and from above. To be worthy of the crown of success he must meet and effect a working relationship with the Mother and the Father, represented respectively by the Earth-cow and Indra.' See 'The Legend of Prithu, a study in the process of individuation', *Purāṇa*, vol. 2, no. 1 – 2 (July

1969), p. 200. For the full psychological implication of the legend only touched upon here, the reader is referred to this article.

23 AV 8,10,1: 'Virāj verily was this [universe] in the beginning; of her when born everything was afraid [thinking]: this one indeed will become this [universe].'

Virāj is subsequently shown as ascending and descending in the fire of the householder, of the offerings, in the assembly (*sabhā*), in the gathering (*samiti*), etc. Verse 9 goes: 'Of her gods and men said: she verily knoweth that upon which we of both classes may subsist; let us call to her . . .' Then she is shown as going to the forest trees which slay her and within a year she comes into being [again]; she then goes to the world of the Fathers who also slay her and in a month she comes back into being again; that is the reason for the monthly oblations to the Fathers (verse 19). The gods, too, slay her and she revives in a half month; therefore gods get fortnightly oblations (20). Slain by men, she is back at once and therefore men need feeding every day. (Cf. 'The Legend of Vena and the Atharva Veda', *Quarterly J. of the Mythic Society of Bangalore* 1932, p. 292.) From the verse 22 onwards the milking of Virāj is described in much the same way as later in the Purāṇas, only Pṛthu, called here Pṛthī, is not the leader of the creatures, but takes his place with humans. Also the milker, the milk pail and the milk are represented in a similar way.

24 Full quotation: *ayam eve'dam agra ākāśa āsīt sa u evā'pi etarhi sa yas sa ākāśo vāg eva sā tasmād ākāśād vāg vadati*. 'This [universe] in the beginning was this space here and that is so even now. What this space is, that is speech. Therefore speech speaks from space.' See Hanns Oertel, 'Jaiminīya Upaniṣad Brāhmana', JAOS 16 (1894), no. 1, pp. 79 – 259.

The relationship between 'space' and 'speech' in the sense indicated in our interpretation does not come across clearly in Oertel's translation. One also has to bear in mind the noumenal character of *ākāśa*.

25 For mother goddess Aditi and her role and nature see the editor's article in this collection, particularly in connection with the verse RV 1,89,10.

26 Cf. Huntington, op. cit., pp. 196 – 7: 'The legend of Pṛthu relates to that critical phase in the life of the individual which Carl Jung has so often characterized as the time of supreme psychological importance — the individuation process . . . In terms of the microcosm of the psyche, Pṛthu represents the conscious ego-complex capable of the arduous and dangerous dual process of integration-differentiation which is essential to psychic wholeness, i.e. ultimate realization of the self.'

27 For a summary of Indra's function see my *The Vision of Cosmic Order*, pp. 93 – 6. For a fuller investigation of Indra and of oppositional forces such as good and evil, right and left, etc. see O'Flaherty's *Origins*, pp. 102 – 24 and 321 – 69.

28 Panikkar, *Myth*, etc., p. 148. Huntington says: 'He represents all those qualities which are traditionally most prized in men — physical strength, bravery, self-reliance, ambition, developed to their symbolic utmost' (op. cit., p. 207).

29 Brahma explains that the sacrifice is an expression of Indra and therefore injuring Indra would bring disaster on oneself, since the sacrifice is also an

expression of one's self (BP 4,19,30). That which is thwarted by the gods (in this case Indra prevented the completion of the last sacrifice) or by providence, had better be left alone (BP 4,19,34).

30 Panikkar, *Myth*, etc., p. 61.

7

ASPECTS OF THE SYMBOLISM OF FIRE

David Smith

In this paper I shall investigate a particular and perhaps unusual instance of fire symbolism. I will examine the role of fire in a ninth century Sanskrit court epic, the Haravijaya, and hope that it will be of some general relevance to Indian symbolism.

By way of introduction, and to provide some perspective for what follows, I offer a few general reflections on fire. The author of a recent study of fire in the Vedas observed that fire symbolism has a central role in Vedic religion;[1] fire could be said to be the symbol of the Vedas themselves. Dandekar remarks that 'sacrifice became the symbol of the Vedic Aryan culture, and Agni came to be recognized as the symbol of sacrifice.'[2] Fire can even be seen as a symbol of symbolism! Banerjea declares:

> The symbols and images [of *bhakti* sects] analogically did the same sort of service as was done by Fire (Agni) in Vedic ritualism. Fire was especially sacred to the Vedic priests, because it was the carrier of the sacrificer's oblations to their respective gods; in the case of a sect, the image or icon or any such visible symbol for the deity was the handy medium through which he could transfer his one-souled devotion . . . to his god.[3]

Fire is the archetypal, the handiest, medium.[4]

The symbolism of fire comprises symbols representing fire as well as the things which fire symbolized and it can be represented in its entire gamut by a polarity stretching from *brahman* to water, with fire as such in the middle. In one direction, fire becomes less and less visible, more and more refined, passing from the fireplace to the belly, sexuality, and on to superhuman *tapas*, to divinity, to pure intelligence, and ultimately to *brahman*. In the other direction, fire achieves visual representations, most fully perhaps in the well-known Geddes panel now in the Cleveland Museum (Agni — Inventory Number 55.51; ACSAA slide 6396; Mid-Central India, *c.* tenth century A.D., height 73 cm), wherein Agni is a pot-bellied god, bearded, with an amiable expression, an oval mass of flames rising from behind his shoulders; and with side panels portraying the life of a fire-tending *brahmacārya*; and on down the scale, becoming less and less realistic, from white horse, to goat, to bird, to a diagram (the upward pointing triangle), and finally to water (fire's formless opposite — which is considered to contain fire, and thus can serve instead of fire in some rituals).

The ritual, the functional symbolism of fire in daily life, is manifold. Even the domestic fire has great symbolic significance. It frees foodstuffs from impurity, and must itself be preserved from all impure contacts; thus one should not relieve nature near fire. The cooking fire supports life; fire usually also features in the *saṁskāras*, the rites marking out the life stages from conception to death. Here it is cremating fire that has the greatest significance, Agni being requested to take the deceased to heaven, and the body being visibly transformed to ashes. 'It is inauspicious for a brahmin who has his father alive to touch the ordinary domestic fire, as a brahmin carries fire for the first time in his life when he carries it to the pyre on the death of a parent.'[5] Thus the cooking fire can be a reminder of death.

In addition to being the supreme medium and symbol of transformation, fire is also the life-force manifest, representing fertility. Thus husband and wife, newly married, sit by the fire prior to cohabitation; at the marriage ceremony they have already circumambulated the fire and prayed to Agni for children. Fire's connection with fertility requires that it be carried by a married woman, never by an unmarried girl. Fire is also the symbol of spiritual power. At the investiture with the sacred thread, the student lights and feeds his first sacred fire, saying, 'As you, Agni, are inflamed by wood, thus am I inflamed by life, insight, vigour, offspring, cattle and holy lustre.' And when at the *samāvartana*, the ending of his studenthood, he is kept in a room alone during the morning preparatory to his new birth, this is said to prevent the sun being insulted by the student's superior lustre: the sun shines only with the light borrowed from the student.

The lamp is the other form of visible fire in the house; though it may be noticed in passing that houses do themselves catch fire and that so beneficial to man is the general symbolism of fire that to dream of a burning house is considered to bring good fortune! Lamps are used to ward off evil, and to honour — particularly by being waved (*ārtī*). Thus lamps are waved round the bridal couple at various stages in the marriage ceremony; and they are waved at birth, tonsure and the thread investiture. Above all, *ārtī* is performed before the image of a god. The apotropaic power of the lamp is naturally shared by its soot, and thus soot 'formed on a finger put in the flame of an *ārtī* is used to ward off evil eye and spirits'.[6] So much in brief for fire lit by man.

Mention must also be made of that horrendous terrestrial fire, forest fire, often graphically referred to in literature; and, above all, the fierce burning of the Indian sun.

In addition, and of great importance, are those fires which cannot be seen. The heat of the body is explained by the internal fire that is the life-process, the dead body turning cold when that fire goes out; and the burning of that fire is audible when external sounds are shut out. Fire digests food, in a process of transformation that culminates in the production of semen or menstrual blood; Abbott notes, talking of Western India, '*tej* is a common word for fire as it is for the human seed'.[7] By asceticism, by the storing of semen, heat builds up in the body, manifesting and constituting the superhuman power acquired. Then again, the light of sight and the inner light of the intellect presupposes the fire of consciousness. Finally, there is the fiery radiance of the gods themselves, visible on occasions.

Having made some general remarks about fire, I now turn to the main subject of my paper — the fire symbolism in the Sanskrit court epic of Ratnākara, the Haravijaya, which describes Śiva's victory over the demon Andhaka. This long poem has aroused the scorn of the historians of Sanskrit poetry.[8] Indeed, *kāvya* (classical Sanskrit poetry), generally has been neglected by modern scholarship, and it is hardly surprising that students of religion have passed by it. I have myself argued that the classical *mahākāvya* is analogous to ritual in the way it seeks to provide stability and certainty in the insecure world of the Indian court.[9] Be that as it may, Ratnākara's poem does contain in abundance the paraphernalia, as it has been called, of *kāvya*, the incessant references to lotuses, and the face-moons of women, and so on. Yet, though it is a manifestation of the sophistication of what is in the Indian context high art, the work is imbued with a strong religious feeling. In his concluding remarks, the poet tells us that the poem is beautiful because it is about the deeds of Śiva. And that god is, we may remember, the patron of all the arts.

Because the poem is about Śiva, it is also full of fire. In broad terms, Śiva is a fiery god, whereas Viṣṇu is watery. Yet fire need not have been prominent in Ratnākara's work: Kālidāsa's Kumārasaṁbhava, which deals with the events leading to the birth of Śiva's son, Kumāra, gives nothing like the same emphasis to fire. But fire is crucial to the theme of Haravijaya. Ratnākara deals with the destruction of Andhaka, a demon born of Śiva's sweat, and so in some sense another son of his. He sprang from Śiva's forehead when Pārvatī once playfully covered his eyes: this loving act threw the world into darkness, and forced the fire of Śiva's *tapas* to find some other outlet — hence the birth of the demon. Born in the darkness he is blind and this is also the meaning of his name. Born in darkness he is necessarily a demon. The poem concludes with Śiva burning up Andhaka on his trident and this fire returning into Śiva's body.

The prominence of fire in Haravijaya is made all the more interesting because of Ratnākara's personal remarks appended to the poem. Ratnākara's tone here is utterly different from that of Māgha, the *mahākavi* he probably sought to surpass, and whom literary historians who scarcely looked at Ratnākara assert he slavishly imitated. In Māgha's personal statement, his *praśasti*, three of its four verses are concerned with his ancestry, and only the last verse mentions the poet himself and his poem:

> in the vain hope of good poet's fame
> he has written this poem,
> beautiful only
> in that it describes the deed
> of Lakṣmī's Lord, Viṣṇu.[10]

Ratnākara uses a similar phrase with regard to his poem's relation to Śiva, deals with his ancestry in a couple of lines, and expatiates on his own merits. Two of his remarks especially concern us. 'O king', he says, referring to his tutee:

> O king, know then that one
> on whose arising — burning blind darkness —
> the lakes/fools exhibit purity/perfect wisdom,
> know him to be Ratnākara
> who has swallowed the ocean of speech;
> and after him may be added
> the sun, Agastya, and the submarine fire.

And a little later he says:

> It was Bāṇa who first led the way
> with writings great in scope, slow yet bold,
> and, O king, Ratnākara like a fire
> blazes forth, a second such!

Our poet not only alludes to his royal pupil as a fool, but claims superiority to the sun, the sage Agastya and the submarine fire. Ratnākara, whose name signifies ocean, has swallowed the ocean of speech. The sage Agastya swallowed the ocean to enable the gods to get at some demons hiding at the bottom. The other two also drink the ocean: the sun by its rays which evaporate the water; and the submarine fire, a destructive fire biding its time until doomsday, ceaselessly burns, consumes, drinks, the surrounding waters. Ratnākara as poet-tutor causes fools to exhibit perfect wisdom, just as the sun makes the lakes of Kashmir clear when it rises. Both are said to burn blind darkness. We must also remember that the poem concludes with Śiva burning that quintessence of darkness, his son Andhaka, the blind one, born in darkness, and dark in his deeds.

A brief word on the poem as a whole. The Haravijaya, the longest of *mahākāvyas* and called a monster by Schmidt,[11] is similar in structure to the usual post-Kālidāsan *mahākāvya*, with separate sections for descriptions of nature, political debate, love-making, and the destruction of the foe. Ratnākara manages to mention Śiva and fire repeatedly throughout the very disparate subject matter. There are several other important symbolisms in the poem, but they are not relevant here.

To begin with, I shall inquire into what Ratnākara means in respect of himself when he talks of fire. In the RV, Gonda tells us, fire is not only the physical light but also 'the internal light which illumines seers and poets'.[12] He instances a verse wherein the spiritual, priestly and political greatness of the Vāsiṣṭhas is portrayed: 'their light is like the growth of the sun, their greatness deep like that of the ocean' (RV 7,33,8). Here too we have the coincidence of sun and ocean. However, Ratnākara's claim is unprecedented in a classical Indian poet. The linking of light with greatness continues, of course, beyond the Vedas — 'according to common Indian tradition', says Gonda, 'a kind of fiery energy radiates from the bodies of great men'[13] — but the status of poets suffers a decline in later times.

Poetics does not normally talk of genius (*pratibhā*) in terms even of light, let alone fire. It is true that Ratnākara's contemporary, Ānandavardhana, speaks of *mahākavis*' genius as *parisphuran*, but this word means 'throbbing' as well as 'glittering'. Basically it means becoming visible on account of movement. At all events, this kind of notion differs from the illuminating radiance of sun and fire. The normal view of poetic genius was that the standard themes were seen by genius in an ever new light. As one anonymous verse puts it,

> The same old words,
> the same old subjects,
> yet the poem's new
> thanks to the poet's skill
> in composing.[14]

There is also a higher genius, philosophical and yogic *pratibhā*, a direct intuitive knowledge such as the *ṛṣis* themselves enjoyed. It is to this higher *pratibhā* that Ratnākara lays claim when he asserts that he, Ratnākara, is 'rich in the very pure shining intuitive knowledge that reaches the limit of what can be known'. He is, however, careful, to distinguish it from the merely literary *pratibhā*, and in the sixth canto he speaks of Paramaśiva as the one who is 'beyond both sorts of *pratibhā*'.

I am not claiming that Ratnākara was a latter-day *ṛṣi*. He claims for himself attributes analogous to those of a *ṛṣi*, but his work, beyond the two verses quoted and a few others like them, is utterly different from the productions of a Vedic seer.

Ratnākara claims to be, metaphorically, symbolically, fire: is not that fire the fire that dominates his poem? Since Ratnākara has swallowed the ocean of speech, as he has told us, does he not pour forth the content of the poem from within himself? This is how Bhaṭṭa Nāyaka (tenth century Kashmiri poetician) sees the poetic process: 'The poet does not regurgitate *rasa* (the aesthetic emotion, the essential content of a poem) until he is completely filled with it.'[15] The same view is expressed more fully by Uttaṅgodaya (14th cent.), with the addition that, unique in Indian poetics, the poet is a man out of his ordinary senses:

> First, by the stream that is *rasa* his own heart which is like a great and immeasurably deep lake becomes filled, then he becomes as if possessed by a planet, as if mad, and finally he pours out his poetry, and turns the listener, the sensitive reader (*sahṛdaya*), into the same [sort of madman as he has become].[16]

Does not Ratnākara exhibit megalomania in his claim to surpass the sun? And more to the point, does he conceive of himself containing fire within himself, and further is it that fire which is to be found so prominently in the poem?

Clearly, poets could be said to relate to the *rasa* in their poem, and it is particularly interesting for our line of inquiry that Ratnākara punningly parallels *rasa* to fire in a verse in praise of Śiva from the mouth of the *gaṇa* Naṇḍiṣeṇa:

> When Śiva's third eye,
> ⟨unfailingly ready to take fire⟩/
> ⟨fully indicating the determinants of *rasa*⟩,
> set ⟨Kāma⟩/⟨love⟩ ablaze,
> it attained the beauty of a poem
> with manifest erotic *rasa* in all its variety (15,49).

Conventionally, a classical Sanskrit poem aimed at producing erotic *rasa*, suggesting the essential aesthetic emotion of love, to be savoured by the audience; court epics like the Haravijaya sought to produce a variety of *rasas*, though only one in each canto. But Ratnākara's punning connection of *rasa* and fire is a statement, albeit perhaps unconscious, of what is to be found in his poem. He aims at producing the *rasas* of love and heroism, but at the same time his poem is full of references to fire, to the fire of Śiva's third eye, and other fires, which by their frequency acquire what is from the point of view of the standard poetics undue weight.

Much of the fire in the poem has its origin directly in Śiva. Fire from his third eye burns up Kāma and the universe; Śiva shoots the fiery arrow that destroys Tripura, the triple city of the demons; he is closely connected with the submarine fire, the fire of doomsday waiting its time; he also absorbs the *kālakūṭa* poison which is the doomsday fire in another guise; his flaming trident will burn up Andhaka. The quasi-human characters of the poem also have to do with fire — I refer to Śiva's followers (the *gaṇas*) and the divine nymphs. The *gaṇas* are multiforms of Śiva, and while the nymphs are simply young and beautiful, their male counterparts spit fire, melt their own golden armlets with the fire of their angry glances, and have such names as Agnidaṁṣṭra (Fire-tooth) and Vahnigarbha (Fire-full). The nameless nymphs burn in the fire of separation when their lovers are away. Thus:

> The buzzing of the bees on the prominent filaments
> of the blooming lotuses that formed her bed
> sounded like the crackling of her body
> in the fire of separation (24,33).

And another example of the fire which burns lonely women:

> Under the guise of tawny particles of pollen
> from the lotus couch battered by her sighs,
> one woman seemed as if the atoms of her yellow body
> were fleeing
> in fear of the fire of separation (24,36).

When lovers meet, the heat of their passion welds them together (25,70). But apart from one or two such images, the lover is a shadowy figure. In love it is only the condition of the woman that interests the poet.

The union of man and woman finds its symbolic expression in the centre of the poem, where in the middle canto Śiva joins with Pārvatī to form the Man-Woman, Ardhanārīśvara. This union is calm, without fire. It is followed by a description of the ocean. At first sight, this long description is not justified by the structure of the poem, until we realize that the poet, whose name, Ratnākara, signifies the ocean as the 'mine of jewels', is thereby juxtaposing himself to his god. It might be thought, from this summary, that the ocean would represent, assuming that it represents anything, the calm bliss of the divine couple. Not at all. The ocean seethes with contending emotions; it even has stomach-ache, its wave hands reach out to the shore for a medicinal herb to revive the fire of digestion in its stomach which had faded as a result of drinking too much water (22,43). And not least, the ocean has within itself the submarine fire, burning it up.

But it is not only here that the submarine fire is referred to by Ratnākara. Indeed, something of the intensity of Ratnākara's reference to fire can be gauged from the fact that Kālidāsa refers to the submarine fire once in each of his *mahākāvyas*, Māgha five times, and Ratnākara almost a hundred times. Māgha's usage is purely formal and visual, as when Kṛṣṇa's city with its golden ramparts beside the sea is compared to a flame of the submarine fire rising up from the water. As befits Viṣṇu, the fire is non-destructive, merely ornamental. Kālidāsa, however, the master, makes psychological use of the image. In the Raghuvaṁśa, when Daśaratha is cursed by the ascetic for killing his son, the poet tells us:

> he left the forest,
> his serenity shattered by his sin.
> The curse, cause of his own destruction,
> had established itself in his heart.
> He bore it as the ocean bears Aurva's fire, the submarine fire (9,82).

And at the very end of the Kumārasaṁbhava:

> Śiva did not lose his thirst for amorous pleasures,
> as the fire inside the ocean is never satiated
> with its rolling waters.

Ratnākara never uses the submarine fire like this to refer directly to sexuality; it is almost always used by him in connection 'with serenity shattered' as in the case of the unfortunate Daśaratha. But note that

Śiva's lust is not satiated. Kālidāsa uses the submarine fire as a psychological metaphor for anxiety and for unsatiated sexual passion. Ratnākara, as we shall see, uses it in a generally similar way, but his insistent mention of the submarine fire raises it from metaphor to symbol. In Ratnākara's poem, the non-human world suffers in terms of fire as much as or more than do those archetypal humans, the *gaṇas* and *apsarases*. Thus, as I have said, the ocean which is described by Ratnākara in the canto adjoining the account of Śiva's body merging with Pārvatīs is no limpid pool or silent mass of waters. It seethes and suffers torment.

The ocean's waves rise up as if in longing for the cold touch of the moon to allay the burning heat of the submarine fire (22,57). The ocean's foam looks like a coating of sandalwood paste brought by the rivers to allay the violent heat of the submarine fire (22,48). The ocean's eyes are pearl shells — troubled by the smoke from the submarine fire, the ocean shed pearl tears (22,33). More complex is the verse in the description of the ocean that declares that the ocean fittingly has the blues, that is, it has the smoky flame of the submarine fire as its (punningly) black, depressed heart because it cannot wipe away with its wave hands the stain from the moon which had arisen from its lap, which was its own offspring. The smoke of the fire is the frustration of not being able to reach and clean its baby. The submarine fire is similarly associated with frustration in this verse in which the waves rise right up into the sky, carrying the mermen with them:

> The mermen, lusting when they get to see
> the heavenly nymphs in their celestial cars
> buffeted in the sky by the waves
> at once jumped into the submarine fire,
> as if in overwhelming despair
> at not possessing them (22,17).

There is likewise a connotation of frustration, of overreaching and subsequent humiliation in later verses from the same canto, where the ocean tide, having showered pearls and uprooted the neighbouring kings that are the trees along the shore, then fell back into the submarine fire.

Ratnākara often uses the submarine fire with reference to heroic ardour. Thus a demon is said to burn up the ocean of the foe with the flames of the submarine fire of his valour (16,57). And thus one *gaṇa* tells another that a fiery person like him cannot calm himself without first slaying the foe: the submarine fire never ceases to burn the ocean

(10,45). The raging fury of the submarine fire is brought out when the forces of nature are likened to the force of Viṣṇu in his dread man-lion incarnation:

> Like the Man-lion
> the ocean was roaring loudly,
> its wave paws
> with oyster shells for claws
> contemptuously ripping the rampart chests
> of the mountain demons on its shores,
> its bristling mane
> the flames of the submarine fire (22,27).

This heroic ardour, this unbridled fury pertains, we must note, to the unachieved act. Even in the example just given, where the submarine fire is only a part of the ocean considered as man-lion whose wave-paws rip the mountain-chests of the mountain-demons on its shores — no damage is actually done to the mountains. Action here is metaphorical, its reality only potential. The actual achievement of heroic deeds is symbolized in Ratnākara and in classical Sanskrit poetry in general by the white light of fame that suffuses the horizon.[17] Fire is the impulsion to act, light signals the successful act.

It is not clear in the Haravijaya whether or not the submarine fire emanates from Śiva. In a *gaṇa*'s account of the blazing up of the submarine fire to destroy the world, an extended reference some ten verses long, the fire concludes its burning of the universe by smearing Śiva with ashes, an act of obeisance. O'Flaherty in her study of the submarine fire can only give one or two references where Śiva himself, with the blaze of his third eye, engenders the submarine fire.[18] The *gaṇa* just mentioned, Prabhāmaya, shortly afterwards describes the fire of Śiva's upper eye burning Kāma, and thereafter the whole world. It would therefore be safe to say that Ratnākara considered the submarine fire to be implicitly Śiva's fire. And both the fire of Tripura and the fire of his third eye are likened to it in the poem.

Prabhamāya's whole speech is of interest to us. His argument is that the existence of Śiva in combined form with Viṣṇu, as Hari-Hara, means that there is nothing for them, the *gaṇas* in the assembly hall, to worry about — Śiva will find the solution to the problem of Andhaka. The *gaṇa* describes first Śiva's half of the joint body, then Viṣṇu's. There follows the account of the destructive blazing of the submarine fire, with no explanation of its origin; but its culmination is said to be in applying ash to Śiva. Thereafter, Viṣṇu's role in the churning of the ocean is mentioned at length; this episode closes with Śiva's drinking up the poison that is also produced from it.

Prabhamāya then turns to Śiva's destruction of the triple city of the demons, with some slight help from Viṣṇu. He details the forming of Śiva's chariot from the sun, moon, the Vedas, and the earth. Mount Mandara is the bow, the king of snakes the bowstring, Viṣṇu the arrow, and Agni the blazing barb. The demons will be burned up and their widows will suffer the torment of loneliness. Finally, he tells of the burning of Kāma and the universe by Śiva's eye-fire.

Note how in the destruction of the triple city the force of the god's aggression falls upon the women. It might be said that this is merely a convention of *kāvya*, that a warrior's attack has as its result the tears of wives — but this convention itself is deeply significant. Fire from the dark snake of his sword made tears appear on the wives. The rationale of the myth, Śiva's destruction of the demons for a particular reason, is of no interest whatsoever to Ratnākara, beyond its being a deed of Śiva's; its value for the poet is as an occasion for fire and suffering. And thus the inconvenience to the serpent king of being tied on Mount Mandara as the bowstring is Ratnākara's main theme in several verses, and the sparks the unhappy creature sends forth are of more interest to him than the fate of the demon city. And another instance: when the sun sets, its rays redden Śiva's city, as his arrows did the demons' cities. The *cakravāka* love-birds who are invariably parted by sunset are burnt by the pangs of unfulfilled love as were the demons by the fire (19,67). Here the demons, not their wives, are mentioned, but their sufferings are equated with those that normally arise in that event, namely frustrated sexual passions, which indeed in the climate of the Haravijaya is what the sorrows of widowhood boil down to.

In the whole range of Śiva's myths — to leave for a moment the hothouse world of the Haravijaya — Śiva is very seldom a genuine saviour god, in the sense that Viṣṇu is. In the case of Tripura, the demons themselves ask to be killed by Śiva, and the alignment of the three cities allowing them to be shot by a single arrow clearly has connotations of astronomy. Śiva properly undertakes the role of saviour when he absorbs the *kālakūṭa* poison that is the corollary of nectar in the churning of the ocean. Yet even this act of redemption is not straightforward, for he ends up containing within himself that from which he saved the world and thus partially embodying it. It is with this image that the poem begins:

> Let heavy-haired Śiva,
> whose beautiful throat,
> where the deep coloured poison
> resembles a lovely garland of blue lotus blooms,

seems smoky coloured from imbibing
the offerings of incense,
let him impart to you every happiness.

There is a starkness, a baldness in this opening verse. The darkness of the poison is unrelieved by any contrast. The blue lotuses and the smoke of offerings serve only to intensify the darkness of the *kālakūṭa*. Here there is something of the neutral attitude to gods that is found in *kāvya* in general: Śiva is reduced to colour alone, and the darkest of colours at that.[19] Yet, there is ample significance in the mark that the poison left on Śiva's throat. Śiva swallowed the poison churned up from the ocean in the search for nectar, a fiery poison that threatened to destroy the whole world. Ratnākara frequently refers to the poison, though only once does he spell out its fiery nature:

The flood of poison,
flame of the fire that burns up the universe,
settled on his neck
as if thinking
'There's no room for me
in that heart
soaked in the nectar of love for Pārvatī' (1,50).

Thus we see that even the black or dark blue mark on Śiva's throat is a form of fire. And Andhaka, the blind demon of darkness that emanates from Śiva, returns inside him at the poem's close as a ball of fire, having been impaled on Śiva's fiery trident. Śiva is said to swallow the *kālakūṭa* poison that is Andhaka. The darkness is again shown to be a form of fire.

The fire that erupts from his third eye and destroys Kāma, the god of love, as the Indian Cupid is about to fire his flowery arrow at the meditating Śiva, is the form of fire most intimately connected with Śiva. It arises from the fact that his asceticism builds up within him. It is a manifestation of *tapas*. But at the same time, Śiva is an erotic god, and there is ambivalence in the situation, as is well known from O'Flaherty's brilliant study.[20] Ratnākara is aware of ambiguity in this myth. Thus the tawny filaments of a lotus, blazing like the flame of the fire from Śiva's third eye, inflame a woman's desire (18,19). Thus the red blooms of an *aśoka* tree send women eagerly to their lovers; red as the fire of Śiva's eye the blooms punningly aroused love/burnt up Love (3,45).

Sometimes there is sheer delight on the poet's part in the manifestation of fire:

> When Śiva was about to dance, his eye-fire
> reducing the sun to a lustreless circle
> with its flames that yellow the faces of the quarters
> threw out before him
> a stage-curtain of hot light (2,28).

But above all, like the other fires we have looked at, this fire has negative associations. The hissing snakes that form Śiva's ear ornaments blow sparks that evaporate Gaṅgā on his head — Pārvatī, who is jealous of this other woman, the river, observes this with satisfaction (2,4). The moon of Śiva's head becomes depressed because it is not as beautiful as the moon of Pārvatī's face and seems ready to jump into the fire of the upper eye (2,6). When Śiva is about to dance the snakes on his wrists writhe in agony because of the heat of his fiery looks, and so show their yellow bellies — this gives them the beauty of golden bracelets (2,52). And the submarine fire is compared to the third eye because both the ocean and Kāma are said to have a *makara* sea monster as their banner. Ratnākara is able to say punningly:

> The blazing fire of the submarine fire,
> like Śiva's upper eye,
> burnt the ocean/Kāma, the *makara*-bannered,
> when it/he put the water/arrow
> on the bowstring of its waves (22,47).

But the force of love is no more reduced than is the ocean by the submarine fire. We must note that Ratnākara makes no reference to Śiva's *tapas*. Simply, a fiery energy breaks forth from Śiva, an energy that destroys love, and yet it is a fire that is parallel to the eroticism of nature (the lotus filaments and the *aśoka* tree) that causes love to burn in women. Like the submarine fire it comes forth from within.

Clearly, what is to be found in the Haravijaya is an interiorization of fire, and a psychologizing of fire. This is perhaps hardly surprising in the context of a conscious and highly developed art. This inner fire, which is partly a reflection of the inner person, and partly the inner person's actual being, is circumscribed by the circular movement of fire that is the poem's context and pretext. The inner fire of all creatures described throughout the poem is set against its narrative momentum, the fire that comes inadvertently from Śiva in the form of Andhaka, the blind one, the heated sweat of Śiva, and which Śiva's fiery power reduces again to fire and brings back to him. Within this circular movement is the inner fire of the poet, and the inner fire of the *gaṇas*, and the women. All this from a poet who declares himself to be fire!

It is tempting to conclude that just as the serpent when squashed by the weight of the world above spits forth fire from the depth below, so does Ratnākara. And yet the symbolism of fire thus found in the Haravijaya cannot stand alone; it must, to some degree, relate back to general fire symbolism in Hinduism, and to some degree throw light upon it.

There does seem to be a change in attitudes to fire after the time of the Vedas. This change is dramatically stated by Nirad Chaudhuri:

> Down to the epic age from the Vedic, we see an honest wood-fire . . . But in the age which followed, that of classical Hindu attitudes, a benevolent but erratic daimon threw a handful of magnesium into that yellow fire, to change the flames into a dazzling, blinding and cascading mass of white light. Then it went out, and what was left behind were beds of dirty red cinders, smouldering and hissing, and there clung to them an obstinate odour of burnt flesh and hair which always lingers in the atmosphere of our burning ghats and crematoriums . . . It was a world of death, in which fire itself was death.[21]

In the Haravijaya we have a fire which for the greater part is internal, negative and destructive, the inverse of the outer, life-giving, life-enhancing fire of both popular symbolism and ancient Vedic esotericism. How widespread was this change?

NOTES

1. Knipe, *In the Image of Fire*, Delhi, 1975, p. 19.
2 R. N. Dandekar, 'Some Aspects of the Agni-Mythology in the Veda', JOIB, vol. 11 (1962), p. 370.
3 J. N. Banerjea, *The Development of Indian Iconography*, Delhi, 1974, p. 78.
4 Cf. G. Bachelard, *The Psychoanalysis of Fire*, Boston, 1964, p. 7: Fire is a 'privileged phenomenon which can explain anything . . . the ultraliving element . . . Among all phenomena, it is really the one to which there can be so definitely attributed the opposing values of good and evil . . . It can contradict itself; thus it is one of the principles of universal explanation.'
5 J. Abbott, *The Keys of Power*, London, 1923, p. 177.
6 Ibid., p. 184.
7 Ibid., p. 175.
8 For full details, see my *Ratnakara's Haravijaya: an Introduction to the Sanskrit Court Epic*, Delhi, 1985.
9 Ibid., chap. 3, 'Kings, courts and poets'.
10 All translations from Sanskrit are mine unless stated otherwise.

11 R. Schmidt, 'Neue oder im PW noch nicht belegte Wörter aus Ratnākara's Haravijaya', WZKM, vol. 29 (1915), p. 260.
12 J. Gonda, *The Vision of the Vedic Poets*, The Hague, 1963, p. 272.
13 Ibid., p. 269.
14 Quoted as a 'well-known saying' by T. N. Sreekantaiya, ' "Imagination" in Indian Poetics', IHQ, vol. 13 (1937), p. 73.
15 Quoted in Locana, ed. Pathak, p. 88; transl. by J. L. Masson and M. V. Patwardhan, *Santarasa and Abhinavagupta's Philosophy of Aesthetics*, Poona, 1969, p. 85.
16 Kaumudī (a commentary on the Locana) in Kuppuswami Sastri's edition of the first Uddyota of the Dhvanyāloka, Madras, 1944, p. 170. *Santarasa*, p. XII.
17 Cf. my book (note 8), p. 281ff.
18 W. D. O'Flaherty, 'The Submarine Fire in the Mythology of Śiva', JRAS 1971, pp. 9–27.
19 *Tamas* is, of course, the quality (*guṇa*) of Śiva; but this is so primarily from the perspective of Vaiṣṇavas.
20 W. D. O'Flaherty, *Asceticism and Eroticism in the Mythology of Śiva*, London, 1973.
21 Nirad Chaudhuri, *The Continent of Circe*, London, 1965, p. 210. Quoted in O'Flaherty's *Asceticism . . .*, p. 92, as an 'interesting example of fire imagery in modern Indian mythology'.

8

WEAPONS AS SYMBOLS IN HINDU ART

Valerie J. Roebuck

In this paper I propose to examine the use of weapons as symbols in Hindu art, and the kinds of meaning that they can carry. I hope that it may provide a contribution to the discussion of the whole issue of symbolism in Indian culture and the ways in which it resembles or differs from symbolism used in the West.

One issue that has emerged strongly in the course of this study is the question of 'realism' and innovation in Indian religious art: how far the artists were copying traditional shapes and how far they were free to introduce contemporary objects into their work. Some of the answers may prove surprising and perhaps even shed some new light on the relationship between the individual and the tradition in Indian art.

ATTITUDES TO WAR

A large number, perhaps the majority, of figures in Hindu works of art carry weapons of war or attributes derived from them, yet there appears to have been no general study of the ways in which this symbolism is used, perhaps because of assumptions about the non-violence of Indian culture.[1]

In fact until modern times, mainstream Hindu thought has rarely taken non-violence to preclude either warfare or capital punishment.[2] The BhG (II,31 – 7) teaches that fighting is the duty of the *kṣatriya*. Perhaps it was not until Mahatma Gandhi that its text was reinterpreted in a non-violent sense. In many ways Hindu civilization has tended to take a more pragmatic approach to war than the West, at least in theory. This can also be seen in the relative values attached to different types of weapon.

It is a fair generalization that in the West weapons used for fighting at close quarters have usually been considered more honourable than those that kill from a distance, a feeling that goes back as far as Homer: the bow is the weapon of the wily Odysseus and the cowardly Paris; it is also used by Apollo and Artemis, deities with some frightening aspects. Heroes of the more straightforward kind, however, rely on the spear and the sword.

Related to this feeling is the current thought that technologically advanced weapons are more sinister than the older ones. Even when the crossbow was introduced in Europe, its use was considered an atrocity: it was forbidden by the second Lateran Council in 1139 and condemned again later that century by Pope Innocent III, except against Muslims.[3]

With the crossbow the reasons for banning it were partly pragmatic from the point of view of the nobility, as it enabled foot-soldiers to kill armoured knights. Nevertheless the feeling that older and less effective weapons are somehow more honourable was probably there, too. It certainly persists into our century, strengthened by further advances in warfare technology. Orwell wrote in 1946:'. . . writing that aims at glorifying war usually takes on an archaic colour, its characteristic words being *realm*, *throne*, *chariot*, *mailed fist*, *trident*, *sword*, *shield*, *buckler*, *banner*, *jackboot*, *clarion*.'[4] Today the sword forms part of the ceremonial uniform of high-ranking officers in the British army and even in the SAS and the Parachute regiment.

The traditional order of values in India was more or less the exact opposite.[5] Various types of bows were the most valued weapons, and when guns were introduced, they seem to have met with no prejudice at all. Next in value came weapons for throwing such as the *cakra* (discus). Swords and daggers were valued least. The pragmatism of this approach lies in doing maximum damage to the enemy while incurring minimum risk. But there may be here also some feeling that weapons used in hand-to-hand fighting are particularly bloodthirsty.

Hindu gods and goddesses are represented in art with almost every kind of weapon known in Indian history. This does not present a moral problem within the Hindu religion, as when they are shown using them, it is invariably against demons and other enemies of the right. Moreover, tradition has it that being slain by one of the great gods leads to immediate salvation. Demons may actually choose this path to liberation.[6]

However, the weapons of the gods hardly ever function as mere weapons; they have taken on layers of symbolic meaning which sometimes take over from their warlike use, though the latter is never quite forgotten. The shape of the symbolic weapon can then change in artistic representation, especially when the weapon concerned becomes intimately associated with one particular deity, as with the *cakra* and mace of Viṣṇu and the *triśūla* of Śiva, as the weapon becomes obsolete or rare in human warfare. On the other hand, when the weapon is of a type used by many different deities, and well known in human use, its warlike significance tends to remain prominent.

THE BOW

Probably the best example of the latter is the bow which has been the prominent weapon in battles during most of Indian history. During the Vedic period the aristocratic warrior was a chariot-borne archer and the epics still envisage it as the main technique of warfare (Mhb 5,149). Later, the chariot was superseded by elephant-borne troops and cavalry, but the bow remained the main weapon.

Two main types of bow are known to have been used, the self bow and the composite bow, while the crossbow seems never to have been used widely and I have not seen it represented in Indian art.[7]

A self bow is made from a single piece of wood like the English yew longbow. In India it was made of bamboo, a less effective material, and it was gradually replaced by the composite bow adopted from nomadic invaders from Central Asia. Composite bows are built from layers of different woods and horn, and can be made more powerful yet much shorter in length. This made them particularly suitable as a cavalry weapon.[8]

Composite bows can be recognized in art, because they are 'four-curved' – the ends curve back to form the familiar 'Cupid's bow' shape. When unstrung they may be more or less circular, curving in the opposite direction from that which they take when strung. Some of the surviving examples are beautifully painted.[9] Self bows form a single curve, and in Indian art the bamboo from which they are made may be clearly depicted. Surviving arrows are of a wide variety of types known also from art and literature.[10] Distinctly Indian is the crescent-shaped arrow-head, but many other shapes are found.

The change from the self bow to the composite bow began probably with the Saka invasion of North India (first century A.D.) and gradually spread east and south, but it was never complete: the self bow occurs in South Indian works of art of the eighteenth and nineteenth centuries, and in remote tribal areas it was never superseded.[11] It is possible that even in North India the composite bow remained largely the weapon of the cavalry.

The distinction is interesting for our purposes, because it provides an indicator of how far Indian artists were depicting weapons current in their own time, but there seems to be no difference in iconographic meaning between the different kinds of bow when depicted in the hands of the gods — apart from the sugar-cane bow of Kāma.

It appears that until the introduction of firearms, almost every Indian fighting man was an archer, whether an aristocratic cavalryman with a beautifully made composite bow or an infantryman with a simple longbow and little else. Similarly with the deities: some gods and heroes are archers *par excellence*, notably Kāma, the god of love, Uṣas and Pratyuṣas, the dawn goddesses, and of course Rāma and Lakṣmaṇa; but almost any deity, it seems, can appear as an archer if need be. Viṣṇu's characteristic weapons are the discus and mace, but when he appears in many-armed forms such as Trivikrama,[12] the bow is one of his attributes. Durgā, too, nearly always carries a bow and arrows among the many weapons with which she attacks the buffalo demon; in the famous seventh century relief in Mahābalipuram she rides into battle like a mounted archer on her lion, shooting at the demon.[13] Śiva's bow, Pināka, features in a number of myths, for example the one in which he appears to Arjuna in the form of a Kirāta tribesman.[14] Most spectacularly of all, Śiva as Tripurāntaka uses the bow Pināka and a single arrow to destroy the triple city of the demons. It is described in the Mhb:

> Then the great god said, 'I will take my bow and arrow and chariot and I will slay in combat those enemies of the inhabitants of heaven. You must see to my chariot and to my bow and arrow so that this very day I will cause the enemy to fall upon the surface of the earth.' 'We will gather all the forms in the triple world from here and there to make your chariot of great strength, O lord of gods,' said the gods, 'and Viśvakarman will make the auspicious chariot, designing it cunningly.' Then they who were like tigers among the gods fashioned that chariot, and they made his arrow out of Viṣṇu and Soma, and the Oblation-eater, Agni, became its shaft, Soma its head and Viṣṇu the point of that supreme arrow . . . They made the body of the chariot out of the goddess Earth . . . Mount Mandāra was its axle . . .[15]

Then follows a long series of correspondences describing how the various parts of the chariot were made from various gods. The description resembles a *maṇḍala*. The type of symbolism used is very fluid. Sometimes there are recognizable correspondences: Mount Mandāra – the axle; sun and moon — the wheels. In some cases, as with the Kṛta Yuga and the yoke, there is a punning connection; sometimes there is a link, as between the base of the chariot and mind. Very often, however, there is no clear resemblance at all, but one feels that certain elements, such as the ocean and the plants, had to be included somewhere in the chariot to make it fit with the poet's picture of the universe. The symbolism of the horses actually changes in the course of the description:

When the supreme chariot had been thus fashioned by the gods to wipe out those that hated them, Śaṅkara placed his own superior weapons in the chariot. He made the sky his chariot staff and placed his bull upon its banner.

Now the Vedas, priests and sacred sounds take their places.

Having made the year embroidered with the six seasons his bow, he made his own shadow the bow string, unbreakable in battle. For the lord Rudra is Time and Death, and the year is his bow, and therefore the Night of Doomsday for men was made the unwithering string of that bow . . . The lord cast on to that arrow his unbearable, sharp anger, the fire of anger, born of the anger of Bhṛgu and Aṅgiras, which is very hard to bear.

Brahma himself acted as charioteer, and Śiva

drew his bow and released against the triple city the arrow which was the essence of the triple world. It burnt the band of demons and hurled them into the western ocean.

In the visual arts Śiva is occasionally depicted as Tripurāntaka, the destroyer of the triple city.[16] Perhaps the most dynamic version is the relief at Elora (eighth or ninth century).[17] The sculpture agrees with the Mhb account in representing Brahma as the charioteer, and there may be a hint of the Earth with her mountains in the shape of the chariot body, but there is no attempt at all to find a visual equivalent for the elaborate symbolism of the epic. The unknown sculptors have conveyed the same kind of cosmic energy by different, almost opposing, means. Instead of seeking to overwhelm with detail, they have simplified the scene so that the figure of Śiva dominates it completely.

The pose of the figure looks like an accurate representation of the action of a chariot-borne archer.[18] As with the figure of Durgā from Mahābalipuram, the symbolic content of the image has proved compatible with a certain amount of realism in the treatment: the bow of Tripurāntaka may be the year and its string the Night of Doomsday, but as far as it is possible now to tell, it still looks like a self bow of its time.

In comparing the treatment of the same subject in art and literature, it is important to bear in mind the skill of Indian artists in using the characteristics of their own particular media. The traditional craft training, handed on through the caste system, encouraged a thorough understanding of the possibilities of tools and materials, allied with a conservative approach to subject-matter and iconography. Writers, on the other hand, were free within certain limits to weave their own fancies, even around the figures of the gods.

A poet included in the Subhāṣita-ratna-kośa gives a different atmosphere to the Tripurāntaka myth by looking at it from the point of view of the female demons who were killed by the fire of Śiva's arrow whose flames seemed to caress them like a lover.[19] The metaphor is not only an erotic one, but also suggests the mystical union between the devotee and the god: a triple meaning beautifully in keeping with the character of Śiva in this myth.

However, this interpretation of the story appears not to be found in the visual art. In fact, the kind of symbolism, so common in the West from Renaissance art to the film poster, in which a weapon of war is linked with male sexuality, seems rather rare in the visual arts of India. Even the bow and arrows of Kāma are rarely depicted, and when they are, their symbolism is softened to sugar-cane and flowers. The theme of sexual violence by the male to the female, so ably discussed by Lucie-Smith,[20] occurs in Indian literature but seems not to have interested Indian painters and sculptors (or their patrons) very much. In fact, if we look at the works of art as visual objects, without reference to their religious content, the female is more often shown threatening the male.

THE WEAPONS OF VIṢṆU

The four main attributes of Viṣṇu in art are the discus or the wheel (*cakra*), mace (*gadā*), conch-shell (*śaṅkha*) and lotus (*padma*). In sculpture the lotus tends to be replaced by a *mudrā*, often *abhayamudrā*, the gesture granting freedom from fear. In South Indian sculpture the same can happen to the mace: in certain forms of the god, such as Śrīnivāsa and Varadarāja, the front left hand is still in the position of the hand resting on the mace, but the gesture is one of *katyavalambitahasta* — hand resting on the thigh — and is then taken to signify that, for devotees of Viṣṇu, the ocean of *saṁsāra* is only thigh-deep, and they can wade across.[21]

The change may have been encouraged by the fact that, in South India, divine attributes such as weapons are not always made as an integral part of the sculpture, their presence may merely be indicated by the gestures of the image. Suitable attributes may be made quite separately and placed in the hands, perhaps by worshippers. I have seen a private collection of small Vijayanagar bronzes in Madras which had recently been provided by their owner with silver weapons where appropriate.

There are other examples in Indian art of visual forms that have persisted and been reinterpreted, taking on different meanings over time. A good example is the 'woman under a tree' motif, used variously in sculpture to represent *yakṣis*, *apsarases* and Mahāmāyā giving birth to the Buddha-to-be.[22] However, the four basic attributes of Viṣṇu have been known throughout the area and period of Hindu art, though they have been treated in strikingly different ways. Three of them have warlike connotations: the discus and the mace are weapons and the conch was used not only as a ritual instrument, but also as a war trumpet, and forms part of the warriors' equipment in the Mhb (e.g. V,149,64). Viṣṇu is the archetypal warrior-king, just as Brahma is the archetypal priest and Śiva the archetypal yogi.

These warlike connotations were never entirely lost, but the set of four attributes is sometimes reinterpreted to connect it with other sets of four, such as elements. The various interpretations may in turn have affected the ways in which the attributes are represented in art.

One natural development was to regard the attributes as symbolizing the powers of the god. Particularly in the case of Viṣṇu these powers then come to be regarded as having characters of their own and may sometimes be personified as attendants of the god.[23] In certain periods, notably in post-Gupta Kashmir, this seems to have become almost the standard way of representing the mace and the discus, but such figures crop up at other times and places as well. In theory their sex should follow the grammatical gender. Thus the mace (*gadā*, fem.) is normally represented by a female (*gadānarī*); the discus (*cakra*, neut.) is invariably shown as a male (*cakrapuruṣa*) and just occasionally the mace is, too.[24]

Personifications of other attributes of Viṣṇu are sometimes found in art, notably in the relief of Viṣṇu Śeṣaśāyin from the Gupta temple at Deogarh, Uttar Pradesh.[25] Here Viṣṇu sleeps, attended by Lakṣmī, Garuda and other divine figures, but below him his powers, in human form, ward off the demons Madhu and Kaiṭabha.

The third and fourth of them are readily identified as the Cakrapuruṣa, with the shape of part of a wheel in his headdress, and Gadānarī, an elegant female figure with a hair-style shaped like the head of a mace. The symbolism of the other two is less clear. The first draws a sword which may be meant to represent the sword of Viṣṇu, but he also wears a large flower on his head-dress and may represent the lotus as a Padmapuruṣa. The second has been thought to symbolize the bow, but it has also been suggested that this *puruṣa*'s crown looks remarkably like the top of a conch-shell and, in fact, the pose of his arms fits the shape of the coils of the shell even better than that of a drawn bow. It is possible, then, that he is indeed a 'Śaṅkhapuruṣa', completing a set of the four regular attributes of Viṣṇu, with the lotus taking an unexpectedly warlike role.[26] One can only admire the wit and grace with which the Gupta sculptor handled this somewhat intractable material.

This way of personifying divine weapons is largely a Vaiṣṇava phenomenon. There is a Kashmiri bronze Harihara in which the Śiva half has a Triśūlapuruṣa to correspond to the Cakrapuruṣa belonging to the Viṣṇu half. A well-known post-Gupta figure of Śiva in the British Museum (BM) (12 – 16 2 OA; colour slide OA 89) is attended by two Triśūlapuruṣas, as well as holding a *triśūla* in his left hand.

There are even a few Buddhist examples among Nepalese images, in stone and metal, convincingly identified as figures of the Bodhisattva Vajrapāṇi accompanied by a 'Vajrapuruṣa'.[27] There may, of course, be other *puruṣas* and *nārīs* not yet identified: often, as in the last two examples, the weapon component of the attendant figures is not at all obvious and can easily be mistaken for part of the head-dress. It seems clear, however, that the overwhelming majority of these figures is Vaiṣṇava in inspiration.

The Cakrapuruṣa of Viṣṇu has developed into a deity in his own right to a far greater extent than any other personification of an attribute.[28] When worshipped individually, often in association with Garuda, he takes on a formidable many-armed form and appears to embody in himself the destructive part of the powers of Viṣṇu.

It is never forgotten that the cakra is a weapon, and it is used as such in a number of myths associated with Viṣṇu and Kṛṣṇa, such as the freeing of the elephant-king. When depicted it may be shown in a relatively realistic way. It remained in use as a battlefield weapon until well into the nineteenth century and consisted of a thin, flat ring of metal with a sharpened outer edge, which could be whirled around the finger and thrown. It seems to have remained particularly popular with the Sikhs, and there are sets of them in the Royal Armouries of the Tower of London and in the Victoria and Albert Museum (V & A) that are made in graduated sizes so that they can be carried on the conical tops of helmet-turbans.[29] The discus of Viṣṇu can be seen in use in the Mughal painting of Kṛṣṇa and Indra fighting for the 'wishing tree'.[30]

However, in more formal representations of Viṣṇu and his *avatāras*, especially in sculpture, the discus tends to take the form of a wheel, often rather decorative and sometimes giving out flames. This form has probably been influenced by the symbolism of the wheel of kingship and of the sun as a wheel.[31]

In such versions the *cakra* may look like a wheel with spokes. In South India the central part of it may consist of a six-pointed star made up of two triangles like the star of David so that the whole *cakra* looks

Fig. 1. *Rangoli* for Dīvālī festival: Viṣṇu's *cakra* with butter-lamps.

like a Solomon's seal. This pattern is used as an auspicious design in South India, for example in the *rangoli* that women make outside their houses on special occasions (see Fig. 1).[32]

It is perhaps legitimate to question here how far we are dealing with a shape derived, rather remotely, from a curious South Asian weapon and how far with a pattern that on some level is satisfying to the human mind. As so often in matters of Indian symbolism, the two strands seem inextricable. As the forms of Hindu art are used as subjects for worship and meditation, their overall visual effect may be at least as important as the information carried through their symbolism.

For example, in those typically Kashmiri images of Viṣṇu in which the two front hands rest on the heads of the Gadānarī and the Cakrapuruṣa, part of the effect on the worshipper comes from what he or she understands of this symbolism, but part surely comes from the visual impact of the figure of the god with the smaller figures of the male and female on either side, perhaps suggesting the opposite aspects contained within him. This kind of experience is hard, if not impossible, to assess, but should not be neglected when considering the meanings of Hindu iconography.

THE WEAPONS OF ŚIVA AND HIS FAMILY

The *triśūla* — trident or three-pronged spear — was used as a battle weapon in India. A rather crude Rajasthani painting of a battle scene (perhaps late eighteenth century) shows *triśūlas* in use alongside bows and guns. The BM (1900, 1 – 13 2 OA) has one which I believe is a genuine battle weapon, on the perhaps subjective grounds that it is too ugly and shapeless to have been used for any sort of ritual purpose. However, memories of the use of the *triśūla* in battle were practically superseded by its association with religious ascetics and with Śiva as their patron.

It is not possible to be certain which was the earlier, but it seems likely that this symbol was adopted as a badge of Śaiva ascetics because it had already become the weapon *par excellence* of Śiva. In turn, this affected the way in which the weapon was viewed as an attribute of the god.[33]

When *triśūla* is shown in action, which occurs often more in painting than in the more formal medium of sculpture, it may appear as a weapon for stabbing or hurling at an enemy.[34] More often it appears as the yogi's emblem in the god's hand or standing in the ground beside a meditating Śiva.[35] This peaceful sort of *triśūla* frequently appears in the Pahārī paintings in which Śiva and Pārvatī are shown visiting the Pañjab hills. In the famous and beautiful eighteenth century painting believed to come from Garhwal and now in the Museum of Fine Arts, Boston,[36] in which the two deities are depicted as lovers in a hill landscape at night, the *triśūla* is stuck into the ground beside the tiger skin on which they rest. Tied to it are Śiva's drum and two small bundles, presumably containing the couple's belongings as they travel about the earth. This down-to-earth approach to a divine attribute is in keeping with the atmosphere of this painting which combines human and divine qualities by means of its delicacy and gentle wit.

The *triśūla* in its warlike use is seen in almost every figure of Durgā Mahiṣāsuramardiṇī, sculpted or painted, as it is the principal means with which she attacks the Buffalo demon.

Although 'Triśūlapuruṣas' are rare in art, Śaiva and Śākta iconography have their own characteristic ways of giving life to divine weapons. When an object of worship, the *triśūla* may have as a part of it a small image of the appropriate deity. The Musée Guimet has a Chola example in metal, with a figure of a goddess in high relief.[37]

In the Śakti cult of Bengal a particular kind of heavy ritual sword, the *rāmdāo*, is closely associated with the goddess Kālī. In Bengali works of art, such as Kalighat paintings, she carries this weapon as an attribute and to this day it is used to slaughter buffaloes in sacrifice to her. Devotees explain this practice by saying that an animal killed in this way achieves immediate liberation.[38]

Todd (1829) describes a Rajput cult in which a sword was worshipped as a symbol of 'Hurra, the god of war', clearly a reference to Hara, Śiva as destroyer.[39] As the Rajputs are warriors, there is probably a link here with the practice of doing reverence to the tools of one's trade so that a carpenter will worship his hammer and saw and a musician his instruments. In the religious atmosphere of India this is a natural development of the respect that any conscientious worker has for his means of livelihood. As a warrior's weapons are often all that lies between him and death, there are particularly urgent reasons for propitiating them.

Various other kinds of edged weapons are associated with forms of Śaktī and outside Bengal Kālī is depicted with other types of sword than *rāmdāo*.[40]

The axe (*paraśu*) has strong Śaiva connections. It is the normal weapon of Gaṇeśa (along with the *aṅkuśa*, the elephant-goad), and in Chola art and related styles it is a standard attribute of Śiva himself in place of the *triśūla*. Nearly all Pallava, Chola and Vijayanagara metal images of the god, other than as Natarāja with its own special iconography, carry in their back two hands an axe and a tiny jumping deer (see Fig. 2). But often the shape of the axe may be so stylized that

Fig. 2. Śiva Viṣāpaharaṇa (Destroyer of poison). Copper alloy. Chola, Tamil Nadu, tenth century.

In his back hands, Śiva holds his normal South Indian attributes of the axe and the deer. The front left hand holds a snake symbolizing the 'world poison' (*halāhala, kālakūta*) that Śiva destroyed by swallowing it. The front right hand forms *abhayamudrā*, granting freedom from fear.

Reproduced by courtesy of the Trustees of the British Museum. (1970, 9–21 1 OA) it would be quite hard to recognize if one were not familiar with the tradition.[41]

The axe and the deer are explained mythologically as weapons created by a group of hostile sages in order to attack the god, but Śiva caught them and adopted them as his attributes.[42] With mythological explanations, there are often unanswered questions. Here it remains unexplained why the sages chose a deer as one of the weapons for the intended murder. I would guess that the visual imagery is older than the myth and that the deer is connected with the symbolism of Śiva as Paśupati, the Lord of animals.

Perhaps because of its connection with Śiva, the axe is also found in South India as an attribute of *śaktis* such as Māheśvarī, one of the seven Mātṛkās.[43] On the Vaiṣṇava side the axe is, as his name implies, the distinctive weapon of Paraśurāma. But of all the incarnations of Viṣṇu he is particularly believed to have been a devotee of Śiva. Rajput battleaxes are sometimes found to be decorated in relief with figures of Kṛṣṇa and Rādhā. There seems no clear symbolic reason for this choice which may come from a desire to adorn the weapon or to invoke a blessing on it. Perhaps the owners of these weapons were devotees of Kṛṣṇa. On the whole, pointed or bladed weapons are linked with Śiva and his family.

The characteristic weapon of the war god Kārttikeya is the spear (*śakti*) called *veḷ* in Tamil South India, where the tradition of worshipping this god under the name of Murugan is very strong. It is a recognized sign of allegiance to him and in some modern prints this god and his consorts (Mahāvallī and Devasenā) appear within the shape of the head of the *veḷ*. In Chola and related metal images the god holds a thunderbolt (*vajra*) as well as a spear.[44] The cult of Kārttikeya survives in Bengal, too: here, however, he is now usually represented as armed with a bow. Although largely neglected in Western accounts of Hinduism, with their generally North Indian and Vaiṣṇava bias, he is an important deity to a great many Hindus and his rather complex symbolism seems to require further study.

FIGURES ARMED WITH A MULTIPLICITY OF WEAPONS

In certain cases, particularly in some representations of many-armed demons, the artist seems to have aimed for an overall effect of a figure bristling with all kinds of weapons which seems more important than the symbolism of individual attributes that may vary.

A frequent subject of sets of paintings in the eighteenth and nineteenth centuries, particularly in Rajasthan, was the portraying of the ten *avatāras* of Viṣṇu, treated in a rather standardized way.

Paraśurāma was invariably shown conquering Arjuna Kārtavīrya, and Rāma with his brother Lakṣmaṇa, both armed with bows, were shown fighting the ten-headed, twenty-armed Rāvaṇa. Both the formidable demon kings were generally depicted with a weapon in each hand, normally a selection of swords and daggers of different shapes and sizes, giving the effect of a forest of weapons. Here there is no particular symbolic value in the weapons depicted other than to suggest the ferocity of the opposition, so the artist was free to vary the details within the overall pattern. In a Rajasthani painting of this kind in V & A (IM 293 – 1913), Rāma and Lakṣmaṇa are aiming their bows at a Rāvaṇa who, apart from the usual edged weapons, also has a gun.

What is perhaps more surprising is that the same kind of variations can take place in such an important and sacred figure as that of the goddess Durgā, depicted as the slayer of demons. In such subjects she is shown armed with a whole arsenal of weapons, which contrasts with the beauty and gentleness of her face. A rather crude painting of Durgā Mahiṣāsuramardiṇī in V & A (IS 246 – 1955), considered by Robert Skelton (to whom I am grateful for finding this and the previous example for me) to have been painted in Bengal in the 1930s, shows her holding a gun, resembling an old flintlock, in one of her eighteen hands.

Obviously, there was no objection to non-traditional weapons in these subjects, so long as they did not interfere with the traditional composition. To show them firing the gun would have altered the whole conception of the standardized icon which would be unacceptable. As we have seen earlier, however, it was possible to show her shooting at a demon with a bow.

Most later versions of the subject conform to a basic idea: Durgā stands on or over the Buffalo demon and kills him by stabbing with a *triśūla* and beheading him with a sword, releasing him thus from his animal form. Being born of the combined energies of all the gods, she carries replicas of their weapons.[45] Most prominent are those of Śiva, her husband, and Viṣṇu, her brother. The others vary. Some attributes belong logically together and are normally placed in corresponding hands: a sword in the front right hand and a shield or buckler in the front left; when there is a bow in her back left hand, the back right holds or is reaching for an arrow. In sculpted versions the goddess is the dominant figure and the demon is reduced, sometimes to the point where he seems to be little more than another attribute identifying her. Paintings, with their story-telling element, show greater interest in showing the conflict between the two.

A magnificent example is a painting in V & A attributed to the late eighteenth century Chamba school (see Fig. 3).[46] The iconography conforms to the myth, but the treatment is modern in terms of the time

Fig. 3. Durgā Mahiṣāsuramardinī. Gouache. Pahārī, perhaps Chamba, late eighteenth century. *Reproduced by courtesy of the V & A Museum. (IS 150–1951)*

when it was painted, with the goddess' coat of mail showing Mughal influence. Her round shield is an accurate depiction, down to decorative details, of numerous surviving specimens. Her sword, axe and club can be paralleled from collections of Indian arms and armour, except for a white object with six prongs which might represent the *vajra*, sometimes depicted in Pahari paintings in curious ways.

Distinctively Indian is the weapon with which the goddess strikes at the demon's face. It is a type of dagger called *katar*, which has a double hilt with a cross-bar between. It is held by this cross-bar, and used in a punching action. These contemporary weapons are mingled with the traditional attributes, the conch, *triśūla*, lotus, *cakra* and mace, all of which are treated in a rather realistic way. Overall, the impression given is that the artist(s) were trying to make the scene as immediate and contemporary as possible, as if to involve the viewer in the struggle between good and evil. There is further evidence of the willingness of Indian artists to change in the fact that the *vāhana* of Durgā is shown as a tiger, which has largely, though not entirely, replaced the lion in her iconography over the last century or two as lions have become rare in India.

Even in the most traditional treatments of the subject of Durgā Mahiṣāsuramardinī, we find details that can be explained only by assuming that they come from observation of contemporary life. This is particularly clear in the case of the weapons shown in use.

In a typically ornate and stylized Hoysala sculpture which is in V & A (see Fig. 4)[47] there is a realistic touch in the way in which the bowstring is carved: the sculptor has shown clearly the way in which it has been made from a number of different strands, and looped over the ends of the limbs. It is of interest, too, as a representation of a composite bow (see note 8), which may have been a quite recent introduction in the Southern Deccan in the thirteenth century, the probable date of this work.

Therefore when we see unusual weapons in Indian art that cannot be explained in terms of iconographic tradition, it may well be that they are accurate representations of weapons that were current at the time but soon fell out of use. An example may perhaps be seen in the fine, though damaged, thirteenth century Orissan sculpture of Durgā in the BM (see Fig. 5). Three of the eight hands have been broken off, but from those that remain it seems clear that this version followed the same basic iconography as the Hoysala one cited above. The swords and daggers shown as used by the goddess and the demon are recognizably the ancestors of known Indian types (e.g. the goddess' sword is a forerunner of the *khanda*).[48] The oddity is the small oblong shield that terminates in a dagger-like stabbing point. The evidence of the other Mahiṣāsuramardinī figures we have examined suggests that

Fig. 4. Durgā Mahiṣāsuramardinī. Potstone. Hoysala, Karnataka, *c.* thirteenth century. *Reproduced by courtesy of the V & A Museum. (IS 77–1965)*

Fig. 5. Durgā Mahiṣāsuramardiṇī. Basalt. Orissa, *c.* thirteenth century. *Reproduced by courtesy of the Trustees of the British Museum. (1872, 7–1 78 OA)*

this may well have been a weapon in use at the time when this sculpture was made.

It is very likely that there were weapons in use in various parts of India of which no examples have survived: practically all surviving Indian arms and armour date from the late eighteenth century or after, by which time many types had been drastically modified or replaced altogether, under Islamic influence. (It is perhaps worth mentioning here that until the 'Mary Rose' was raised, there was very little archaeological evidence for the English longbow.)

MODERN WEAPONS IN TRADITIONAL SUBJECTS: INDIAN AND WESTERN ATTITUDES TO HISTORY

It would not have been out of keeping for a traditional Indian artist to depict modern weapons and other objects in a work on a religious subject. This approach may be compared with that seen in some Medieval European art in which biblical and historical events are presented in what must have then been entirely modern terms. A good example is the illustrated Bible manuscript in the Pierpoint Morgan Library, believed to be fourteenth century French.[49] Here, for example, the young David struggles realistically with a borrowed coat of mail before deciding to fight Goliath armed only with his sling. Uriah the Hittite appears as a knight falling from his horse, shot down by a crossbowman. Koch reproduced a fifteenth century illustration showing Cyrus the Great with troops armed with guns as well as pikes and bows, and an incident from Caesar's Gallic wars as a battle between two armies led by armoured knights. In cases like these, it seems highly probable that the artist has simply not realized how different warfare must have been in the ancient world.

Other cases are more problematic. In the sixteenth century German woodcut of the apocryphal story of Judith and Holophernes there seems to be some awareness that things had changed: no firearms are depicted. But otherwise all the participants are sixteenth century Germans, and Koch has included the reproduction in his book as an illustration of the military tactics of the *Landsknechts*.[50]

In Flemish and German religious paintings and prints of that period, the events of the Bible and scenes from the lives of saints were commonly depicted with the costumes and weapons of the artists' own time. Saint Sebastian, for example, was often shown being shot with crossbows. Paintings of the Crucifixion are populated by figures with contemporary clothes, weapons and banners.[51] In such examples, it seems unlikely that the artists were totally unaware of the differences between contemporary and ancient ways of life. It is probable that they were simply not interested in recreating a historical scene, but wanted to bring home to people of their own time the meaning of the stories of their religion. In the same way, the donors of the paintings are not always depicted on separate panels, but are sometimes virtually included in the events depicted.[52] Such works can still act powerfully on the emotions of the viewer, and their impact must have been even greater when the people in the painted martyrdom looked exactly like one's friends and neighbours.

Of course, judgements like these are bound to be subjective to some extent when no documentation exists to show how much a particular artist knew about history or what he had in mind when approaching a traditional theme. Only in the case of recent painters of Christian subjects, such as Stanley Spencer, can one be quite sure that the anachronisms are intentional.

Even in Western art the quest for historical accuracy, in the sense of an attempt to imagine what a past scene might have looked like if one could have been transported back in time, is fairly recent.[53] In pre-Raj Indian art it did not exist, because the idea of history was different. Indian cosmologies could envisage vast expanses of time and space beyond anything imagined in the West before the twentieth century, but it was never supposed that society could, or should, change very much. In Hindu myths, set many aeons into the past or the future, it is assumed, for example, that the brahmins are still the guardians of the Vedas and the natural heads of society.

Moreover, this history (if that is the proper word for it) is cyclic and the patterns of events within it are repeated in every cycle. By contrast, Christianity has always seen the events of the Bible as having happened uniquely, at particular points in historical time. Above all, the life of Christ has been seen as the central event to which time before or after looked forward or backward. The Western historical approach to religious art seems to have reached its extreme in the late nineteenth century. It can be seen, for example, in the work of the pre-Raphaelite painter Holman Hunt who visited the Middle East in order to achieve greater authenticity in his religious paintings, and even attempted to procure the correct kind of wood-shavings for a painting of Christ in his carpenter's shop.[54]

Although many of the Hindu myths are traditionally placed in different periods of history, and some, such as those associated with Kṛṣṇa and Rāma, seem to have an historical content, they have never in practice been tied down to a particular place and time. In an important sense, the myths are always taking place in the present, within the temple and within the mind of the worshipper. Rāma and Sītā are believed to have been king and queen of ancient Ayodhyā, but what is really important to the worshipper is their presence now. The victory of good over evil in the battle of Durgā and the Buffalo demon is re-enacted every year in festivals.[55] In fact the myths are timeless, so that when the Bengali folk artist paints Durgā holding a gun we cannot call it an anachronism when the troops of Judith and Holophernes are represented as sixteenth century German mercenaries, whether we think that the Book of Judith is historical or not.

This is one of the main reasons for the variety of the ways in which weapons are treated in Hindu religious art. Where the forms of attributes were not dictated by tradition, artists were free to draw upon their own experience; and when they had to create figures armed with large numbers of weapons, they depicted the ones that they saw around them. In a sense it was because they were working in a strong and living tradition that they were able to introduce modern objects into their work: there was no need for them to look to an earlier time.

Today, under Western influence, the situation has changed, and modern Hindu religious prints often seem to imitate costumes, weapons and architecture of the past. In a print I bought at Mahābalipuram in 1975, Māriamman, the South Indian goddess of smallpox, is portrayed sitting on a throne, with offerings before her of the kind that would be given in temples: food, betel, flowers, lights and so on. The attributes in her four hands are a drum with a snake coiled round it, another snake, a sword and a medicinal fruit. The sword is now treated in a schematized way which suggests that the artist has never seen a sword but is trying to imagine a weapon of the past. In most of the works examined above, the weapons depicted have an air of reality as though they were objects with which the artists were familiar.

INDIAN ARTISTS AND WAR

This air of reality leads us to speculate whether some of the artists of traditional India could have experienced warfare at first hand, as numerous Western artists have done. A well-known example is Henry Lamb (1883 – 1960) who drew upon his service in the 1914 – 18 war in creating such works as 'Advanced Dressing Station on the Struma' (1920).[56] At an earlier date Urs Graf (*c.* 1485 – 1527/8), a Swiss artist, goldsmith and mercenary, used his (evidently chequered) experience in his drawings and prints.[57] Others, such as Winslow Homer (1836 – 1910) in the American Civil War, have been employed as war artists.[58]

Evidence about artists is notoriously difficult to find in India. On the rare occasions when works of art were engraved with the names of individuals, these were practically always the names of the donors: it was not the practice for the artists to sign their work. The entire body of Indian painting and sculpture, at least until Mughal times, is in effect anonymous.

One of the very rare exceptions is the art of the Hoysala period in Karnataka. S. Settar discusses the inscriptions left by Hoysala sculptors/architects, in which some of them give their names and other information about themselves.[59] One sculptor set up a monument to his brother who died fighting in a military action. From this solitary piece of evidence we know, at least, that a member of the sculptor caste, whose family was still engaged in its traditional occupation, could serve as a soldier, so it does not seem impossible that there were some who had experience of both trades.

Painters who served as court artists must frequently have accompanied their employers to their wars. Clearly, there was little scope in the Indian tradition for the direct recording of military life, though we find hints of it in certain Pahārī paintings such as the portraits of Balwant Singh going about his daily activities in his camp,[60] or the Kangra painting of a warrior returning home to his wife, with his servant carrying his camp-bed and other equipment (BM, 1948, 10 – 9 0122 OA). As in the religious subjects, the realistic details are subordinated to a traditional theme: the portrait of a ruler or the separation and reunion of lovers.

CONCLUSIONS

To summarize, there is no one way in which weapons may feature in Hindu art, but a great variety of ways. Certain weapons, such as the *cakra*, of Viṣṇu and the *triśūla* of Śiva and Devī, become so intimately connected with particular deities that they can symbolize them or embody part of their character. They may themselves become gods attendant on the deities with whom they are associated. The warlike character of such attributes seems never to be entirely forgotten, but it may become secondary to other kinds of symbolism. The shapes of these weapons seem to be invested with a power of their own, and they can be given a wide variety of interpretations.

At the other extreme, there are figures, divine or demonic, that are armed with many weapons held in numerous hands. Not all the weapons shown are necessarily dictated by tradition. They may be used as much to give an impression of warlike power as to convey a detailed symbolism. In representations of demons they add to the impression of ferocity, while in images of Durgā they are contrasted with the beauty of her face and body to convey a sense of her heroic power in conquering demons and protecting her devotees. In figures of this kind artists would sometimes introduce contemporary weapons alongside traditional ones.

In any case, there seems not to have been any objection to a degree of modernity or realism in Hindu art so long as iconographic correctness was maintained. The events of Hindu myth were treated as happening in a timeless present, not in an historic past. It is perhaps only under the influence of Western ideas about time that Hindus have felt the need to depict their myths as ancient events, with archaic costumes, weapons and architecture.[61]

Why are weapons so important in Hindu art? They are among the most commonly depicted kinds of divine attribute, perhaps the commonest after jewellery and flowers. Often the attribute by which a deity is immediately recognized is a weapon or a form derived from one.

It is clear that weapons are closely connected with divine power: most obviously with the power to overcome evil and to protect the good, mythologically expressed as the power to kill demons. There is also a sense in which the transformations brought about by religious practice can be seen as a kind of death in which the old self is destroyed. The weapons of the gods can then be seen as the means to bring this transformation about. This symbolism is clearly present in certain images of Śiva and Kālī. But there is no sharp division between any of these different kinds of symbolism.

In making this study, I have been brought to a renewed sense of the power and subtlety of Hindu symbolism and have been surprised on occasion by its adaptability and readiness to draw on everyday life, which are greater than is generally assumed. It has left me with deeper respect than ever for the artists of India, who have developed this symbolism and given it concrete form. I hope that it will inspire further discussion of one important aspect of symbolism in Hindu art, and so perhaps make a contribution to the understanding of the many and complex ways in which symbolism is used in Indian religion.

NOTES

1 I owe this suggestion to Prof. Deborah Klimberg-Salter of the University of California Art Department.

2 Cf. A. L. Basham, *The Wonder that was India*, London, 3rd ed. 1982, pp. 122 – 3.

3 Sir Ralph Payne-Gallwey, *The Crossbow*, Holland Press, 1903, repr. 1976, pp. 3–5.

4 George Orwell, 'Politics and the English Language', *Inside the Whale and Other Essays*, Harmondsworth, 1957, p. 147.

5 This tradition appears to go back to the Dhanur Veda of which I have been unable to trace a copy. However, in the RV the bow is already the pre-eminent weapon; see e.g. the hymns 'To Arms', Wendy O'Flaherty, *The Rig Veda*, Harmondsworth, 1981, pp. 236–9.

6 E.g. in the Tripurāntaka myth; *The Subhāṣitaratnakoṣa, compiled by Vidyākara*, ed. D. D., Kosambi & V. V. Gokhale (Harvard Oriental Series, vol. 42), Cambridge, Mass., 1957. Tr.: Daniel H. Ingalls, *An Anthology of Sanskrit Court Poetry*, Harvard UP, 1965. See the Introduction, pp. 72–3.

7 William Irvine, *The Army of the Indian Moghuls*, repr. Delhi, 1963, p. 92 & 95 mentions the use of crossbows.

8 For composite bows see E. McEwen, 'The Chahār Kham or Four-curved Bow of India', *Islamic Arms and Armour*, ed. R. Elgood, London, 1979. I owe my thanks to Mr. McEwen, and Mrs. A. Wendy Hodkinson, Hon. Keeper of the Simon Archery Foundation, for their help on matters connected with bows and archery.

9 E.g. British Museum, OA + 2750; Simon Archery Foundation (Manchester Museum), SAF 101, SAF 374, SAF 156.

10 E.g. BM, OA unnumbered; cf. G. C. Stone, *A Glossary of the Construction, Decoration and Use of Arms and Armor*, repr. New York, 1961 (first edn. 1934).

11 For bamboo self bows in use in the 20th century see J. S. Lee, 'A Santhal bow and arrows from Bihar, India', and 'The Bhumea and Baiga archers of Madhya Pradesh, Central India', *Society of Archer-Antiquaries Journal*, 3 (1960), pp. 19–22.

12 E.g. in the relief from Badami: H. Zimmer, *The Art of Indian Asia*, New York, 1955, vol. 2, pl. 125, III.

13 Ibid., ppl. 284–5; Stella Kramrisch, *The Art of India*, London, 1954, pl. 86.

14 For this theme see M. S. Nagaraja Rao, *Kirātārjunīyam in Indian Art*, Delhi, 1979.

15 Wendy O'Flaherty, *Hindu Myths*, Harmondsworth, 1975, pp. 126–37.

16 On the iconography of Śiva Tripurāntaka see T. A. Gopinatha Rao, *Elements of Hindu Iconography*, Madras, 1914, repr. New York, n.d., vol. II, part 1, pp. 164–71.

A fine South Indian bronze pair of Tripurāntaka with his consort (Pārvatī as Tripurasundarī) is reproduced by Douglas Barrett in *Early Chola Bronzes*, Bhulabhai Memorial Institute, Bombay, 1965.

17 Zimmer, op. cit., vol. 2, pl. 226.

18 Cf. a Gupta terracotta panel depicting a chariot battle, G. N. Pant, *Studies in Indian Weapons and Warfare*, Delhi, 1970, pl. IV.

19 Kosambi & Gokhale, op. cit., p. 10 (no. 4.20); Ingalls, op. cit. Section 4, no. 49 (see note 6). The meaning of this and other poems on the same

theme is discussed in the Introduction, pp. 72 – 3. (My thanks to Dr J. D. Smith for help in locating the poem.)

20 E. Lucie-Smith, *Eroticism in Western Art*, London, 1972. See esp. pp. 190 – 4 & 213 – 4.

21 On South Indian iconography see F. H. Gravely & T. N. Ramachandran, *Catalogue of the South Indian Hindu Metal Images in the Madras Government Museum*, Bulletin of the Madras Government Museum, New Series – General Section, vol. 1, part 2 (1932), pp. 5 – 20. This section is particularly useful, because it summarizes material from the *dhyānas* ('meditations'), verses used by traditional artists in order to memorize the correct forms for images of deities in their different aspects.

22 In paintings the motif comes to be used for 'portraits' of queens (e.g. that of Khanzada Humayun, see Douglas Barrett, *Painting of the Deccan, XVI – XVII Century*, Faber Gallery of Oriental Art, 1958, pl. 1, pp. 6 – 7; for Rāgamālā or Rasamañjarī themes see Kramrisch, op. cit., pl. VI, p. 35 and note p. 213.

23 W. E. Begley, *Viṣṇu's Flaming Wheel: The Iconography of the Sudarśaṇa-Cakra*, New York UP, 1973; indispensable for the study of the weapons of Viṣṇu, and much drawn on by me.

In this context, *puruṣa*, man, and *nārī*, woman, are used for male and female personifications of divine weapons (*āyudha-puruṣas*). T. A. G. Rao, op. cit., vol. 1, part 1, pp. 287 – 96 gives a traditional, highly theoretical account of these figures, including many which seem not to occur in art.

24 C. Sivaramurti, *South Indian Bronzes*, Delhi, 1963, publishes a Chola pair of discus and mace, both male.

25 Kramrisch, op. cit., ppl. 51 – 2.

26 Kramrisch, op. cit., p. 202, seems to hint at this interpretation, too, when she says that 'the four remaining figures are personifications of the potency of Viṣṇu's four hands'. It occurred to me to wonder whether the hand that holds the lotus is the same one that would hold the sword. However, it appears that the arrangement of the four main attributes is so variable, depending upon which aspect of the god is depicted, that it is not possible to make a categorical statement about it.

27 Pratapaditya Pal, *The Arts of Nepal*, vol. 1, Leiden, 1974, pp. 41 & 71. I am grateful to Dr F. R. Allchin for information on this topic.

28 Begley, op. cit.

29 'Dastar bungga' (helmet with a set of *cakras*), Royal Armouries, RA inv. 26.60A. For an example in the V & A Museum see W. Egerton of Tatton, *Handbook of Indian Arms*, London, 1880, no. 613, pp. 128ff. On the use of *cakra* by Sikhs, see Captain Mundy, *Journal of a Tour of India*, London, 1827, p. 131.

30 Harivaṁśa album commissioned by the Emperor Akbar around 1590, see V & A Museum, IS 5 – 1970, colour slide VAS 84.

31 Cf. the Buddhist symbolism of the Dhamma-wheel and of the Wheel-turning monarch. — However, for a sculpture of a wheel-like *cakra* in use see Zimmer, op. cit., pl. 110, a relief from Deogarth, showing Viṣṇu's rescue of the elephant king (Gajendra-mokṣa). Here the *cakra* is held

sideways on in the hand. As the mace in this relief looks rather realistic, it is just possible that this *cakra*, too, is based on an alternative type in battlefield use.

32 My drawing from memory in Fig. 1 shows a *rangoli* made in Madras for the Dīvālī festival.

33 Threefold symbolism seems to have a special connexion with Śiva. See J. Gonda, *Viṣṇuism and Śivaism: A Comparison*, London, 1970, repr. Delhi, 1976: p. 14 on the name Tryambaka; pp. 111 – 12 on the *bilva* tree whose 'trifoliate leaf "symbolizes" the three functions — creation, preservation and destruction — of the Lord as well as his three eyes'.

34 Rao, op. cit., vol. II, part I, pl. XXXV, Fig. 1, reproduces a sculpture of Śiva as Kālāri in which he kicks Kāla while stabbing him with his *triśūla*. Cf. also a Kangra painting in the BM 1923, 7 – 16 02 OA, showing a battle between Śiva and Kṛṣṇa and their entourages. Here the *triśūla* is depicted as a throwing weapon.

35 E.g. BM, 1924, 4 – 1 01 OA (Kangra Painting) — and many modern prints of the god.

36 Zimmer, op. cit., vol. I, pl. C11; Veronica Ions, *Indian Mythology*, London, 1967, p. 45.

37 Ions, op. cit., p. 97. The seated female figure that forms part of this *triśūla* appears to represent Maheśvarī rather than Śītalā as suggested in the caption. Two more examples of *triśūlas* with figures of deities attached can be seen in Sivaramamurti, op. cit., pl. 65a – b, showing high relief figures of a form of Devī (described as Śūla-Pidāri) and of Śiva accompanied by the bull Nandin (Vṛṣabhāntika) respectively.

38 Jeanne Openshaw (on personal communication).

39 James Todd, *Annals and Antiquities of Rajasthan*, London, 1829, p. 587.

40 Cf. the 18th century painting, attributed to the Chamba school, of Kālī in the burning ground, V & A, IS 126 – 1951; published in the catalogue *In the Image of Man*, London, 1982, p. 220, no. 459. Here the goddess holds a *talwar*, with a hand-guard and a curving blade, which was introduced from Central Asia but by the 18th century had become the standard Indian sword; see Stone, op. cit., pp. 601 – 2.

41 There are numerous other examples in Barrett (see note 16), Sivaramamurti (note 24), Graveley and Ramachandran (note 21).

42 Rao, op. cit., vol. II, part I, pp. 113 – 14.

43 Similarly, Vaiṣṇavī carries the discus and mace, Brahmāṇī has four heads etc., taking attributes of their husbands. Rao, op. cit., p. 616.

44 I have omitted the *vajra* from discussion in this survey as it does not correspond to a human weapon. On the iconography of Kārttikeya (Subrāhmaṇya) see Rao, op. cit., vol. II, pp. 415 – 51.

45 O'Flaherty, *Hindu Myths*, pp. 238 – 49, esp. p. 241.

46 The same picture is reproduced in colour in Veronica Ions, op. cit., p. 74, where, regrettably, it has not been carefully researched: the caption describes the goddess wrongly as with ten arms! (Other examples of similar misrepresentations in the same work are: the feminine left head of Śiva at Elephanta is described as masculine on p. 25, and on p. 95 a perfectly normal metal image of the crawling baby Kṛṣṇa is captioned as

'A Dakini, female fiend attendant upon Kali, who . . . takes pleasure in drinking blood and eating human flesh' and dated about nine centuries too soon.)

47 IS 77 – 1965. Reproduced also in V & A's *Large Picture Book no. 36: Indian Art*, HMSO, 1969, pl. 17; and in: *Arts Council of Great Britain*, op. cit., no. 450, p. 219.

48 Cf. Egerton, op. cit. pp. 104, 117, no. 521T; Stone, op. cit., pp. 351 – 2.

49 Sydney C. Cockerell, *Old Testament Miniatures: a medieval picture book with 283 paintings from the Creation to the Story of David*, Phaidon, n.d., pp. 135, 191. My thanks to Ailsa Bertram for help on this subject.

50 H.W. Koch, *Medieval Warfare*, Bison, 1978, pp. 152 – 3; p. 188; p. 175.

51 E.g. the one in the National Gallery attributed to the Master of Delft, see Albert Châtelet, *Early Dutch Painting*, Phaidon, 1981, pp. 155 – 7, 237.

52 E.g. the Pieta by Van der Weyden in the National Gallery; see Martin Davies, *Rogier Van Der Weyden*, Phaidon, 1972, pl. 72.

53 This topic, mainly in connexion with British history paintings of the 19th century, has been explored by Roy Strong, *And When Did You Last See Your Father? The Victorian Painter and British History*, London, 1978.

54 Holman Hunt, *Autobiography*, 1905, vol. 2, p. 276. He says: 'I made it my business to find out traditional carpenters' tools,' and describes how he made 'a study of wood shavings'. The painting, 'The Shadow of Death', is in Manchester City Art Gallery, and I am grateful to Mr Maurice Davies of that Gallery for information on this subject.

55 Ninian Smart, *Background to the Long Search*, BBC, London, 1977, unnumbered page (in fact p. 84), has a fine illustration of a festival of Durgā in which a festival image of Mahiṣāsuramardinī is being plunged into a river after procession. (It is wrongly captioned as representing Sarasvatī.)

56 Keith Clements, *Henry Lamb: the Artist and his Friends*, Redcliffe, 1985, pp. 218 – 20, and pl. facing pp. 210 – 11. Also: *Henry Lamb* (exhibition Catalogue), Manchester City Art Gallery, 1984, pp. 7 – 8, 44 – 5, and ppl. 32 – 3.

57 Emil Major and Erwin Gradmann, *Urs Graf*, Basel, n.d., pl. 46 – 8, 123 – 4, and throughout.

58 John Wilmerding, *Winslow Homer*, Praeger, 1972, pp. 33 – 4, 41 – 6, col. ppl. 2, 4 (pp. 23 – 4) and ppl. 2 – 1 to 2 – 16.

59 S. Settar, *The Hoysala Style of Temple Architecture and Sculpture, XIth to XIVth Century*, Ph.D. thesis, University of Cambridge, August 1970.

60 D. Barrett and B. Gray, *Indian Paintings*, London, 1978, pp. 176 and 179.

61 A useful source for the way in which Hindu myths are seen today is the series of children's books in comic-strip format: *Amar Chitra Katha*, published by India Book House Education Trust, Bombay. Strongly recommended are: *Ganesha* (no. 89), *Sati and Shiva* (no. 11), *Tales of Shiva* (no. 164), *Shiva Parvati* (no. 29), *Tales of Vishnu* (no. 160), *Karttikeya* (no. 252) and *Tales of Durga* (no. 176).

9

MEANING AND SYMBOLISM IN THE WORK OF ANANDA COOMARASWAMY

Jonathan Sutton

In this paper I propose to consider some of the questions that most preoccupied Coomaraswamy during his lifetime of writing and extensive research. I will trace the general process of thought that led him to his insistence on the need for scrupulous study of, and then adherence to, traditional symbolism.

Before embarking on this task I would like to say that the artist, his purpose and his creative work are all subjects that are prominent in Coomaraswamy's writings, and these must feature in even the briefest account of his outlook. This is not to say that Coomaraswamy sought to set up the artist apart from other men or that he valued the artist's work at the expense of other men's work. In fact, he was opposed to such exclusive elevation of the artist, regarding him as one among many men, each of whom followed a vocation with appropriate duties and responsibilities. I am here concerned with the artist's endeavour to convey, through symbols, meaning and values in his works. However, it will be immediately evident that a large proportion of the comparatively modern works of art to which we are commonly exposed in galleries have little bearing on a discussion of the Indian religions and their symbolism or, indeed of religion as such. Their subject matter is quite plainly secular, and frequently enough it has been the artist's avowed intention to dissociate himself and his works from the 'spiritual' perspective and from spiritual concerns altogether. Coomaraswamy, however, acted upon the premise that for discussion of works of art to be truly valid, it necessarily entailed constant reference to religious 'ends'. As Lipsey points out: 'There are two paradigms of the work of art in Coomaraswamy's thought: the religious icon and the useful object.'[1]

My observations regarding Coomaraswamy's ideas will be taken under the following three headings:

(i) his affirmation of meaning in art, and his view of art's purpose as the transmission of values;

(ii) his insistence that beauty and utility have to be taken in conjunction, in any worthwhile assessment of works of art;
(iii) his demonstration of the consistency of authentic symbolism, and his explanation of symbols as means to the attainment of an 'active wisdom'.

It is not my intention to confine discussion exclusively to the artist and to his choice of symbolic subjects for his paintings or sculptures. Discernment in the artist's choice of subjects is, itself, most commendable, and it answers one of Coomaraswamy's foremost requirements for the reinstatement of works of art which may properly be said to be 'significant'. But if we are to be consistent in applying his standards, we should go considerably further and should underline the point that the monk, the layman and householder, the marriage partner, the warrior, the sacrificial priest and the temporal ruler of a kingdom each bear responsibility akin to that of the artist in their own sphere of activity. This traditional view of vocational responsibilities is certainly prominent in a monograph by Coomaraswamy considered further on in this paper.[2]

My account of Coomaraswamy's ideas begins with the following short but particularly instructive quotation from another work of his:

> The study of art, if it is to have any cultural value, will demand . . . in the first place an understanding and acceptance of the whole point of view from which the necessity for the work arose, and in the second place a bringing to life in ourselves of the form in which the artist conceived the work and by which he judged it.[3]

For Coomaraswamy it was axiomatic that human needs prompt the making of beautiful objects. He wrote from a deep conviction about the truth of the above quotation concerning the art historian's 'understanding and acceptance of the whole point of view from which the necessity for the work arose'. He was acutely aware of the researcher's tendency to attribute wholly inapplicable intentions to the artist, a problem which arises from importing one's own standards when evaluating what is produced in a substantially different culture.

We must be clear about what Coomaraswamy intends when speaking of the 'human needs' that are served by the making of beautiful objects. In fact even this paper, in common with all the other papers in this collection, will in effect examine the human needs that are served by the making of beautiful, symbolically eloquent objects.

Coomaraswamy commends the essentially Platonic view of value:

> It is one of Plato's virtues, and of all traditional doctrine about art, that *value* is never taken to mean an exclusively spiritual or exclusively physical value.[4]

This is one of the most prominent themes in Coomaraswamy's writings. It is illustrated by a wealth of extensive references to scriptural sources of the various great religions. It would be worthwhile to mention, for instance, that the well-known Christian precept 'Man cannot live by bread alone' is seen by him as applicable in the context of art: our concern for physical value may eclipse recognition of the spiritual needs that should be met by artistic and other activities. Certainly the Christian Church has ceased to exert a decisive influence as the artist's patron, and gives every appearance of being resigned to the divorce between utilitarian or commercially-minded artists and its own purposes.

Where Coomaraswamy takes up questions of cultural history, and particularly the cultural history of Western Europe, he alludes constantly to our readiness to uphold a rigid distinction between the 'fine' arts and, on the other hand, the 'applied' arts. A measure of our acceptance of these opposed categories can be seen, he holds, in the fact that nowadays one does not readily associate 'beauty' with useful objects. He argues that the notion of beauty and utility have in former times been intimately connected:

> For Socrates the distinction of beauty from use is a logical distinction, but not a real one, not objective; a thing can only be beautiful in the context for which it is designed.[5]

That we came to accept that distinction and that it influenced our habitual perceptions and thought in such a profound manner represents a decline. Coomaraswamy calls it 'an impoverished perception of reality'.

Of course, it is not the beauty/use distinction that alone accounts for our 'impoverished' perception; Coomaraswamy frequently cites the modern preference for the arbitrary and subjective in works of art, particularly the preoccupation with self-assertive expression, as directly conducive to this decline. His overall thesis is that this 'impoverished perception of reality' was very evidently *not* suffered by those who adhered to traditional canons of artistic production and evaluation. He believed that a characteristic 'traditional' approach to artistic production *could* be defined; he provided both general features of the traditional viewpoint and detailed supporting evidence gathered from anthropological and other studies. He further believed that the approach to art properly called 'traditional' represented a highly coherent view in itself. He focused on three broad notions:

1. Everyone in the traditional community acknowledged that the objects to be made (i.e. commissioned by the patron) were, ultimately, 'supports of contemplation'. Given that this was the end in view, naturalistic representation was unsuited and alien to the traditional artist whose work was iconographic.
2. Self-assertion of the individual artist as such was not sought or valued in the traditional community; the personal characteristics and psychology of the individual are the accidental and least enduring aspects of his existence; so to give them prominent expression in a work of art could with good reason be considered arbitrary, unwarranted and irresponsible. Coomaraswamy underlines the traditional artist's concern with conformity to archetypes, where certitude and precision of expression become possible.
3. According to the traditional view, argues Coomaraswamy, the spectator's response to a work of art is not confined to enjoyment, or to gratification of the sense. This all-important point is affirmed by him thus: 'In traditional philosophy the work of art is a reminder; the summons of its beauty is to a thesis, as to something to be understood, rather than merely enjoyed.'[6]

Coomaraswamy has been charged on occasion with idealizing the virtues of the pre-industrial, feudal type of community and the values which inspired traditional craftsmanship. This alleged idealization is taken to derive from the powerful influence of William Morris's ideas in his student years. It is misleading, however, to characterize Coomaraswamy's own ideas as a type of confused romanticism or sentimentality about tradition and craftsmanship. In the first place, he deplored the gratuitous mimicry of medieval and other art forms by those who no longer grasped their intended meaning as 'supports of contemplation'. He held confusion of this sort to be particularly harmful, especially where it was masked by complacency or conformity to fashion. Being acutely aware of the scale of confusion constituted by this failure to recognize contemplative and spiritual ends, he consciously undertook to provide in his writings a reclarification of the terms of the traditional philosophy of art.

In another essay Coomaraswamy defines 'significant and liberating art' quite directly as 'the art of those who in their performances are celebrating God . . . in both His natures, immanent and transcendent . . .'[7] It is a definition consistent with the various religious traditions of East and West, and a definition very evidently suited to the Hindu perception of life. The *celebratory* aspect of creative activity is eloquently affirmed by the dance of Śiva and by the notion of *līlā*, or Play. Coomaraswamy further quotes also the authority of the BhG: 'In this world people are fettered by action, unless it is performed as a [worshipful] sacrifice.'

The essay just quoted is, in a number of ways, a definitive statement on questions regarding the true status of the artist and the nature of his work. It emerges from it that Coomaraswamy viewed the artist's life and activity as nothing less than a discipline of self-transcendence. The artist's operation

> is not a meaningless labour, but quite literally a sacred and significant rite, and quite as much as the product itself an adequate symbol of a spiritual reality. It is therefore a way, or rather *the* way, by which the artist, whether potter or painter, poet or king, can best erect or edify *himself* at the same time as he 'trues' or corrects his work.[8]

Ideally, a 'renunciation of works' is required of the artist:

> This renunciation is essentially the abandonment of the notion 'I am the doer', and a reference of the works to their real author, whose skill is infallible.[9]

Self-forgetfulness of this high order has been an ideal expressed in most scriptural traditions, not least in the Russian and Greek Orthodox ones whose iconographic art is so universally acclaimed.

It is perhaps Zen Buddhism that recently and forcefully introduced to the West the notion that by following one activity with a sufficiently concentrated attitude of mind — even the seemingly saṁsāric activities of archery, flower-arranging or sweeping a courtyard — one's own insight might be deepened and enlightenment attained. Certainly, some of the Japanese masters displayed a genius for showing, albeit obliquely, how the mundane incidents in life provided true occasions for learning — learning, possibly, that we already hold the Pure Land within our hearts, could we but recognize it. Such is the theme of Hakuin's Zazen Wasan, or Song of Zazen.

Coomaraswamy's writings bear out such insights and point insistently to recognition of the Pure Land situated within the heart. His painstaking and scholarly application of scriptural teachings, parable and symbolic myth to all possible levels of reference may in some measure counterbalance the bias against intellectual rigour which marks some expositions of Zen Buddhism.

As already stated, Coomaraswamy sought to clarify terms that had become obscure through bad or thoughtless usage. Notably, he shows how we tend to refer to 'art' when we have in mind 'works of art'. The following quotation reveals a significant difference of emphasis, given the correct usage of words:

> Art is nothing tangible. We cannot call a painting 'art'. As the words 'artefact' and 'artificial' imply, the thing made is a work of art, made *by* art, but not art itself; the art remains in the artist, and is the knowledge by which things are made.[10]

A further instructive example of reclarification of terms occurs when Coomaraswamy cites, in his essay 'Ornament', the medieval usage of the words 'ornament' and 'to adorn': such expressions as 'the mind is adorned by learning' and 'a sword adorns a soldier' were then current. Here the idea of ornament signifies the attributes of someone or something that makes them 'complete', that which allows them to operate effectively, as in the case of the soldier and his sword. This is quite clearly counter to the impoverished idea of ornament today, when it means something frivolous, extraneous, something entirely unconnected with the utility of an object. Coomaraswamy commends the former usage of the word and particularly the emphasis on ornament as necessary for 'effective operation'.

One might catalogue numerous cases where he has researched the etymological sources of terms that we now misuse, terms whose true import he conveys by giving specific examples of their correct application in Hindu, early Christian, Judaic or other cultures. In this context one could usefully consider essays such as his 'Imitation, Expression, Participation', 'The Intellectual Operation in Indian Art', 'Recollection, Indian and Platonic' and 'The Traditional Conception of Ideal Portraiture'.

Coomaraswamy has also written extensively on the place of iconoclasm in the various traditions, taking into account the Islamic avoidance of representational art, the early indication of the Buddha by his footprints (or 'traces') alone, and — at the other end of the spectrum — some of the regrettably naturalistic depictions of Christ. Varied and wide as his essays may be, their burden is really this — that the artist's choice of subject matter, his attitude of mind, and his skill in the execution of his work are far from being arbitrary matters.

As indicated above, it is not solely the artist's responsibilities that concern us in this paper. I am more concerned to follow the symbolic representation of ideas expressed in scriptures, and I will duly proceed to this theme. Relying upon scriptural writings of the various religious traditions, there is great justification for the view that authentic religious symbolism is not of an arbitrary character, but is marked by the highest possible degree of consistency. Indeed, Coomaraswamy himself took the degree of consistency in symbolic expression as a reliable measure of its authenticity.

By taking up some prominent symbolic themes developed by Coomaraswamy in his commentary on the Rājasūya ceremony (as it appears in the AB), I mean to show that in his scholarly exegesis of texts he convincingly demonstrated the consistency and instructive character of authentic religious symbolism.

First I would make a few explanatory remarks in order to point out how certain forms of literary symbolism should be set apart from the symbolism that concerns us here.

Due to the pronouncements of a school of literary theorists and poets who called themselves 'symbolists' and enjoyed a certain popularity in Western Europe and Russia late in the nineteenth and early in the twentieth century, symbols have in popular parlance come to denote that which is obscure, vague and largely undefined. This view is diametrically opposed to Coomaraswamy's understanding of the nature of symbols. Years of scholarly research on the world religions and on their traditional expressions of spiritual teaching led him to discern, and to convey in his writings, the consistency and precision of authentic symbolism. His many essays were intended to illustrate, with a wealth of examples, that where symbols are concerned, one should expect to find the very same degree of precision, order and clarity as is evident in mathematics.

Precision in the gestures of the (sculpted) object and appreciative understanding on the part of the observer can be noted in the following description of a Buddha image by Marco Pallis. And of this image it can rightly be said that 'the summons of its beauty is to a thesis, as to something to be understood rather than merely enjoyed'.

> We must . . . examine one concrete means of grace, mentioned before, which perhaps more than all others has helped to keep remembrance of enlightenment alive among man. This is the image of the Buddha making the 'earth-touching' (*bhūmisparśa*) gesture. No corner of the Buddhist world but knows and loves this image; both Theravāda and Mahāyāna have produced marvellous examples of it . . .
>
> Before going into the various details of the image itself, it were well to refresh our memory about the episode in the Buddha's life which this particular posture is meant to perpetuate. Everyone will remember that shortly before his enlightenment the Buddha-to-be proceeded into the great primeval forest near the place in Bihar now called Bodh-Gaya and there found a spreading pipal tree (Ficus religiosa) at the foot of which a seat stood ready prepared for one destined to become the Light of the World; the tree itself obviously stands for the world's axis, the Tree of Life as Genesis calls it. Just as he was about to take his seat there, Māra the tempter appeared before him,

challenging his right to the adamantine throne: 'I am the prince of this world,' Māra said, 'so the throne belongs to me.' Then the Bodhisattva stretched forth his right hand and touched the earth, mother of all creatures, calling on her to witness that the throne was his by right, and earth testified that this was so.

In the classical form of this image the Buddha is always shown sitting upon a lotus; the choice of this water plant is itself significant inasmuch as in the traditional lore 'the waters' always symbolize existence with its teeming possibilities, that *saṁsāra* that the Buddha was to show the way to overcome, not by mere denial, but by showing forth its true nature. As for the figure itself, its right hand points downward to touch the earth as in the story while its left hand is turned upward to support the begging bowl, sign of a *bhikkhu*'s estate. Just as the *bhikkhu* in his bowl catches whatever the passer-by may choose to cast into it, be it much or little, not asking for more but letting it serve his own sustenance for the day, so also man has to accept the heavenly grace as the free gift it is. In the two gestures displayed by the Buddha image the whole programme of man's spiritual exigencies is summed up.

Toward the earth, that is to say toward the world to which he belongs by his existence, man's gesture is *active*; such an active attitude is always needed where the world and its manifold temptations and distractions are concerned. Toward heaven and its gifts, on the other hand, the spiritual man is *passive*; he is content to receive the dew of grace as and when it falls and to refresh his more or less flagging powers with its aid. As for the ignorant man, he does just the reverse, showing himself soft and accommodating toward the world while making all kinds of conditions of his own choosing where the things of heaven are concerned, if indeed he deigns to give them any thought at all. For the truly mindful man, even his own *karma* can be both grace and *guru*, not merely in the sense of reward or sanction imposed by a cosmic law, but because *karma* is a potent and inescapable reminder of enlightenment as the crying need of man and as the only unequivocally reasonable object of his desires. Accepted in this sense, *karma*, be it good or evil, can be welcomed as Sāvitrī once welcomed Death when he came to claim her husband and by her resignation overcame him. Contemplated rightly, the Buddha's sacramental image tells us all these things. For us it is the means of grace *par excellence*.[11]

Coomaraswamy on frequent occasions used the terms 'the symbolism which knows' and 'the symbolism which seeks' so as to distinguish between the reliable and the unreliable forms of symbolic representation. He used them to highlight the arbitrary nature of contemporary, self-expressive literature as compared with the 'measured' nature and tone of canonical art. He argued that the former could evoke a limited, 'local' interest only, and curiosity rather than informed interest, especially where the artist, *as* an individual, aspired to 'make his mark' and to be 'original'.

Without actually embarking on an extensive examination of the literary movement of Symbolism, it will be useful to point to the highly eclectic nature of the ideas that its proponents cherished.

Further, one can say that at least where the Russian wing of the movement was concerned, many Symbolists were notorious for their dilettante excursions into the occult, and that not a few of these were self-avowed 'Decadents'. Apocalyptic interpretations of the 1905 revolution were in vogue, the fruit of understandable political aspirations and a keen sense of history. However, this flux of ideas, rich as it may have been in terms of a generalized sense of anticipation, yielded notably less in terms of defining goals and practical courses of action, on the individual and collective level. The literature of the period was abundant in literary manifestos, political programmes, utopian declarations, tracts, and statements of belief, definitions and redefinitions, virtually all of which reflect the uncompromising seriousness with which ideas were taken, even quite outlandish ones. Given this climate, it would be unrealistic to expect any unanimity of purpose among the leading figures, whose various writings were often accorded almost oracular significance. And in the absence of unanimity one would not expect to find a 'symbolism which *knows*'.

In the view of Coomaraswamy and other exponents of Perennial Philosophy, the scriptural mode of expression is eminently suited to the gradual transmission of spiritual insights, which accords with the level of understanding attained by the disciple.[12] Many teachings come in the form of parables, because a less oblique expression of truth would not serve the purposes of instruction as readily. And yet, while the parable achieves simplicity of a unique kind at the literal level of interpretation, every tradition, whether Christian, Buddhist or Hindu, regards as indispensable guidance and instruction from someone who has verified for himself what is treated in the scriptural literature. The instructor can determine the lesson to be taught, but a whole range of means of transmission is available to him within his tradition. Rather than having to impose the truth in any external manner, he may, by a judicious choice of means, be simply the *occasion* for the growth or deepening of insight in the disciple. Answering also the Socratic ideal of 'education' (drawing out), he plays the role of the *midwife* in this process.[13]

In the light of the foregoing considerations, I now propose to examine Coomaraswamy's work *Spiritual Authority and Temporal Power in the Indian Theory of Government*. His treatment of the Rājasūya ceremony is particularly suited to demonstration of the consistency of authentic religious symbolism. It merits serious consideration, first, as an account of consistent symbolism that accords with traditional scriptural authority. Second, it strikes one as presenting a useful and instructive analogy between on the one hand the government of a state by the religious and temporal authorities, the high priest and the king; and on the other hand the individual man's need to resolve internal conflict produced by differing sides of his nature.

The point of comparison is that of *effective rule* — rule over the collective body of a king's subjects, and rule over mutually opposed elements in the individual man. In terms of quite practical worth, what is referred to as the 'royal road' to self-mastery provides a more useful goal for man than the elevation of self-expression as virtually an end in itself, which the modern sense of individualism promotes.

As the title of the book indicates, its central theme is the nature of the relationship between the representatives of spiritual authority and of temporal power in a state, the high priest and the king. The priest's sphere of operation is here termed Sacerdotium, and the king's sphere the Regnum. We shall see that from the very outset the relationship between them is equated with marital union. The status of these partners is clarified, and its significance reinforced, by an extensive range of parallel relationships, where the mythic and other partners would be very familiar to the participant in the ceremony. Later we will see how the overall pattern of parallels and mutual references gives substantial weight to the central teaching which the text imparts. Coomaraswamy introduces his study thus (p. 1):

> It may be said that the whole of Indian political theory is implied and subsumed in the words of the marriage formula 'I am That, thou art This, I am Sky, thou art Earth' addressed by the Brahman Priest, the Purohita, to the King in AB VIII,27.

Though it will be made clear by subsequent illustration, Coomaraswamy asserts at the beginning that the king 'is unquestionably the ''feminine'' party in the marriage' of the Sacerdotium and the Regnum (p. 2).[14]

Ideally what is sought is the two partners' unanimity of purpose, and their harmonious co-operation to secure or realize that purpose which is to ensure the welfare of all in the kingdom, because that is what the king is specifically charged to do. That is his calling or *svadharma*, and it is the end for which he is entrusted with power.

These considerations may appear self-evident, but the presence of a person in the state who is endowed with power that does not derive from the king's power, or that is of different order from his, has provoked numerous historical instances of dissent and rivalry. In the course of European history the respective status of the monarch and the head of the church has been contested in various ways, fought over and legally disputed, though Judaic and other models of a theocratic state do exist. In India their mutual relationship is referred to in the RV and defined in the Brāhmaṇas.

Virtually at the start Coomaraswamy introduces the notion that Mitra and Agni serve as divine archetypes of the Sacerdotium, and Varuṇa and Indra of the Regnum. The position of the king as *agent* in relation to the high priest is established early on, and the claim is supported by Coomaraswamy's reference (pp. 3 – 5) to RV 100,1:

> The feudal relationship of the Regnum to the Sacerdotium is explicit in Agni's words addressed to Indra — 'I in person go before thee . . . and if thou givest me my share (or due), then shalt thou through me, O Indra, perform heroic deeds'.[15]

In his relationship to the king and in other respects the priest's role is essentially a 'directive' one. Coomaraswamy underlines the point that the king is not only the 'feminine' in the pair, but he represents the 'part' as distinct from the 'whole'; the king stands in need of 'completion'. Here the figures of Mitra and Varuṇa assume significance, and it becomes clear that the priest and king do not stand on equal terms. Coomaraswamy provides an explanation of the metaphysical principles involved:

> The Infinite . ... always includes the Finite as 'its own', of which it cannot be deprived whether logically or really . . . It is the Finite nature that can be logically if not really isolated from the Infinite and therefore stands in need of 'completion' (p. 8).

He then notes the following words of the AB:

> Whatever deed (*karma*) Varuṇa did that was not quickened by Mitra, the Sacerdotium, was not successful. So Varuṇa, the Regnum, called upon Mitra, the Sacerdotium, saying: 'Turn you unto me that we may unite; I assign to you the precedence; quickened by thee, I shall do deeds'. (Ibid.)

He further notes, in keeping with the spirit of AB, that the term *purohita* itself means 'one who takes precedence'. He further explains that the priest invokes the deities, notably Savitṛ, specifically as 'king-quickeners' (*rājasvaḥ*), and that the Rājasūya itself is 'the sacrificial and initiatory ritual of the king's quickening' (p. 9).

The symbolism is very exact: the king is brought forth 'new-born' and the officiating priests are in a sense the 'fathers' who beget him. After the rite, which entails aspersion as its most essential element, the king is clothed in entirely new robes. He discards his old robes like the old, worn skin from which the snake emerges.

The king's immersion in water has a twofold significance: that of a symbolic death of the 'old' man, and that of a baptism for the newly-emerged man, free from sin and from 'all that pertains to Varuṇa' (p. 11). This motif is echoed in the AV 14,2,44: 'Clothing myself anew . . . as a bird from an egg, I am freed from all sin.'

Before proceeding any further with Coomaraswamy's account of the symbolic values attached to the king's initiation rites, the Rājasūya itself, it will be useful to note some of the 'pairs' which reflect the relationship between king and priest.

The counterparts of Heaven and Earth in male and female roles are central to the Indian conception of existence. The recurrence of this Heaven/Earth polarity in virtually all mythologies and scriptural traditions is so plain and striking that it has been studied very extensively, not least by Coomaraswamy himself.[16]

In the work of his under discussion he again acknowledges the central place of the Heaven/Earth polarity, and shows it as the reciprocal relationship by which all other 'pairs' are judged or measured. Coomaraswamy underlines the import of some of these complementary pairs, although they feature less frequently and less prominently in mythological and religious studies than the fundamental pairs of Heaven/Earth and male/female.

I shall briefly catalogue some of these complementary pairs. Consistent with the symbolism of sacrifice expressed in AB, the high priest was regarded as director and the king represented the executive branch of government. This relationship is brought out by alluding to the complementary pair contemplation/action. The complementarity of the contemplative life and the active life is an established notion in Indian tradition.[17] Coomaraswamy notes:

> Inasmuch as the King is the Executive (*kartṛ*) his is essentially the *karmamārga*, the 'active life', as distinguished from the *jñānamārga*, the 'contemplative life', of the Brahman (p. 5).

A further pair is that of *manas/vāc*, or intellect/voice. *Vāc* has the status of messenger or agent here, and is only genuinely 'eloquent' when speaking on behalf of *manas* rather than for itself. As the ŚB III says: 'Intellect takes precedence of voice . . . and were it not for intellect, the voice would only babble.'

There is a direct connection between the pair *manas/vāc* and another pair, *sāman/ṛc*, the chant and the verse. Just as the voice in the absence of intellect only babbles, so — points out Coomaraswamy — the words of the chant without the chant itself produce a mere cacophony and not a harmony.

The recurrence of symbols connected with audition is not a random affair in Indian tradition. Its bearing on the theme of rule and kingship is a direct one: the king is the 'voice' that 'gives effect to the purposes of the spiritual authority, and thus does the will of god on earth'. He *enunciates* the will of the higher authority that delegated power to him, and his sceptre is quite specifically a symbol of delegated power (p. 3). He may rightly be termed a 'viceroy', but he is a necessary element in the process of government: without his participation or 'support' the will of the higher authority could not be enunciated or put into effect (pp. 12 – 13).

The idea of audition and auditory revelation is also expressed in the pairing of *śabda brahma/aśabda brahma* and of the preaching Buddha and the silent Buddha.

Further pairing equivalents are thought to be found in the terminology and philosophy of art: for instance, the priest can be equated with the patron who determines what the artist creates, while the king and the artist are in like manner responsible for the actual execution of an idea.[18] A second instance is the traditional explanation of artistic production as a twofold operation, that is, a matter of intellectual *conception*, which corresponds to the figure of high priest, followed by technical *execution* of the idea conceived, corresponding to the king.[19]

Returning now to the specific matter of the king's status and his acceptance of the power delegated to him, we already know that the ceremony entailed the discarding of the old garments by the yet uninitiated prince, and an immersion and 'drowning' of the 'old' man, a sacrificial death preceding the birth and 'baptism' of the 'new' man, now king. Coomaraswamy notes (p. 10): 'All that is said elsewhere of the ritual death and rebirth of the Sacrificer can be applied to the King, *a fortiori*.'

The fact that the new king received the sceptre or visible symbol of his kingship from the high priest makes him weaker with respect to the high priest (and feminine, receptive); but at the very same time the king is considered to be *male* in relation to his kingdom — he is 'espoused' to it, and his is said to be a virile power for that reason. He shoots arrows to the four quarters as a symbolic representation of this relationship of dominion. But, as Coomaraswamy notes subsequently (p. 16), 'The King is only a true King in so far as he is in possession of his "Royal art", in so far as he does not fail of the end, and does not "miss his mark".'[20]

Here it can be brought out that the traditional conception of kingship (in India and likewise in Europe) entailed *skill*. Effective government required the employment of skill, and it was indeed considered to be 'artful'. Certainly these terms apply eminently, for example, to the reign of king Aśoka.

It becomes increasingly plain from the nature of the references traced so far, that the model of kingship here studied by Coomaraswamy is at no point divorced from an ideal of spiritual attainment. This is of absolutely central importance. The principle of 'as above so below' determines the procedure of high priest and king, as it determines the delegation of power from the former to the latter.

More generally, one might make some observation about 'skill' or 'skilful action'. The Sanskrit word *kauśala* signifying 'skill' is applicable not only to the artist or craftsman and his creative work, but to the 'creative' skill of right government or statesmanship, and in a quite clear way it also refers to spiritual endeavour — it is an 'active wisdom'. The triple application of the word *kauśala* in this way might serve well to indicate the degree of discernment and insight ideally sought in the Hindu artist, ruler and ascetic and in their Buddhist, Christian, Islamic or other counterparts.

We have seen earlier that the Rājasūya ceremony entails a sacrificial death of the king's old persona, a casting off of his old 'skin' so that a new, better and purified self may emerge. It is in this context that the figures of Mitra and Varuṇa assume importance. Says Coomaraswamy: 'The intention is to enthrone as King not a "Varuṇa", but a "Mitra" ' (p. 10).

In a variety of ways Varuṇa represents a force or principle *hostile* to men. He lies in the waters, facing the current, with his jaws open and ready to consume men who come in his path. In other contexts he is the god of privation and drought. And, as Coomaraswamy explains, he is also conceived of as holding or tying up men with a noose or rope. Noting the assimilation of Varuṇa and Vṛtra, mentioned in AV 3,13,1 – 2, Coomaraswamy explains that Varuṇa ' "seizes" the waters and makes them stagnant, while it is the flowing "living waters", divine and fit for sacrificial use, that Indra frees from Vṛtra' (p. 30).

However, men's necessary course of action is to *befriend* Varuṇa, to act so as to turn him from an enemy into a friend and to effect a *conversion* in him. If this conversion is a genuine one, it will entail 'death' and disappearance of the enemy and the 'birth' of a friend. Only upon that basis are men going to achieve liberation from Varuṇa's binding knot or noose.

I can summarize Coomaraswamy's exposition of the symbolism associated with Varuṇa only briefly. He himself, in all his writings, treated this and all the other themes with which he was concerned most thoroughly; in order to present the sceptical academic readership, very positivistic in attitude and even hostile to his message, with incontrovertible evidence.[21] Moreover, the enumeration of tracing of symbols was not for him an end in itself. Far from being content with merely 'literary', i.e. passive, appreciation of traditional religious symbolism (which in his view amounts to *lack* of appreciation), he emphasized the close and necessary link between the *understanding* of symbols, and the philosophical bases which underpin specific spiritual disciplines or paths. He took pains to show symbols both as *means* to increased understanding and as 'points of departure for a spiritual discipline'.

Taking the symbol of Varuṇa's noose that ties men down, Coomaraswamy asks the crucial question, about what release from it might ultimately mean. He answers himself thus: 'To be wholly free is to be released from Name and Shape (*nāma-rūpa*)' (p. 31).

This accords with AAr 1,6 which holds that 'names themselves are knots' and with ŚB 4,6,5,3 that 'everything here is gripped by name'. This end or ultimate purpose is the very same end towards which a wide range of Indian spiritual and contemplative discipline — Hindu, Buddhist, Jain and others — aim, namely to get beyond contingent being, beyond the conditioned and named.

The meaning of the conversion of Varuṇa into a friend is, for Coomaraswamy, an actual 'conversion' within the heart of men, the second 'birth', to be valued most highly, far above the mere physical birth from a woman.

As said before, only unanimity in aim and action between the high priest and the king can ensure the welfare of all the king's subjects. The high priest's authority and the king's authority are not identical, but the bond between the two figures must be very close and is, as we know, likened to marital union. Of special relevance to the definition of this relation is Coomaraswamy's observation that 'marriage implies *trans*-formation of the second party by assimilation' (p. 37). This and other relationships are directly elucidated by the theme of the marriage between Sky and Earth and they can be measured in terms of it. Coomaraswamy further observes:

> Amongst the syzygies to which we have referred, it is that of Two Worlds, Sky and Earth, the Universal Parents upon whose harmony depend the posterity and fertility of the entire universe, which is chiefly taken to be the norm and archetype of all marriage (p. 39).

The network of mutually reinforcing images is as great as could be: not only is the Sky masculine in its relation to the Earth, but it is also feminine in relation to the Sun. Mitra represents the Sun which inseminates Varuṇa, the Sky; and, consistent with this, Mitra is designated as seed and Varuṇa as the womb. Coomaraswamy affirms that 'effective and productive coupling' depends on 'a conjunction (*mithuna*) of contrasted forms' (p. 40). Subsequently he writes:

We are now in a better position to understand the mutual choice or 'wooing' of one another by the High Priest and the King, and to understand the marriage formula with which the alliance of their 'houses' is effected in AB VIII,27 (p. 51).

The critical respect in which the king must 'provide for' his people is, points out Coomaraswamy, to ensure that the sacrifice can be performed, i.e. he must 'provide for' the sacrifice:

Unless the King fulfils his primary function as Patron of the Sacrifice, the circulation of the 'shower of wealth, the limitless, inexhaustible food of the Gods' that falls from the Sky as rain and is returned from the Earth to the Sky in the smoke of the burnt offering, will be interrupted (p. 68; cf. ŚB 3,3,15,16).

The truly and completely effective ruler is able to 'provide for' his subjects' immortal *and* their mortal natures. Such is the burden of the traditional Indian theory of government. But it does not present a king who is self-sufficient or even self-assertive, although, of course, the king may choose not to follow the *purohita*. Coomaraswamy clarifies the position in the AB:

In our text it is clear that the choice *has* been made, and the spoken words are those of the Purohita expressing his acceptance of the King, whom he will 'cause to perform right acts', and therefore to prosper (p. 62).

The king's efficacy is a 'grace', a freely given *gift*. The gift cannot be duly valued or appreciated by an unreceptive ruler who wishes to govern in his own right.

It is wholly consistent with the fundamental idea of 'government' or 'rule' that it applies to the individual no less than to the nation. As Coomaraswamy puts it:

This doctrine has also a self-referrant (*adhyātman*) application; the question is not only of a universal and a national or civic order, but also of an *internal economy* (p. 71).

The self-assertion of man's ego or self can be likened to the rule, or rather the misrule, of a tyrant who has appropriated the power of another. Coomaraswamy attributes this self-assertive way of action to ignorance (*avidyā*):

We are naturally at war with ourselves and often not merely at war with 'what is divine in us', but ignorant of it because of our notion that 'I am the doer' (pp. 78 – 9).

The relationship between our outer, active and 'feminine' self and our inner, contemplative and 'masculine' self is, to a greater or lesser extent, disordered or disturbed. These selves need to be 'wedded', and when they are truly so, their union will mirror the relationship of Sky and Earth, Mitra and Varuṇa, Kṛṣṇa and Arjuna, the *aśabda brahman* and *śabda brahman*. That is, it will be 'not indeed an equality, but a true reciprocity' (p. 69). The central teaching here is that this 'marriage' is an indispensable condition for *efficacious action*:

There is nothing that can be truly and well done except by the man in whom the marriage of the Sacerdotium and the Regnum has been consummated, nor can any peace be made except by those who have made their peace with themselves (p. 87).

Though this study on spiritual authority and temporal power in Indian theory implies a picture of society as a highly ordered hierarchy, it is in no sense consistent with the idea of exclusive or tyrannical rule. Indeed, one of Coomaraswamy's most important and telling conclusions is:

The Kingship envisaged by the Indian and traditional doctrine is as far removed as could well be from what we mean when we speak of an Absolute Monarchy or of 'individualism' (p. 86).

As in the Islamic context the Jihad or holy war is understood to refer most truly to the inner battle between our two selves rather than to actual war, so here *skill in ruling* refers most eminently to self-rule and self-conquest as distinct from rule over the 'body politic', the state. And the *way* towards attainment of composure and control is even referred to, on occasions, as 'the royal road' to self-mastery.

All the foregoing examination of inter-related symbols of 'government' provides Coomaraswamy with sure evidence for his conclusion, namely that, 'The essence of the traditional politics amounts to this, that "self-government" (*svarāj*) depends upon self-control (*ātmasamyama*), rule on ruliness' (p. 85).[22]

CONCLUSION

The Rājasūya ceremony endows a king with temporal power, and this fulfils a need both practical and ritual for the community of his subjects. The general welfare of the community is the king's direct responsibility, and what is required is his public acceptance of that responsibility, his undertaking to provide for his people and rule effectively.

The words or formulas of the ceremony affirm the worth of numerous so-called 'royal' qualities: the exercise of a benevolent will, sobriety and restraint, a skill in just administration, and others. But the ceremony affirms the ultimate value of *svarāj*, self-conquest. Through the symbolic motif of temporal rule of a kingdom, the far-reaching effects of self-conquest are presented in a way that is at once graphic and instructive. Conversely, of course, the lack of self-rule in an individual can be recognized as harmful in its effects by comparison with the lack of rule at a national and at a cosmic level.

The symbols that recur in this ceremony, and in the scriptural sources from which it derives its authority, impart knowledge and awareness of the need to 'bring one's house in order'. It is for each individual to resolve the conflict between his 'outer king' and his 'inner sage', Coomaraswamy's Regnum and Sacerdotium.

Coomaraswamy presents the central idea in his study as an inwardly coherent teaching that requires no extension, and certainly no dilution. As is always his approach with the canonical literature of Hinduism, Buddhism and the other traditions, he refrains entirely from statements of a purely personal view, because personal opinions have negligible bearing on the essential impact of teachings in the scriptures. His intention always was to draw together scriptural passages that affirm the worth and significance inherent in endeavours of self-discovery. Certainly he presents a persuasive argument for the view that the actions of men are *not* random, arbitrary or 'meaning'-less in their effects. Coomaraswamy's various writings establish the idea that scriptural literature and iconographically 'true' works of art redirect the sufficiently receptive observer away from distractions and towards recognition of 'what he *is*'. But this rediscovery of oneself requires more than what we commonly understand by 'observation'. It requires a decisive *reorientation* that one should call 'participation' in the truth expressed by an icon rather than mere 'observation' of it.

I hope to have accounted adequately for, and illustrated sufficiently, Coomaraswamy's recognition of the decisive function that symbols fulfil within any authentic religious tradition. It seems to me that his recognition of this function informed his whole mode of thought and his writings. Certainly his books and essays could not rightly be considered *apart* from his full acceptance of each of the major religious traditions as paths of spiritual attainment and liberation.

NOTES

1 Ananda K. Coomaraswamy, *Selected Works I–II* (Commemorative Edition), edited by Roger Lipsey, Princeton U.P., 1977 (Bollingen Series LXXXIX), vol. I: *Selected Papers*, editor's Introduction, p. XXXIII.
2 Ananda K. Coomaraswamy, *Spiritual Authority and Temporal Power in the Indian Theory of Government*, New Haven, USA, 1942.
3 Ananda K. Coomaraswamy, *Christian and Oriental Philosophy of Art*, Dover Books, 1956, p. 30.
4 'Figures of Speech, or Figures of Thought', an essay in *Selected Papers*, p. 27ff.
5 Ibid., p. 19.
6 *Selected Papers*, p. 241, the essay 'Ornament'.
7 'Figures of Speech, or Figures of Thought'. *Selected Papers*, p. 40.
8 Ibid., p. 30.
9 Ibid., p. 39 (notes).
10 *Christian and Oriental Philosophy of Art*, p. 18.
11 Marco Pallis, 'Is there room for "Grace" in Buddhism?', SCR, vol. 2, no. 4 (autumn 1968).
12 See T. R. V. Murti, *The Central Philosophy of Buddhism*, London, 1955, repr. (paperback) 1980, pp. 42–3, 45, 207, 247, 278, *et al.*
13 Cf. M. Conrad Hyer, *Zen and the Comic Spirit*, London, 1974.
14 The Russian religious philosopher Vladimir Solovyov (1853–1900) devised a formula for theocratic government that included three figures, the high priest, king and prophet. See his *Istoriya i Budushchnost' Teokratii* (The history and future of theocracy, 1885–87), *Collected Works*, vol. IV, 241–633, Brussels, 1966.
15 For definitions of theocracy, see ERE, vol. XII, pp. 287–9; also *Encyclopaedia Britannica*, 11th ed., vol. XXVI, p. 760.
16 In his two essays: 'The Symbolism of the Dome' and 'The Inverted Tree', included in the *Selected Papers*.
17 Cf. M. Hiriyana, *Indian Conception of Values*, Mysore, 1975, p. 224. — For extensive materials on the reciprocity of contemplation and action, see *Traditional Modes of Contemplation and Action* (Papers from a Colloquium held at Houston, Texas, 1973), ed. Y. Ibish, London, 1976.
18 The subject of true patronage is more extensively treated in other Coomaraswamy's works, such as the already quoted *Christian and Oriental Philosophy of Art*, and this is a matter about which he felt very

strongly, in part because the modern concern with the artist's self-expression does not accommodate the valid notion of patronage.

19 This twofold procedure is explained from the Indian and from the European scholastic points of view in Coomaraswamy's essay 'The Intellectual Operation in Indian Art', *Selected Papers*, pp. 131 – 46.

20 On kingship in India see Ahjita Kumāra Sen, *Studies in Hindu Political Theory*, Calcutta, 1926, ch. 4; A. S. Altekar, *State and Government in Ancient India*, Delhi, 1949, ch. 5; Vishvanath Prasad Varma, *Studies in Hindu Political Thought and its Metaphysical Foundation*, Delhi, 1959, esp. ch. 4.

21 This point was suggested by a former pupil of Coomaraswamy in the U.S.A., Whittal. N. Perry, in his review article 'The Bollingen Coomaraswamy Papers and Biography', SCR, Autumn 1977, p. 208.

22 For further new material on the thought and influence of Coomaraswamy, see *Paroksa: Coomaraswamy Centenary Seminar Papers*, Lalit Kala Akademi, Delhi, 1984. Contributions by Roger Lipsey and many others, from a seminar in New Delhi on 19 – 20 December 1977.

10

THE POSSIBILITY OF SYMBOLISM IN INDIAN RELIGIONS

David Bastow

I wish to sketch a theory about the possibility of symbolism in general, based on the question 'What must be the relation between X and Y, for X to be a possible symbol for Y?' The theory will claim that if X is to be a fruitful symbol for Y, one capable of creative exploration, X and Y must be ontologically related; at the deepest level, the relation will be metaphysical. One primary role which symbols play in religions is to mediate between the religious believer and the focus of the religion; religions also typically provide a world view or metaphysics, to which one might look for deep links between symbol and the symbolized focus. I shall, further, explore how this works in Indian religions, making particular reference to the examples of symbolism provided by the other contributors to this book.

SECTION 1: A DEFINITION OF 'SYMBOL'

This will be a stipulative definition; that is, it does not aim to describe current English usage of the word 'symbol', which is vague and ambiguous, but to provide a reasonably sharp tool which will be useful for my purpose. The definition is this: a symbol is a sign which is semantically non-arbitrary.

In this definition, a sign is anything that can have meaning; a symbol is a special kind of sign. Signs may be semantically arbitrary, or non-arbitrary, or to some extent arbitrary; so a sign can be to some extent a symbol. This concept of arbitrariness comes from de Saussure. He explains it thus:

> The idea of 'sister' is not linked by any inner relationship to the succession of sounds *s-o-r* which serves as its signifier in French; that it could be represented equally by just any other sequence is proved by differences among languages and by the very existence of different languages.[1]

It is generally agreed that such semantically arbitrary signs as 'sister' have meaning because of the existence of interpersonal conventions. De Saussure says that the arbitrariness (in this sense) of linguistic signs is a reason for not using the word 'symbol' for them, because

> One characteristic of the symbol is that it is never wholly arbitrary; it is not empty, for there is the rudiment of a natural bond between the signifier and the signified. The symbol of justice, a pair of scales, could not be replaced by just any other symbol, such as a chariot.[2]

De Saussure talks of 'inner relationship' and 'natural bond'; I shall show later how Indian religions provide such relationships or bonds between their symbols and what they symbolize.

The link between arbitrary signs and their meaning is explained by reference to conventions. It is true that many features of these conventions are far from arbitrary; the grammarian shows the systematic interrelation of the conventions; the etymologist shows how the conventions originated. Nevertheless, de Saussure is right to point to the sense in which an idea, conventionally represented (in a given language) by a certain succession of sounds, 'could be represented equally by any other succession of sounds'. How then are we to explain the link between symbols, non-arbitrary signs, and their meaning? I shall answer this question in general terms first, and then apply my answer to particular cases of religious symbolism.

Symbolism works in virtue of some feature of the thing which is being used as a symbol which links it to the thing symbolized. The more deep-seated is this real relation between the thing used as a symbol and the thing which it is being used to symbolize, the richer, the more productive, is the symbolism.

We may consider an example from Shakespeare's Sonnet 2, in which he likens the wrinkles of old age to the trenches dug by a besieging army:

> When fortie Winters shall besiege thy brow,
> And digge deep trenches in thy beauties field . . .

The topic of the poem is old age (and ways of combatting it); the military image constitutes an attempt to say something about old age, and in fact is used as a symbol for it. It seems to me that this symbolization is justified by two quite different levels or degrees of relation between the things being compared.

The specific comparison between trenches and wrinkles is justified by a rough similarity of shape, which the poet finds useful for the moment, but which cannot be further explored or elaborated. Other features of military trenches — that soldiers crouch in them to shelter from enemy fire, etc. — are quite unrelated to any other feature of wrinkles on a person's face. In fact, in this case most of us are more familiar with wrinkles than with trenches, so the comparison does not improve our knowledge of the physical nature of wrinkles. It works in the poem, if it does work, because of its unexpectedness; its superficiality makes it witty; it is a conceit, a *jeu d'esprit*. Here the symbol may be said to be shallow or superficial, because it rests on only one point of similarity between symbol and thing symbolized.

Other almost equally superficial metaphors may be more useful; such as the Buddhist idea that doctrinal beliefs are like a raft in that they are essential for the journey along the path to liberation, but are to be abandoned once their purpose has been served. This image makes the idea of provisionality easily graspable, and so memorable; but those who, thinking more deeply about the provisionality claim, realize its difficulties and its profound implications, will get no further help from thinking more deeply about the nature of rafts. The raft-image is itself raft-like, in being of only provisional and limited use. The related comparison between *saṁsāra* and a river, though, is more profound, given the Buddhist 'philosophy of flux'. According to the doctrines of *anicca* and *anatta*, every worldly thing, even the most apparently substantial, has no more essential identity or thingness than does a river. The river is an appropriate symbol for *saṁsāra*, because it exhibits openly a metaphysical nature which it has in common with other worldly things, but which in these other things is, for the worldly onlooker, hidden.

In Shakespeare's sonnet, the trench/wrinkle image, which I have so far treated in isolation, could be seen in the context of a wider image, which is sketched in the surrounding lines of Sonnet 2, and appears again in the second quatrain of Sonnet 65. This is the comparison between the attacks of a besieging army and the onset of old age.

This way of thinking about old age is very far from superficial. It contains the implication that old age is to be seen as an attack on the integrity of the person, coming from the outside; not part of the nature of personhood, but a contingent and catastrophic threat to it. It is an enemy, to be resisted for as long as one's strength holds out. And to go further back, or to explore the image more deeply, war and old age do not just happen to have these many and profound characteristics in common, we do not have here just a more elaborate conceit. War and old age both partake of the essential nature of human suffering: having its origins far beyond the control of the individual person, threatening his very survival, to be resisted doggedly but perhaps in the end hopelessly.

This last sentence of mine contains what may be called a theory of the nature of suffering. It is of course controversial; it is for example very different from the account of suffering given within the Indian doctrine of *karma*. But I am claiming that it is in the light of this theory, or something like it, that war and old age are deeply linked, so that war can act as a powerful symbol for old age.

The question of the truth of such theories does not often arise in our reading of literature. The modern Western view of the nature of art (very different from the traditional view described in Sutton's paper on Coomaraswamy) is such that on the whole we are content to value literature for the *possible* views of the world which it presents. We ask of these views only that they should be plausible, illuminating; not that they should be true in a way which excludes the truth of contrasting or conflicting views. But religions do have their own world-views; it is these, I am suggesting, which provide the grounding relation between symbol and focus.

So something used as a symbol is non-arbitrarily related to what it symbolizes; this relation may be more or less superficial or deep. Sometimes it seems that the relationship is so profound that the light the symbol throws on what is symbolized can be explored without end — as can the meaning of a great work of art. Many writers have pointed out that some imagery invites creative interpretation; it provides an occasion for the reader or 'understander' to explore for himself the symbolic relationship. Such an exploration may go beyond what the poet or artist or religious symbol-finder 'had in mind'. In fact the poet's thoughts are hardly relevant, for the relationship is in no sense the poet's creation; it exists, one may say, in the nature of things. In the poetic use of a shallow relationship, the point of similarity certainly exists independently of the poet — it is the case that trenches and wrinkles are both indentations — but here the bringing together of the two is the poet's doing. In a deep relationship the closeness is already there.

Even a symbol which is deeply grounded will be rich and fruitful only in some directions. In the typical case, not every aspect of the symbol will throw light on what is symbolized; in the image of old age as being besieged by an enemy in war, the fact that soldiers wear uniforms is of no symbolic significance. Similarly, arguments from analogy, which can only be valid if they rest on some real connection between the two terms of the analogy, always have to be used with caution; for they operate surrounded, as it were, by disanalogies. Otherwise the two terms would not be distinct in the first place.

SECTION 2. RELIGIOUS USES OF SYMBOLISM

Symbols may play many roles in religions; but a primary one will obviously be to bring the believer closer to, or into harmony with, the focus of religion.[3] This closeness may be a matter of knowledge or understanding, such as may be achieved for example by the study of theology; but more religiously important will be a harmony of wills, or the realization of a kind of identity, or the kind of self change which is required on the Buddhist path. How can symbols play this role? By mediating between the focus and the believer. That is, the religion postulates, the believer accepts and experiences, some kind of gulf between the believer and the focus. This gulf is, from the believer's point of view, unsatisfactory. He looks to his religion for salvation or liberation or enlightenment, to be achieved by the crossing of the gulf. The symbol acts as a bridge, to help in this gulf-crossing.

I shall suggest a model of how this may happen; the model is too simple for many actual cases, but will provide a useful point of reference. The focus is, by the nature of the gulf, inaccessible to the believer; perhaps its transcendence makes it unapproachable or incomprehensible. The symbol of the focus is, though, comprehensible; this implies that it must be in some way worldly, to be suited to the believer's understanding. But to be a bridge the symbol must be related to both sides of the gulf, so it must have some type of relationship to the focus. At this point the general theory of symbolism which I expounded in Section 1 becomes relevant. I argued there that symbols may be more or less rich and fruitful; this will depend on the degree of real relationship there is between the thing which is used as a symbol and that which it symbolizes. It would seem to follow that if the religious symbol is to play a crucial and fruitful role in gulf-bridging, it must be deeply related to the religious focus. Since the symbol will itself be worldly, the world or part of it must have a close relationship to the focus. One relationship which may provide the necessary closeness is that the world is the *creation* of the focus; I shall discuss others later on.

It is sometimes important to address the question: who is the user of the symbol? If the cosmology is such as to provide a full and comprehensive relation between world and focus — as when for example the natural world in all its details is to be seen as the creation of the focus — then a rich source of symbolism is available to the religious tradition; it may be used by religious teachers, or by ordinary believers seeking to express their religious situation, to the religious benefit of themselves or their fellow believers. But sometimes a central religious symbol is seen as the result of a specially intended act of self-presentation on the part of the focus — a special 'revelation'.

Such epiphanies may themselves make deep or shallow use of their symbols, or worldly vehicles. In the story of the burning bush (Exodus 3,2) it seems that it is only the strangeness of the bush which burns and is not consumed, which is used by the angel of God to attract Moses' attention. This strangeness symbolizes the 'otherness' of God; 'the place on which you are standing is holy ground'. But nothing more is made of the specific nature of the symbol. At the other extreme, nothing could be more profound than the sense in which God is in Christ.

The situation in the great epiphany of the BhG XI is complex (and controversial). The Lord shows to Arjuna his 'divine form' (*rūpam aiśvaram*); to see this is to see the Lord, presumably as to see a person's body is to see that person, not a symbol of the person. But the contents of the vision include images which do seem symbolic; the 'mouths with jagged ghastly tusks' which consume the warriors, the flaming mouths which devour 'worlds, universes, everything' (V,30), represent, as Arjuna surmises and Kṛṣṇa confirms, Time the destroyer. Is the Lord here graciously making use of a symbol, presenting himself through it, for Arjuna's benefit? Or perhaps this visual symbol of Time is introduced for the benefit of us, the readers of the BhG, who do not have the 'heavenly eye' which Arjuna was given.

The model of religious symbolism as it has been developed so far assumes that the symbols used in a religion are recognized within the religious tradition to be symbols. The members of the religion know of something that it is a symbol — has a meaning in virtue of which it points to something other than itself; and are aware that what it tells them about is the focus of the religion. So there are religious concepts of symbolism, that is concepts used within the religion which show awareness that symbolic (in my sense of the term) relationships are operating. Examples of such concepts are: parable, ritual, sacramental object such as god-image, incarnation, skilful means.

This assumption is in general true of the examples of religious symbolism discussed elsewhere in this book. It is not clear to me whether it is true of Jungian interpretations, such as those suggested by Miller in her account of the Vena-Pṛthu sequence of stories. The interaction between Pṛthu and the Earth Cow certainly has the character of a founding myth, specifying the original and essential relation between man and nature. But for Miller the Earth Cow represents, psychologically, the unconscious, from which the surface consciousness feeds. When the cow is pursued from world to world it implies, in Miller's understanding, gradual penetration into all levels of the unconscious by the conscious ego-complex which thus gains control over it and may achieve release of pent-up energies.

The terminology here is modern; is the suggestion that the psychological concepts were in some sense available at the time when the myth was first current; is the interpretation internal or external to the religious tradition itself?

Miller also suggests, at the end of Part I of her paper, an interpretation which is more obviously religious in the sense in which I have been using the term: she asks whether Vena symbolizes mankind in its corrupt state, but still capable of redemption as shown by the new race personified in Pṛthu, born through 'divine grace', who redeems his fallen parent.

The teaching device of 'personification' to point out a religious moral — that is a moral about how a man may become closer to the focus of his religion — was famously used by John Bunyan in *Pilgrim's Progress*. The possibility of this device rests perhaps not on any particular psychological theory such as that of Jung, nor on any specifically religious cosmology such as those to be described in my next section; but rather on the common experience that debates within oneself are not essentially different in form from debates between oneself and other people.

Miller argues convincingly that the Vena story shows the nature and consequences of a life lived in wilful opposition to *dharma*. It shows the truth that the wise man lives a dharmic life by being an instance or example of it. The story has a vivid particularity which is much more effective than an abstract statement of *dharma* as duty; though of course not every particular element of the story can be taken as revealing an aspect of the general truth.

SECTION 3. SYMBOLISM IN INDIAN RELIGIONS

It follows, I have argued, from my general theory of symbolism, that when, in religions, symbols are used to bring the believer closer to the religious focus, there must be some real (non-arbitrary) relationship between what is used as symbol and the focus itself. If the symbol is to be a deep and fruitful one, subject to creative interpretation, the relationship on which it is grounded must be correspondingly profound.

Several of the papers in this book argue for the centrality in the Indian tradition of what may be called a multi-level emanationism. This makes possible a particularly rich and varied symbolic structure, which I shall examine later.

My discussion of examples starts, however, with the possibilities for symbolism made available by the doctrine of creation. Creation sometimes appears as a strand in Indian thought, but usually within an emanationist context. I shall briefly sketch the implications of a creation doctrine such as that of Christianity, which is more purely dualistic.

If the world is created by the focus then it should, one may at first think, reveal its nature as clearly as a potter is revealed by his handiwork; the world as a whole and in its details should be an inexhaustible source of symbols for the creator; the more so if the creation is *ex nihilo*. But as the relationship between the creator god and the world is seen to be more complex (as in the Christian doctrine of the fall), so the availability of symbols becomes more problematic. Hence the need for special revelation becomes more pressing; to be satisfied for example by doctrines of *avatāra* or incarnation.

In general, the closer the creator is to his creation (either because creation merges into emanationism, or because the created world is uncorrupted by any wilful deviation from the creator's purposes for it), the more appropriate will it be to look within the created world for symbols of God. The persistent Christian tradition of seeing God in the objects of nature must rest on the idea that God participates in the world, so that he who most deeply contemplates and seeks to understand the natural world, even in its most particular detail, will be made more and more aware of God's presence and his nature. On this way of seeing the world, its divine significance is inexhaustible; an indication, on my earlier argument, that we have here examples of deep symbolism, and of essential relationships. At extremes of deism, on the other hand, the relationship between creator and creation will not allow such rich symbolic uses of nature; the deist can, looking at the world, draw abstract propositional conclusions about God's attributes from the formal structure of the universe, but thunder, lightning, flowers and mountains are not in themselves seen as symbolic, revelatory.

Another strand of Christian thinking focuses on the transcendence of God, his distance from the sin-corrupted world. So the world is correspondingly less suited to be a source of symbols of God; though if the doctrine of creation survives the world must still be capable to some extent of pointing to God. Certainly if the natural world were the creation of the devil, we would look to it in vain for deep symbols of God. It is of course the sinfulness of the world which makes necessary God's special revelation in Jesus Christ; he for Christianity is the central symbol of and way of approach to God. He is the deepest of all symbols; his endless fruitfulness as a symbol of God is grounded on the closest of all relationships: identity, though a mysterious kind of identity. Similarly in the *avatāra* doctrine, Viṣṇu's incarnation is necessary when the world has strayed far from its essential created pattern.

> Whenever there is a decline of righteousness and rise of unrighteousness, O Bhārata, then I send myself forth. For the protection of the good, for the destruction of the wicked, and for the establishment of righteousness, I come into being from age to age (BhG, IV,7–8).

Rawson claims in his paper that the basic Indian symbols are 'the generative and fertilizing waters; organic juice as energy; sex and its physical attributes; the inverted tree; descent and ascent through tiers; speech and the alphabet'. Many of these symbols are brought together in his later description and analysis of the Indian temple, which he represents as a model of all that is, in which energy and reality descend from the absolute, symbolized by a central dot or seed, through the realms of the gods to the ordinary world.

The same idea is presented more abstractly in the Upaniṣadic doctrine that the *ātman* (self) or *brahman* brought forth the world (*sarvam idam*) in such a way that he himself became what was thus brought forth or emanated; he 'entered into it right up to the fingertips' (BU 1,4,7). The implication of this is that 'everything here is real, and it is real because it is an expression of Brahman'.[4] Or, everything here is capable of symbolizing *brahman*.

The symbolic *ascent*, from symbol to symbolized focus, may be direct. As Yājñavalkya says: 'Mark well, it is not for the love of a husband . . . that a husband is dearly loved' (BU 2,4,5). Husbands and all contingent beings are to be valued as symbols of the absolute which informs and sustains them, constitutes their reality. But in the examples given in this book the symbolic ascent is more complex, with more stopping places. And often, as in the case of the temple as a complete structure, what is symbolized is not simply something higher up the (inverted) tree of emanated being, closer to the source, but rather the whole dynamic structure, cosmogony rather than cosmology, to use Irwin's distinction.

The symbol, the temple made of earthly elements, in its parts stands for various higher realms of being. The stone iconic statue symbolizes the god, *via* the god's iconographic form: his bodily shape, facial expression, *vāhana*, weapon etc. But understood as a whole the temple comments on such partial symbolic ascents, warns against purely *ādhidaivika* interpretations, which mistake the celestial for the transcendent. It does this by its total vertical structure; but this is further reinforced, Rawson points out, by the details of its style which shows the bodies of the divine 'inflated like bubbles into total convexity, which suggests that they are illusory . . . and only appear at the meeting place of original energy encountering original desires'.

So the worshipper's understanding of the temple as a whole will show him a cosmology, but also a cosmogony; that is he will be aware of the source of the reality of the whole. Thus the prime religious purpose will be served; the believer will be helped in his desire for closeness with the source, he will appreciate for example that theistic devotion may be a suitable though transcendable means to that end.

The editor of this book analyses in his paper a particular case in which *ādhidaivika* must be complemented by *ādhyātmika* interpretation. He argues that the goddess Aditi, as described in the Vedic hymns, expresses the mystical vision of the *ṛṣis*. But this is not simply a vision of the absolute; it is a more complex experience including the mystic's own relation of dependence on the absolute, and therefore his sense of unity with the whole emanated world.

Aditi represents the triple dimension of the divine absolute: (1) boundlessness and infinity and therefore freedom; (2) the fact that, although transcendent, the absolute is the source of the manifest; and at the same time (3) it also is this manifested reality itself. And this insight is understood as not just a metaphysical postulate, but as stemming from the seers' experience of their unity with reality in all its aspects, those manifested within time as well as its timeless source.

So, to return to Rawson's way of putting it, the mystic's vision is of 'the whole of the temple', that is of the whole scheme of reality for which the temple is a symbol.

But in this particular Vedic context the symbol is Aditi herself. A figure from the celestial realm of being is taken as a symbol of the higher transcendental realm, and also of the downward pervasion of the absolute. How is this possible? Is there a deep relation between the symbol and what it symbolizes? Obviously the rich concept of emanation or manifestation itself provides such a relation. The realm of the gods is ontologically related in one direction to the absolute, and also in the other direction to the grosser manifested world.

At a lower level Aditi may herself be the object of symbolism; she is pointed to by the worldly symbols of mother (and son) and cow. So for the ordinary worshipper she is quite properly to be thought of, through these and other symbolic concepts and images, as 'a mighty goddess who can grant freedom and relief from suffering'. Again the symbolism rests on an ontological ground; the realm of the gods itself pervades the ordinary world.

This is confirmed, as Sutton shows us, by Coomaraswamy's work on the *Rājasūya* ceremony. Coomaraswamy's analysis explicitly links several levels of reality. The target level is that of social existence, the ritual expressing primarily the correct relationship between Sacerdotium and Regnum. But this is linked 'upwards' to the cosmic polarity of heaven and earth, and to relationships between the gods. 'Mitra and Agni serve as divine archetypes of the Sacerdotium and Varuṇa and Indra of the Regnum.' That is, when the political balance of power is as it should be, then the gods are active in the world.

The social level also relates closely to the interpersonal relationship of marriage, and even to the intrapersonal realm. The self-assertion of man's ego is like a ruler become tyrant; and both point to a disturbed relationship between the outer-active-feminine self and the inner-contemplative-masculine self. To put things right, these selves must be 'wedded'; and then they will mirror the relationship of Sky/Earth, Mitra/Varuṇa, Kṛṣṇa/Arjuna, *aśabda brahman/śabda brahman*.

It is remarkable how in Sutton's exposition these many realms and polarities provide ways of talking about and understanding each other; they constitute a complex set of mutual symbols. This can only be because they are all *really* linked in the Indian cosmogonic system.

In the papers by Irwin and Harvey we are given two complementary but contrasting explorations of the significance of the Buddhist stūpa. I should like to argue that they exemplify two different ways in which symbolism may work, related to the distinction made at the beginning of this paper between deep and superficial symbolism. This was itself based on differences in the depth of the relationship between the object used as a symbol, and what it was used to symbolize. An emanationist cosmogony links together, at the deepest level, different levels of reality, from the phenomenal physical world through the divine realms to the absolute. Irwin sees the stūpa as Rawson sees the temple, as a symbol of this descent of reality; and therefore as a means whereby the believer can understand and affirm and realize his own relationship with higher reality. And so Irwin can see in the ancient world's concern with cosmogony, expressed in metaphoric language, a need to relate to the sacred world as the source of the Cosmic Order on which, so archaic man felt, his existence wholly depended. This order was the result of the creative act of separating out the determinate polarities; this act being represented by the *axis mundi* which in turn is symbolized in the ancient myth by the Indra's spear, which separated heaven and earth, and in the stūpa by the central post.

How is this symbolism possible; what is the relation between the stone dome with its central stone or wooden pillar, and the many-levelled 'sacred world' which it symbolizes? The relation is given by the cosmogony itself: the dome and the pillar are themselves products of the primeval but ever-present act of creative emanation. As expressed in the editor's summary of Irwin's work, 'the worshipped aniconic representations now as in ancient times are not what we call "symbols" of the divine, but actual manifestations of sacred power'. Here, I think, the concept of 'symbol' is used in its restricted sense suggesting a superficial relation between symbol and what is symbolized; which contrasts with the real relation behind deep symbolism.

In Harvey's discussion of the symbolism of the stūpa he concentrates on Buddhist meanings, that is meanings given by (in Irwin's terms) doctrinal rather than cultic Buddhism. For example, the Bodhi tree symbolizes the enlightenment, the Dhamma-wheel the preaching of the doctrine, and the stūpa the *parinibbāna*. Harvey shows how the stūpa as a whole incorporates all these symbols, and others such as the lotus, the vase of plenty, the *kumbha*, and so on. It seems to me that his explanations of how some of these symbols work show them to be 'superficial' in the sense which my theory gives to that term. The Bodhi tree symbolizes the Buddha's enlightenment for the obvious reason that the enlightenment took place under such a tree. (This is the 'doctrinal' reason; by contrast, Marco Pallis — as quoted by Sutton — gives an explanation and justification which associates cultic Buddhism with its Indian cultural background, and with the widespread cosmogonic beliefs of 'ancient prehistoric man' of which Irwin and Coomaraswamy speak, when he says that the pipal tree under which the Buddha-to-be was to achieve enlightenment 'obviously stands for the world's axis, the Tree of Life as Genesis calls it'.)

The stūpa (to return to 'doctrinal' justifications) symbolizes the Buddha's entry into *parinibbāna* because originally stūpas contained the relics of the Buddha's body, and so were associated with his 'death', which itself is doctrinally linked to his *parinibbāna*. These 'associative' links, if we take them just as I have described them, certainly point to a non-arbitrary relation between the symbol and what it symbolizes; but this relation is not a deep one; it is more 'raft-like' to use my earlier example. That is, no more can be learnt about the nature of enlightenment by looking into the essential nature of trees. The same applies to the symbolism of the lotus blossom which grows up from the mud just as an enlightened mind develops out of the ranks of ordinary beings, and from which drops of water roll off, suggesting the non-attachment of the liberated mind to conditioned phenomena.

The relationships here are like similes, in that the points of similarity are specifiable and limited. No *cosmological* relationship between the lotus and the enlightened mind, or between enlightenment and the

Bodhi tree, is presupposed in this kind of symbolism. Of course I am not suggesting that this type of symbolism is in any way inferior to what I have called deep symbolism; but it does seem to be the case that the two types work in a different way. It is worth suggesting, I think, that the difference reflects a different attitude to and concern with cosmology in the two religions. Creationist or emanationist cosmogonies are particularly suited to the grounding of deep symbolism whereby the transcendent focus of a religion is symbolized by something 'lower'. Theravāda Buddhism certainly has its cosmology, its range of heavens and hells etc.; but these are in many ways interchangeable with psychological states, and the principle of their cosmogony is karmic, rather than a link with the transcendent source of all reality, god or *brahman*. In fact this points to a basic question about the possibility of (deep) symbolism in religions where the cosmogony is negative rather than positive, that is in religious traditions where the emphasis is on *nirguṇa brahman*, or on some version of the *via negativa*.

If *brahman* is *nirguṇa*, the discriminated nature of the world of ordinary experience — and indeed of the higher worlds of the gods — tells against their ultimate reality. At its extreme, this way of thinking implies that the world is an illusion. The position is formally similar to the possibility mentioned earlier, that the world is the creation of the devil. How, in these cases, could the world be the source of deep symbolism for the religious focus? For the world has no ontological relation to the focus, the ground of being; or even has a kind of negative relation.

I cannot give this problem adequate discussion here.[5] As my final example I shall discuss one version of it which arises in Mahāyāna Buddhism. According to the Lotus Sūtra, as explained by Pye,[6] the religious use of symbolism may be said to be the teaching of Mahāyāna Buddhism. For example, the Buddha addresses Śāriputra:

> The *buddhas* in times past, by infinite, numberless tactful ways [skilful means] and with various reasonings and parabolic expressions, expounded the laws [*dharma*] for the sake of all living beings. All these laws are for the One Buddha-vehicle, [so that] all those living beings, who have heard the Law from the *buddhas*, might all finally obtain perfect knowledge.[7]

That is, Buddhism contains many apparently different and even incompatible teachings. In particular, three are mentioned; that of the *śrāvakas*, that of the *pratyeka buddhas*, and that of the *bodhisattvas*. All are teachings of the Buddha (of one and all of the infinite number of *buddhas*); and the hearer is right to listen to and follow the teaching which comes to him, with his personality and in his context — for example to aim at and achieve arahatship. But the teachings received by the Hīnayāna and Mahāyāna schools are different from each other only in appearance; really there is only 'one Buddha-vehicle'. The nature of this one vehicle is inexpressible, is understood only by the *buddhas*; nevertheless, this transcendent truth is the purpose of the Lotus Sūtra. The truth is, precisely, that the truth is transcendent, that all the teachings of Buddhism are skilful means. The *arahat* (or for that matter the *bodhisattva*) is not really what he claims to be unless he realizes this, and thus transcends his arahatship, sees it as of merely provisional relative worth, does not cling to it. His achievement stands only if he is aware that it cannot stand, is insubstantial.

Thus the innumerable skilful means used by the *buddhas* point towards, symbolize, the final truth expounded by the Lotus Sūtra. To raise the question which has been central to this paper: how can they do this, how can the merely worldly be a deep symbol of the focus? By their very nature as symbols are they fitted to be symbols of the Buddha knowledge; in their inner nature they are mere symbols, only appearances, empty of final truth. But emptiness is itself the final truth; skilful means, the fact that only symbols are or can be used, is the highest truth of Buddhism.

NOTES

1 Ferdinand de Saussure, *Course in General Linguistics*, tr. Wade Baskin, London, 1960, pp. 67 – 8.
2 Ibid., p. 68.
3 'Focus' is a term introduced by Ninian Smart, for example in *The Phenomenon of Religion*, London, 1973, pp. 5 & 7ff, to refer to what a religion is centred round or directed towards. This may be a being: god in Christ in Christianity; or a group of beings; or a state: *nibbāna* in Theravāda Buddhism; or an absolute such as *ātman-brahman* in Vedāntism.
4 Pratima Bowes, *The Hindu Religious Tradition*, London, 1977, chap. 5.
5 For a discussion of the complex ways in which Śankara's Advaita Vedānta tries to deal with these issues, see an earlier version of this paper, published as 'The possibility of Religious Symbolism', in *Religious Studies* 20 (1984), pp. 559 – 77.
6 Michael Pye, *Skilful Means*, London, 1978, chapters 1 – 3.
7 See *The Threefold Lotus Sūtra*, tr. Bunno Kato *et al.*, New York, 1975, p. 60 (chap. 2).

GLOSSARY

abhaya — fearlessness, freedom from fear.

ādhidaivika — with respect to gods; theological.

ādhyātmika — concerning the self or essence; absolute; ultimate.

ādi — beginning; (in compounds:) original, primeval, archetypal.

Aditi (= infinity) — one of the most ancient Vedic deities seen as the Divine Mother who has given birth to the whole world and all beings in it, including the gods, in accordance with the eternal law (*ṛta*).

Agni (= fire) — god of fire, especially of the sacrificial fire; the priest of the gods and the mediator between the gods and human worshippers.

ahaṅkāra — 'I-maker', 'I-am-ness'; egoity; the principle of individuality.

ākāśa — space, ether; sometimes added as fifth to the four 'great elements' (*mahābhūtas*: earth, water, air, fire) which form the material reality.

amṛta (Pāli: *amata*) — immortality, the immortal; in Hindu mythology the drink ('nectar') of immortality; in the Pāli Canon usually interpreted as 'the deathless' or 'deathlessness' and equalled to *nibbāna*.

anatta — unsubstantial; without self; the doctrine of *anatta* asserts the unsubstantiality of all saṁsāric entities or phenomena; some schools of Buddhism, such as Theravāda, assert non-existence of any self, essence or substance in the ultimate sense, claiming that even *nibbāna* is *anatta*.

anicca — non-eternal, impermanent; impermanence; the doctrine of *anicca* asserts the impermanence of all saṁsāric processes or phenomena, but it does not apply it to *nibbāna* where 'there is no coming or going'.

apsaras — heavenly nymph; Vedic references point to the aquatic origins of this category of lower female deities, thereby connecting them with water nymphs of other IE mythologies; their male counterparts are *gandharvas*, but already in Vedic times they occasionally befriended humans and gave birth to their children; they wait on gods and humans reborn in heaven, delighting them with song and dance.

arahant, *arahat* — the 'worthy one'; in early and Theravāda Buddhism a term for the accomplished disciple of the Buddha who has followed his teaching and has reached, as an individual, the final goal, i.e. liberation; it is also used in Jainism.

artha — purpose, goal, sake; means, wealth, achievement, success; one of the four goals in a Hindu's life combined with the scheme of four stages of life known as *āśramas*: (1) *brahmacāri*, i.e. student, disciple or apprentice, (2) *gṛhastha*, i.e. householder, (3) *vānaprastha*, i.e. hermit, and (4) *parivrājaka* or *sannyāsi*, i.e. mendicant, homeless wanderer; the scheme is highly theoretical and has never been universally adopted, most Hindus preferring worldly life till death (and those caring for liberation renouncing it even in youth); *artha* in the narrower sense, i.e. as one of the four goals in life (*puruṣārthas*), corresponds to the second or mature stage which involves material and worldly success (wealth, fame etc.); in the broader sense it also designates all the four goals of human life, as described in Miller's paper, note 19.

ārya (Pāli: *ariya*) — noble; originally a designation which the Vedic Indians used to refer to themselves as did the ancient Iranians and probably all or most of the IE nations (cf. the Celtic Eire); in Buddhism the term acquired the meaning of 'supramundane' or 'holy'.

asat — non-being; correlative term to *sat*, being; according to the RV 10,129,1 both 'being' and 'non-being' apply to the manifested world, while the pre-manifest dimension of latency is free from this dichotomy: 'then there was neither being nor non-being'; confusingly, later texts, from the Brāhmaṇas onwards, often use the term *asat* to denote the pre-manifest dimension and maintain that *sat*, being, emerged from *asat*.

asuras — originally a class of higher deities, Varuṇa being the chief among them (cf. Avestan *ahura*), they later came to be regarded as 'antigods', adversaries, although occasionally also collaborators or temporary allies, of *devas* in Brahmanic and Hindu mythology; they are comparable to the Greek 'titans'.

aśvamedha — horse sacrifice; an elaborate rite which could be performed only by a powerful king who was able to ensure protection to the sacrificial horse wherever it went while allowed to roam freely for a year.

ātman (Pāli: *atta*) — self (as reflexive pronoun); the self; the inmost essence of man, in the Upaniṣads seen as identical with *brahman*, the inner essence or source of the whole of reality; in the RV its meaning was 'breath' or 'breath of life'; in Buddhism it is used only negatively in statements denying self, essence or substance to saṁsāric phenomena, but it is never positively defined, asserted or denied.

avatāra — descent, advent; descent of god to earth; divine incarnation.

avidyā (Pāli: *avijjā*) — ignorance; lack of (adequate, substantial) knowledge about the nature of existence, and therefore the cause of bondage to *saṁsāra* or the limited and conditioned form of existence.

bhikṣu (Pāli: *bhikkhu*) — mendicant; wandering ascetic living on alms food; monk; Buddhist monk.

bodhi — enlightenment, awakening; in the context of Buddhism it usually implies the three higher knowledges, viz. the knowledge of one's past lives, the knowledge of the 'comings and goings' of other saṁsāric beings and the full knowledge of the destruction of one's own cankers, i.e. the absolute certainty of one's liberation; since not all these three knowledges, except the third one, were usually acquired in full by the liberated disciples of the Buddha, the term has been virtually reserved for him, at least in early Buddhism and the most early schools; later Theravāda sources, however, did introduce the term *sāvaka-bodhi* for the attainment of the liberated disciples, but it has never gained wider circulation.

bodhisattva (Pāli: *bodhisatta*) — 'enlightenment being'; in the Pāli Canon the term designates a being preparing himself for the career of a Buddha as the world teacher over many lives by developing 'perfections of conduct, insight and wisdom'; in Mahāyāna it may also mean a 'permanent' *bodhisattva*, a being who has developed his perfections fully and is virtually enlightened but who remains active in the world for the sake of assisting in the enlightenment of others, without ever taking the role of a world teacher as a historical Buddha; another special category of helper is a kind of 'transcendental' *bodhisattva* who may never have been an incarnate being and is an emanation of cosmic buddhahood or of a particular Dhyāni Buddha.

Brahma — at one stage (coinciding with the early Buddhist time) perhaps the chief god of Brahmanism, certainly a high god of paramount importance; with Brahmanic revival, when the domination of Buddhism peaked off, which marks the beginning of what is known as Hinduism proper, he becomes the first god of the Hindu Trinity (*trimurti*) as the 'creator', followed by Viṣṇu and Śiva who both eventually overshadowed him; reduced to a subordinate position as the 'craftsman-fashioner' (demiurge) with hardly any following, he is usually thought of as sunk in cosmic slumber or deep meditation once he finished the task of fashioning the universe at the beginning of the world period.

brahmacāri — pupil, disciple, apprentice; *brahmacārya*, meaning 'divine faring', is the first of the four stages in the ancient scheme of life of Āryan people, usually lasting twelve years and spent in the house of the teacher; one of the duties of a brahmin apprentice would be to look after the sacrificial fire.

brahman — the divine source and the inmost essence of the universe identical with the inmost self of each individual (*ātman*), to be realized by direct personal experience as a result of spiritual practice; this Upaniṣadic teaching underlies much of Indian philosophical and religious thinking even outside its specific Vedāntic tradition and is detectable also in the background of the epic and Purāṇic literature; originally, in the RV, this expression stood for the 'sacred word', the prayer, the magic formula and the magic power of these; it was appropriated by priests as 'possessors of *brahman*' via the knowledge of the sacred texts and rituals and they derived from it the designation for themselves, namely *brāhmaṇa*; hence the expressions 'brahman' and 'brahmin' in the general meaning 'priest'; from it is further derived the designation for the literary treatises on liturgy and its mythological and cosmic connection, viz. Brāhmaṇas, i.e. 'priestly books'.

Buddha — the Enlightened One; the Awakened One; beside the Buddha as a world teacher who preaches the doctrine and is known also as *samāsaṁbuddha*, the supremely enlightened one, there are also silent or solitary (*pratyeka*, Pāli: *pacceka*) *buddhas*, fully awakened, but without the teaching vocation.

caitya (Pāli: *cetiya*) — a Buddhist monument or shrine.

cakra (Pāli: *cakka*) — wheel; discus.

cakravartin (Pāli: *cakkavattin*) — 'wheel-turner'; the title used for the ideal world-governing monarch both in the Brahmanic and Buddhist traditions; adopted in Buddhism also for the Buddha as the supreme spiritual guide in the universe.

citta — mind, heart; mentality, character.

deva — god, category of beings inhabiting the celestial planes of existence; they are hierarchically structured, although the divisions among them and positions acquired by individual gods are not rigidly determined and are subject to changes.

devī — goddess; when written Devī it refers to the Śakta cult of the feminine principle embodied in many female deities conceived as dominant figures, particularly in the form of Durgā and Kālī.

dharma (Pāli: *dhamma*) — righteousness, virtue, duty, discipline; reality, truth; in Buddhism also: the teaching about the ultimate reality as presented by the Buddha; the Dharma/Dhamma is revered in Buddhism as the second of the 'three jewels', the first one being the Buddha and the third one the Sangha or community of saints. In Hinduism *dharma* as 'duty' is often rigidly interpreted as adherence to caste rules, but it may be more philosophically understood as the 'righteous course of action' or even the 'appropriate action', i.e. appropriate to the situation, so that it is brought to its natural or logical outcome which, in the highest sense, is nothing less than the realization of the ultimate truth. In the schemes of four *āśramas* (stages of life) and four *puruṣārthas* (see *artha*) it permeates all stages, but corresponds in its narrow sense as 'discipline' to the first stage, i.e. that of discipleship; in the wider sense of duty, virtue and righteousness it corresponds to the second stage in which worldly careers are pursued; in its sense as truth it is meditated on in the third stage; and in the sense of ultimate reality it is the goal to be realized in the fourth stage.

dharmakāya — 'the body of truth', the absolute reality in itself and by itself in Mahāyāna Buddhism. Its personalized counterpart is the Ādi Buddha.

dhātu — element; in Buddhism also the bodily relic left over after the cremation.

dhyāna — state of meditation; meditational absorption; in pl. also: versified rules for depicting images of gods in Hindu iconography.

Dhyāni Buddha — 'cosmic' Buddha; there is a multiplicity of them in the Mahāyāna 'pantheon', often arranged in *maṇḍalas* in groups of five; they belong to the level of *saṁbhogakāya* and may be visualized in meditational absorptions.

gaṇa — multitude, group, troop; a body of followers or attendants, particularly of Śiva, in which case their leader is usually Ganeṣa.

gandharva (Pāli: *gandhabba*) — a lower deity, a spirit being; in Hindu mythology a category of male heavenly beings subordinate to the gods and usually fulfilling the role of heavenly musicians; female counterparts: *apsarases*.

guṇa — attribute, quality; the three *guṇas* of Sāṅkhya (*sattva, rajas* and *tamas*) are aspects or forces of nature (*prakṛti*) through which nature evolves into an inhabited cosmos.

guru — teacher; spiritual preceptor; the term is of pre-Buddhist origin, adopted in Hinduism and some yoga schools; it is seldom used in Buddhism, except in its Vajrayāna or Tantric variety (and consequently it survives in Tibetan Buddhism where, however, it is by no means universal).

Hara and Hari — different names for Śiva and Viṣṇu, respectively; formed into the compound Harihara the name indicates the essential unity of the two deities in particular and the underlying oneness of the divine, manifested in different god figures, in general. Harihara is sometimes depicted in works of iconographic art as one figure composed of two halves, one recognizably representing Viṣṇu and the other Śiva.

harmikā — 'top enclosure', cubic structure on top of a stūpa; a cool summer chamber on the top of a building.

Indra — the prominent warrior god of Āryans when conquering India; in the creation mythology of the RV he represents the active force which set the process of manifestation going by piercing Vṛtra, the demon of inertia, and releasing the captive life-bearing waters/maidens and impregnating them; he then set the sun on high; later he became the king of the gods in the *deva*-world; in Buddhism he is seen as the follower of the Buddha who achieved stream-entry.

īśvara — lord; sovereign; usually applied to God (the Lord) in religious schools and sects with monotheistic tendencies; it is also used for the personal god a Hindu may single out as his chosen or preferred deity (called *iṣṭa devatā*).

jñāna — knowledge; insight; knowledge gained through contemplation or by spiritual vision.

kālakūṭa — deadly poison; one of the names applied to the poison churned out of the cosmic ocean, and drunk by Śiva, before the drink of immortality was obtained.

kāma — desire, pleasure, love; as one of the *puruṣārthas* it has its place in the second *āśrama* (see the entry under *artha*); since *dharma* permeates also this stage, it is a Hindu's sacred duty not only to enjoy himself, but to see to the satisfaction of his partner(s) in love as well; by the same token Kāma Sūtra, the textbook of love, is a religious work. Personified, Kāma is the god of love, carrying a sugar-cane bow and piercing hearts with his arrows.

kapāla (Pāli also: *kappala*) — skull, skull-bone; alms-bowl; cup, jar; frying-pan.

karma (Pāli: *kamma*) — action, deed; often used to refer to the 'doctrine of *karma*' as the natural law of retribution for man's actions operating throughout successive lives in the sense of 'as you have sown so you will reap'.

kauśala (Pāli: *kusala*) — skilful, salutary.

kavi — poet, seer, sage.

kāvya — poem, poetry; poetics; the expression '*kāvya* literature' usually refers to the court poetry of the classical age.

kāya — body; trunk of a tree.

kumbha — pot, jar, urn; the dome of a stūpa.

kuṇḍalinī (= 'the coiled one') — often referred to as *kuṇḍalinī śaktī* or the 'serpent power'; according to Tantric yoga it is the spiritual potency of man and it is identifiable in his 'subtle body'; when dormant, she is coiled like a serpent at the base of his spine; when awakened, she rises along the spine activating spiritual centres along it until she reaches the top of the skull which coincides with spiritual enlightenment. Personified, she is regarded as the Goddess — Kuṇḍalinī Devī.

Lakṣmī — also known as Śrī or Śrī Lakṣmī was born as one of the products of the churning of the world ocean by gods and titans in order to obtain the drink of immortality. She has become the wife of Viṣṇu, taking many incarnations alongside him as *avatāra*, e.g. as Sītā with Rāma or Rādhā with Kṛṣṇa. In her own right she is the goddess of beauty, good luck and plenty and she is also the mother of Kāma, the god of love; as Viṣṇu's *śakti* she is the sustaining force in the universe.

līlā — play; divine play as the explanation of the reason for the world creation in the thought of early Advaita Vedānta; this notion also plays a significant part in the Kṛṣṇa legends.

liṅga — mark, sign, member; male sexual organ; the same as the symbol of Śiva, representing his cosmic supremacy; in this context it is often described as extending into the infinite dimension, the revealed personality of Śiva being its emanation; its association with the 'cosmic pillar' and *axis mundi* is obvious.

lokottaravāda (Pāli: *lokuttaravāda*) — supramundane, transcendental; the Lokottaravāda school of Buddhism, originated after the Mahāsanghika split probably in the second century B.C., stressed the transcendental nature of buddhahood and of the Buddha Gotama himself and generally regarded only supramundane entities as really existing.

mahā — great; usually used as the first component in compounds.

Maitreya (Pāli: Metteya) — the name of the future Buddha at present awaiting, as a *bodhisattva*, the time of his last birth on earth, and thereby the start of his mission as a Buddha, in the Tuṣita heaven.

makara — a mythological sea animal resembling, to some extent, the crocodile; regarded to be the emblem of Kāma, the god of love, the Indian Cupid.

manas — mind, intellect.

mantra — a syllable, a word (which may be a name of god) or a phrase used for chanting or repetition, aloud or internally, during rituals or as a vehicle of meditation.

Māra — 'personified' death in Buddhism regarded as the 'prince' or ruler of the saṁsāric world in which every living being is subject to dying.

mārga — path; way.

mātṛkās — mothers; a group of seven goddesses important in medieval Hinduism, often depicted together in a single icon.

māyā — illusion; magic; divine cosmic power; veil of ignorance hiding the true nature of reality; Māyā, also Mahāmāyā: the name of the Buddha's mother.

medhi — pillar, platform round a pillar; platform round a stūpa.

Mitra — one of the sons of Aditi with solar associations, he stands for friendship, communal life, social contract, laws, and peace; he is the closest associate of Varuṇa, the guardian of the cosmic law, and is later seen as ruling the day, while Varuṇa rules the night.

mokṣa — liberation; final release from the round of rebirths; as the fourth and the highest of the four goals of a Hindu's life it corresponds to the fourth stage of life which few ever enter, although it can be and is pursued by some at any stage of their lives if truly aspired for.

mṛtyu — death.

mudrā — sign, symbol; gesture; ritual gesture; symbolical gesture.

muni — sage; in the RV the expression usually designates sages of non-Brahmanic type as in the case of the 'longhaired ascetic' of the hymn 10,136; it is more current in the AV and it was used also for the Buddha (cf. the expression Śakyamuni); in Hinduism, including the Purāṇic literature, it is used indiscriminately with other terms for renunciates and all categories of holy men.

nirmāṇakāya — the 'symbolical body' of truth or 'truth incarnate' as encountered in the person of a Buddha while still living in his physical body on earth; the 'physical' body of the Buddha.

nirvāṇa (Pāli: *nibbāna*) — the ultimate state of liberation from the round of rebirths (*saṁsāra*) which can be realized also during one's lifetime on earth.

padma — lotus.

parinirvāṇa (Pāli: *parinibbāna*) — the ultimate liberation obtained at the physical death of a liberated person; usually used to refer to the death of the Buddha.

parokṣa — beyond sight, invisible; secret, hidden; beyond sensory perception; higher view; higher perception; understanding by higher insight.

pitṛ — father; an expression used in the plural for the deceased ancestors living in a lower heavenly abode (*pitṛloka*).

Prajāpati — 'lord of progeny', one of the Vedic demiurge deities, later regarded as the forefather of all beings.

prakṛti — 'nature'; the primeval dynamic force which, prompted by the presence and observant attention of the *puruṣa*, proceeds to produce, via its three *guṇas* or constituent attributes, the manifested reality, i.e. the whole universe, including its higher spheres or heavens, and the phenomenal constituents of its beings, i.e. their bodies, senses as well as minds; the lower principle of the dualistic philosophy of Sāṅkhya; the Goddess, Devī, in her various forms in Hinduism is often regarded as the personification of *prakṛti*.

pratibhā — appearance, light, splendour; intellect, understanding, genius; power of poetical insight.

pratyakṣa — perception, apprehension by the senses; common view; lower understanding.

Pṛthivī — lit. 'the broad one'; the name of the earth as deity.

pūjā — ritual worship or worship ritual.

purohita — royal chaplain, the high priest at a king's court.

puruṣa — person; the inmost core of personality; spirit; in the RV 10,90: the primeval reality from one quarter of which the whole manifested universe emerged through the process of sacrifice; in the dualistic Sāṅkhya philosophical system: spirit as the higher principle, nature (*prakṛti*) being the lower principle; in concrete terms, there is, in Sāṅkhya, a plurality of eternal spirits (*puruṣas*) whose exact nature is not explained.

rāja — king.

rajas — the active *guṇa* in Sāṅkhya philosophy, representing the energy or dynamism of nature.

Rājasūya — a higher ritual consecration of the king investing him with high power which used to be performed, in ancient times, annually as a rite of regeneration.

rākṣasa — demon, goblin; a category of evil terrestrial beings inimical to men, appearing in various, often animal, forms.

raṅgoli (also: *raṅgāvalī*) — a form of *yantra* in popular use in South India; meant to welcome guests and friendly deities, they are usually drawn in front of houses by women after cleaning the house as part of their housework; art historians regard them as a traditional art-form in its own right.

rasa — sap, juice; flavour, relish; liking, desire, love; feeling, emotion, pathos, sentiment; aesthetic emotion; essence, pith; essence of poetry.

ṛc, ṛg — verse; hence Ṛg Veda, 'knowledge in verses', the first Vedic collection.

ṛṣi (Pāli: *isi*) — seer; in the RV used for the inspired authors of the hymns, later occasionally also for the authors of the Upaniṣads and still later, in Hindu texts, for any type of sage, renunciate or spiritual teacher.

ṛta — cosmic law of balance operating on both physical and spiritual (including moral) level.

śabda — sound; message; evidence; manifested (expressed) truth; truth expressed in the scriptural form.

śakti — power, potency; divine creative force; creative power of god personified as his female consort, particularly in sectarian Viṣṇuism and Śivaism; in sectarian Śaktism she is the primeval female creative force and the supreme goddess, the Devī.

sāman — chant, song; hence Sāma Veda, 'knowledge in chants', the second Vedic collection, compiled almost exclusively from the Ṛg Veda and used in liturgy.

samatha — peace, tranquillity; in the Theravāda tradition a technical term for a type of meditation (*bhāvanā*) which leads to mental absorptions (*jhānas*), but not necessarily to wisdom and liberation.

saṁbhogakāya — the 'body of experience', the truth as experienced by the enlightened mind; the level of transcendental experience in meditational absorption; the 'subtle' body of the Buddha bearing thirty-two marks indicating his high status.

samrāj (*samrāt*) — universal monarch; emperor.

saṁsāra — 'global flow', the phenomenal process of reality; usually used, in the context of the lives of individuals, in the sense of the 'round of rebirths'.

saṅgha — assembly; community; in the Pāli Canon it means the community of the 'noble' disciples (*ariya sāvakas*), whether ordained monks or lay followers, more precisely referred to as *sāvakasaṅgha*; in a more general usage it is employed to refer to the community of ordained monks (*bhikkhusaṅgha*) regardless of their spiritual achievement or lack of it; in Mahāyāna it may denote the whole cosmic hierarchy of spiritually evolved beings, including the *buddhas* of all times and regions (Buddha-fields) and also *bodhisattvas* of all types.

śarīra (Pāli: *sarīra*) — (physical) body; bodily relics after cremation.

sat — being, existence.

sat-cit-ānanda — existence-consciousness-bliss; a designation applied in the system of Advaita Vedānta for the ultimate experience of the state of liberation in which these three phenomenologically distinct concepts represent a unity of the spiritual essence of reality itself.

sattva — the lucid *guṇa* in Sāṅkhya philosophy, i.e. the reflective or reflecting capacity of nature enabling it to reflect the consciousness of the spirit (*puruṣa*).

sāvaka — disciple; in early Buddhism it denotes one of the four types of the 'noble' disciples (stream-winner, once-returner, non-returner, and *arahant*).

Savitṛ — the brilliant, 'golden' solar god and the lord of vivifying, life-sustaining power.

Śiva — known in the Vedas as Rudra, the storm god, but also as the one god who could drink poison without harm (an allusion to the myth of the churning of the world ocean which produced also poison threatening to stifle all life), he became (with Brahma and Viṣṇu) the third god of the Hindu Trinity as the destroyer who brings about the end of the universe with his cosmic dance; he is further the lord of creatures (Paśupati) and the god of fertility, *liṅga* being his symbol, as well as the great ascetic and the lord of yoga (Yogapati); his sectarian followers regard him as identical with the divine transcendent source of existence.

Śrī — see Lakṣmī.

svadharma — 'own duty'; the life's vocation which one is called upon to fulfil by one's position in society and which determines one's duties.

svarāj — self-rule; self-government; in the spiritual sense: mastery of oneself, self-control.

tamas — the static *guṇa* in Sāṅkhya philosophy, representing the inertia and the disintegrating tendency in nature.

tapas — heat; inner flame; creative power; spiritual energy; also: observance of spiritual discipline and hence sometimes referring to ascetic practices.

tejas (vernacular: *tej*) — light, glow, heat, fire.

trikāya — the three 'bodies' or levels of reality or truth in Mahāyāna (*dharmakāya*, *saṁbhogakāya*, *nirmāṇakāya*).

triratna (Pāli: *tiratana*) — the three jewels as the objects of Buddhist worship, namely the Buddha, the Dharma/Dhamma and the Sangha.

triśūla — trident; three-pronged spear.

uṣṇīṣa — anything wound round the head; turban, diadem, coronet, tiara; hair-do with a top knot or a protuberance on the top of the head (as seen in different styles on Buddha statues).

vāc — speech; in the Vedas it is a cosmic divine force comparable to the Biblical Logos; personified as goddess of speech: Vāc/Vāk.

vāhana — vehicle, conveyance, carrier; an animal used for riding on; virtually every god of the Hindu Pantheon has an animal carrier, e.g. Brahma the goose or swan, Śiva the bull, Ganeṣa the mouse, etc.

vajra (Pāli: *vajira*) — thunderbolt; lightning, diamond; Indra's thunderbolt sceptre and weapon in Vedic mythology; it corresponds to the lightning/spear weapon and emblem of sovereignty of the rulers of gods in other IE mythologies, e.g. the Greek Zeus and Germanic Wotan.

Varuṇa — the high god of the encompassing sky, the first-born son of Aditi and thus the first ruler of the universe and the all-seeing guardian of *ṛta*, the cosmic law, in the sense of the laws of nature and, more particularly, in its aspect of moral law, tying in a noose those who transgress against it; the sky and the expanse of the universal space being seen as the world ocean, he is also the god of waters and rules the seas, thus acquiring an association with the sea creatures; his close associate is Mitra who sometimes spurs him to action; he later declined in status, possibly because of the lingering memory of his ancient status as the foremost *asura*, as *asuras* obtained an increasingly negative image.

Vāyu — the god of wind and the 'breath of the gods', also known as Vāta; he mysteriously penetrates all dimensions of existence and rules the life force; he can prolong life of worshippers and even grant immortality; a clue to this meaning may be his association with breath/life force whose other Vedic name was *ātman* which was later to become the designation for the highest principle.

vedikā — originally a sacrificial altar; an elevated spot of ground, a mound, a seat; an elevated pathway round a stūpa, then a railing enclosing the same.

vijñāna (Pāli: *viññāna*) — consciousness.

vipassanā — insight; a faculty developed in the course of meditation and necessary for gaining final knowledge or wisdom and therefore liberation; in the Theravāda tradition a technical term for a type of meditation (*bhāvanā*) which leads to that achievement, possibly even without the attainment of full *jhānas*.

virāj — king, monarch, sovereign; in the AV: a mysterious (feminine) cosmic force, sometimes identified with the cosmic cow and with Vāk; sun and moon are her calves.

Virocana — a foremost *asura* who, according to CU 8,7,1—8 and ff., approached Prajāpati, at the same time as Indra did, for instruction about *ātman*. Having been told that it is the 'self' which one can see reflected in a pan of water or in a mirror and that one should care for it and adorn it, they both went away; Virocana then passed the doctrine to his fellow *asuras* who thus became protagonists of materialism; Indra, however, dissatisfied with the first answer, returned and received, in stages, the full doctrine about the ultimate nature of *ātman*, thus becoming the archetype of a true seeker of the ultimate truth.

Vṛtra — snake, dragon or demon symbolizing inertia and the precreational chaos; he held captive the fruitful waters/maidens until they were freed by Indra who slew or temporarily overcame Vṛtra, thus enabling the birth of the universe.

yakṣa (Pāli: *yakkha*) — a spirit being; a lower deity in the Brahmanic (and Hindu) system, recognized also in Buddhism.

Yama — the Vedic king of the dead, the first man to die; he rules those who followed him to his celestial region, a place of relative bliss for the righteous ones, probably identical with *pitṛloka*; in later Hindu mythology he acquired a more sinister image as death itself.

yantra — diagram; magic drawing used to ward off evil forces; symbolical depiction of the universe or human personality used for meditation in some types of yoga.

yaṣṭi — stick, staff, pole; column, pillar; symbol of *axis mundi*.

yoga — a systematic discipline aiming at spiritual progress and eventual perfection and liberation; its practice has the development of supernatural powers as its by-product; in Hindu tradition it was first revealed to men by *īśvara* (the Lord) and some gods gained immortality as well as supreme powers by its practice.

yūpa — sacrificial post; symbol of the 'cosmic pillar'.

LIST OF CONTRIBUTORS

DAVID BASTOW
Department of Philosophy, University of Dundee.

PETER HARVEY
Department of Languages and Cultures, Sunderland Polytechnic.

JOHN C. IRWIN
Victoria & Albert Museum (retired).

JEANINE MILLER
British Museum (retired).

PHILIP S. RAWSON
Royal Academy, London (retired); formerly: Gulbenkian Museum of Oriental Art, Durham

VALERIE J. ROEBUCK
British Museum (retired).

GLYN RICHARDS
Department of Philosophy of Religion, University of Stirling.

DAVID SMITH
Department of Religious Studies, University of Lancaster.

JONATHAN SUTTON
Freelance scholar.

KAREL WERNER
School of Oriental Studies, University of Durham.

NOTE ON THE PAPERS AND ACKNOWLEDGEMENTS

'Symbols and Religious Language' was presented in its original version as the introductory paper at the Seventh Symposium on Indian Religions on 3 April 1981 in the Cherwell Centre, Oxford, under the title 'Symbol and Religion'; revised and given its present name it was then published in *Humanities: Christianity and Culture* 18, (International Christian University Publication IV-B, Mitaka-Tokyo, May 1984), pp. 17 – 33. It is reprinted here without change.

'The Symbolism of Indian Art' was newly written for this collection, but it is a free rendering of the original talk which the author gave on 19 March 1977 under the title 'Seminal Symbols in Indian Religions' at the Third Symposium convened in the University College (the Castle), Durham; the conference was moved for the occasion to the Gulbenkian Museum of Oriental Art in Durham of which the author was then the curator.

'Symbolism in the Vedas and its Conceptualisation' was presented already on 22 March 1975 at the First Symposium on Indian Religions in Selwyn College in Cambridge and, further developed, published in *Numen, International Review for the History of Religions XXIV*, (1977), fasc. 3, pp. 223 – 40. It has been substantially revised for this collection.

'Origins of Form and Structure in Monumental Art' has had a difficult history. The author was to deliver a paper on 'New Angles of Vision on the pre-Aśokan Pillar and Lapis Lazuli' on 15 April 1983 at the Ninth Symposium in the Cherwell Centre, Oxford, but was prevented from doing so by an accident. His draft paper was read in his absence and the materials from it were published under different headings. After a discussion the author agreed to produce a restatement of the results of his research as his contribution to the present volume. Advanced in years and with his health failing, he recently suffered a mild heart attack and was unable to finish his paper. In view of the importance of his ideas for the theme of this volume the editor undertook the task of putting together a compilation of the author's work using the unfinished draft and supplementing it with summaries of his most important previous papers. John Irwin was able to read and give his approval to the result and make minor changes in it with the help of his research assistant, Margaret Hall, who also produced the illustrations.

'Venerated Objects and Symbols of Early Buddhism' is a new and substantially enlarged version of the paper published as 'The Symbolism of the Early Stūpa' in the *Journal of the International Association of Buddhist Studies* vol. 7, no. 2 (1984), pp. 67–93, which in turn was a revised version of the paper delivered on 24 April 1982 at the Eighth Symposium in the Cherwell Centre, Oxford, under the title 'Early Buddhist Iconography'.

'Predestiny and Evil in Hindu Mythology — an Inquiry into the Symbolism of the Vena-Pṛthu Legend' was given on 25 March 1984 at the Tenth Symposium in the Cherwell Centre, Oxford, and is published here for the first time.

'Aspects of the Symbolism of Fire in Hinduism' was read on 4 April 1981 at the Seventh Symposium at the Cherwell Centre, Oxford, and is published here for the first time.

'Weapons as Symbols in Hindu Art' originated as a talk accompanied by a slide show and given on 4 April 1981 at the Seventh Symposium in the Cherwell Centre, Oxford, and, revised and enlarged for this collection, receives in it its first publication.

'Meaning and Symbolism in the work of Ananda Coomaraswamy' was read on 5 April 1981 at the Seventh Symposium at the Cherwell Centre, Oxford, and published in *Sri Lanka Journal of the Humanities* (University of Peradeniya), vol. VII (1981), nos. 1 & 2, pp. 1–28.

'The Possibility of Symbolism in Indian Religions' is a new version, prepared for this collection, of the paper 'The Possibility of Religious Symbolism' published in *Religious Studies*, vol. 20 (1984), pp. 559–77, which originated as a talk entitled 'A Footnote on

Symbolism', delivered on 23 April 1982 at the Eighth Symposium in the Cherwell Centre, Oxford. While reading all the other contributions for the sake of revising his own paper for this volume, David Bastow made valuable suggestions and corrections in them which are hereby thankfully acknowledged.